M Parkins

ORGANIZATIONAL BEHAVIOR
FOURTH EDITION

ORGANIZATIONAL BEHAVIOR
FOURTH EDITION

Don Hellriegel
Texas A & M University

John W. Slocum
Southern Methodist University

Richard W. Woodman
Texas A & M University

WEST PUBLISHING COMPANY
St. Paul   New York   Los Angeles   San Francisco

Copyeditor: Jerrold Moore
Artwork: Carlisle Graphics
Composition: Carlisle Graphics

A STUDENT STUDY GUIDE

A study guide containing outlines and summaries of major topics plus review questions for additional practice is available with this text. If you cannot locate a copy of the study guide in your bookstore, please ask your bookstore manager to order a copy for you under the title *Student Study Guide to Accompany Organizational Behavior,* prepared by Roger D. Roderick.

Library of Congress Cataloging-in-Publication Data

Hellriegel, Don.
 Organizational behavior.

 Includes index.
 1. Organizational behavior.   2. Management.
I. Slocum, John W.   II. Woodman, Richard W.   III. Title.
HD58.7.H44   1986   658   85-22704
ISBN 0-314-93186-4
2nd Reprint—1987

To Jill, Kim, and Lori (DH)
Christopher, Bradley, and Jonathan (JWS)
David and Anna (RWW)

Contents

Preface

Written for the introductory course in organizational behavior, this fourth edition of *Organizational Behavior* has been substantially updated, revised, and restructured. Four new chapters and other features have been added to improve the usefulness and timeliness of the book.

Goals of this Edition

As with the third edition, our first major goal was to present the various concepts, models, and issues of organizational behavior in a manner that will help the student to develop the conceptual, interpersonal, and communication skills that are needed for effective management in an organization. The development of individual and managerial competencies is stressed throughout the book. A sampling of these competencies includes: gaining increased self-awareness, managing personal stress, solving problems creatively, establishing effective and supportive communication, motivating and improving job performance, using power and influence, improving group decision making, developing leadership skills, managing conflict, and delegating decision making effectively. Many of these individual and managerial competencies are dealt with in more than one chapter.

Each chapter begins with a *Preview Case* that indicates why and how the material presented in the chapter is important to managerial, professional, and other employees of organizations. The actual behaviors and thinking required of managers are emphasized, rather than abstract principles and theories. Relevant research findings are integrated into the text. Several chapters include diagnostic questionnaires to assist the student in personally relating to and learning from the various concepts and models presented.

Our second major goal for this edition was to introduce an international thread throughout the book. One way we do this is with a new feature called *Across Cultures*. Each selection relates directly to the content of the section of the chapter in which it appears. This new feature is clearly identified in the outline of each chapter. These selections, along with other internationally oriented material in the text, meet the accrediting standard of the American Assembly of Collegiate Schools of Business, which states: "Every student should be exposed to the international dimension through one or more elements of the curriculum." With the movement toward a global economy, the Across Cultures feature is timely, unique, and significant.

Our third major goal for this edition was to capture and sustain the interest of the student. We selected a variety of timely and interesting illustrations of real-world situations and present them as the *Preview Case, In Practice* inserts, and the *Across Cultures* selection in each chapter, and the end-of-chapter *Management Incidents and Cases*. All can be used for analysis and class discussion, but the Management Incidents and Cases are particularly intended for that purpose. These four features present a variety of types of issues and problems from a wide range of institutions, levels within organizations, and industry settings.

Our fourth major goal for this edition was to help develop the student's diagnostic skills, which are essential to understanding why certain events and behavioral processes occur within organizations. Because behavior in organizations is exceedingly complex, we avoided simplistic "cookbook" prescriptions. Such prescriptions, while seemingly practical and easy to implement, are usually short-sighted and do not work well in a variety of situations. However, guidelines and suggestions are presented once the contingencies or situational factors have been identified and diagnosed.

New Material in This Edition

The fourth edition includes four new chapters, new features, and a thorough updating and revision of all chapters. First, with a few exceptions, the Preview Cases, In Practice selections, and end-of-chapter Management Incidents and Cases are new to this edition. The *Across Cultures* feature, as already mentioned, is completely new. Second, this edition contains four new chapters: Chapter 3, Personality and Attitudes; Chapter 4, Perception and Attribution; Chapter 12, Organizational Culture; and Chapter 15, Decision Making and Goal Setting. Third, the organization of the book was substantially improved. Changes in organization were based on the author's own use and the recommendations of other users of the third edition and include:

- The chapter on work motivation was Chapter 12 in Part V; it is now Chapter 7 in Part II, Individual Processes.
- The career planning and development chapter was Chapter 7 in Part II; it now is Chapter 19 in Part VI, Individual and Organizational Change.
- The major divisions of the book have been restructured to provide better balance in the number of chapters in each part, as well as to accommodate the four new chapters.

Supplements to This Edition

Dorothy M. Hai (University of Wisconsin—La Crosse) has developed *Organizational Behavior: Experiences and Cases*, which is highly compatible with the organization and content of this book. Hai's book is also available from West Publishing Company.

Available for the first time is a *Student Study Guide* to accompany *Organizational Behavior*. It was authored by Roger Roderick (University of Baltimore) and provides an effective means of self-instruction for students. Other supplements to the text include: (1) an *Instructor's Resource Guide* (containing supplementary lecture resource materials, visuals, and lists of films and videotapes); (2) a *Test Manual*; and (3) 42 two-color *acetate visuals*. These supplements are thorough, up-to-date, and may be obtained from the publisher.

Framework of this Edition

This fourth edition is divided into six parts, each of which contains a grouping of chapters that relate directly a major aspect of organizational behavior.

Part I: Introduction (two chapters)

Chapter 1, Managers and Organizational Behavior, describes the nature of managerial work, approaches to organizational behavior, and the framework for this book. Chapter 2, Learning about Organizational Behavior, introduces the student to ways in which knowledge about management and organizational behavior can be acquired.

Part II: Individual Processes (five chapters)

Chapter 3, Personality and Attitudes, and Chapter 4, Perception and Attribution, are new to this edition. Chapter 3 covers such topics as: factors that influence the development of personality; key personality characteristics that help explain individual differences within organizations; how attitudes form and influence individual behavior; and key types of attitudes within organizations. The foundation laid for individual processes in Chapter 3 is developed further in Chapter 4, which covers such topics as: the basic elements in the perceptual process; why perceptions—not someone's definition of "objective" reality—are crucial in relating to and understanding others; factors that influence the formation of "biased" perceptions; forces influencing the development of attributions about people, things, and events; and the role of attributions in motivating and shaping behavior. Chapter 5, Managerial Problem Solving Styles, Chapter 6, Learning and Reinforcement, and Chapter 7, Work Motivation, have been thoroughly revised and updated.

Part III: Interpersonal and Group Processes (four chapters)

Each of these chapters has been updated and revised. Included in this part are Chapter 8, Interpersonal Communication, Chapter 9, Dynamics within Groups, Chapter 10, Dynamics between Groups, and Chapter 11, Leadership.

Part IV: Organizational Processes (three chapters)

Chapter 12, Organizational Culture, is a totally new chapter. Its inclusion reflects the considerable interest and attention given this area in the professional and academic literature. This chapter includes such topics as: the basic variables that go into defining an organization's culture; the role of top management in forming and changing organizational cultures; how organizational cultures can influence the efficiency and effectiveness of organizations; and the process of socialization of new and current employees that usually exists where there is a strong organizational culture. Chapter 13, Job Design, was reorganized to improve the flow of presentation. Chapter 14, Organization Design, represents an almost new chapter in the approach taken to this topic and the coverage provided.

Part V: Dynamics in the Work Environment: The Interaction of Individual, Group, and Organizational Processes (four chapters)

These chapters build on the preceding chapters by suggesting a variety of linkages among individual, group, and organizational processes. Chapter 15, Decision Making and Goal Setting, is totally new. This chapter includes such topics as: the five phases of managerial decision making; the scope and functions of organizational goal setting and how it can be used to influence individual effort and performance; how management by objectives can be applied as a management philosophy and system; and the purposes and importance of performance appraisal. Chapter 16, Power and Political Behavior, Chapter 17, Conflict within Organizations, and Chapter 18, Work Stress, were revised and updated to reflect the latest developments in these areas.

Part VI: Individual and Organizational Change (three chapters)

This part was expanded from two to three chapters. It includes Chapter 19, Career Planning and Development, Chapter 20, Nature of Planned Organizational Change, and Chapter 21, Approaches to Planned Organizational Change. Chapters 20 and 21 have been restructured to provide more concise presentations of the nature of and approaches to planned change.

Contributors to This Edition

We are grateful to the large number of individuals who have made significant contributions to all editions of this book. In particular, we express our deep appreciation to the following individuals for their many insights and suggestions, which led to improvements in this edition: Karen Dill Bowerman, California State University—Fresno; Anthony Butterfield, University of Massachusetts, Amherst; Gary L. Gordon, State University of New York—Oswego; James L. Hall, University of Santa Clara; Ralph Katerburg, University of Cincinnati; David M. Leuser, Plymouth State College; Richard Mann, Suffolk University; James C. McElroy, Iowa State University; Eric J. Walton, New York University; and George C. Witteried, University of Missouri—St. Louis.

We thank all the writers of the Management Incidents and Cases, whose names appear in the References at the end of the chapter in which the incident or case appears.

We continue to appreciate the excellent support and assistance from the many professionals at West Publishing Company. Our professional and personal working relationship with Dick Fenton, business editor, now spans 16 consecutive years. Our developmental editor, Esther Craig, was of tremendous help and assistance in handling the numerous tasks that had to be coordinated and expedited. Our production editor, Bill Gabler, was terrific in moving this book through the many steps of the production process at an almost unheard of speed, while maintaining the highest quality of production standards. Our copy editor, Jerrold Moore, was outstanding in improving the readability and flow of the manuscript.

For the prompt and accurate typing and the handling of many other critical administrative tasks associated with this edition smoothly and effectively, we thank administrative assistants Jane Bell (Southern Methodist University) and Janet Macha (Texas A&M University). Their many suggestions and keen insights were instrumental in improving the structure and flow of the book. In their proofing of galleys and pages, they not only found errors we missed, but provided additional suggestions for fine-tuning the text.

We are grateful to Dean William Mobley and Lyle Schoenfeldt, previous Head of the Department of Management at Texas A&M University as well as to Dean Roy Herberger and Mick McGill, Chair of the Department of Organizational Behavior and Administration at Southern Methodist University. They were instrumental in creating and supporting an environment that made the writing of this book possible.

December 1985

Don Hellriegel
Texas A&M University

John W. Slocum Jr.
Southern Methodist University

Richard W. Woodman
Texas A&M University

PART I

INTRODUCTION

Managers and Organizational Behavior

LEARNING OBJECTIVES

When you have finished studying this chapter, you should be able to:

- List the characteristics of successful companies.
- Explain what managers do.
- State the ten roles managers play.
- Name the three approaches to organizational behavior.
- Identify the basic concepts of the contingency approach to organizational behavior.

OUTLINE

Preview Case

Translo Energy Company

Ann Cannon, a recent college graduate from a midwestern university, started her career as a management trainee with Eastbrook Inns, a chain headquartered in Lancaster, Pennsylvania. Ann was first interviewed by a representative of Eastbrook during her senior year. She was impressed with their management training program and the promise of a quick opportunity to manage one of Eastbrook's motels and decided to go to work for the company. During the training program, the trainers noticed her drive to achieve and her ability to get along with others, make decisions, and listen to others. Graduating at the top of her training class, Ann was assigned to a motel outside of Atlanta as an assistant manager. She was told by the company that a typical assignment would last two to three years. After a year and a half as an assistant manager, Ann had grown tired of the job and wanted to do something else. She heard about a business that was looking for a director of sales and called the president. After a brief chat, Ann and the president decided to meet. The meeting went extremely well and the president offered Ann a job on the spot. Ann said that she would have to think about the offer because her husband might not be able to relocate where the company was located. The president asked Ann and her husband to spend some time in the new town. He promised to do his best to help her husband find a new job. After several visits, Ann and her husband decided that she should take the job and that he would take a job in a nearby town.

When Ann arrived on the job, she was impressed with the speed at which things got done at Translo. Few staff meetings were needed to make decisions, and orders were quickly processed and shipped. One of her first jobs was to formulate a sales plan for the company. One of her salespeople, Mike, had been hired recently by Translo and had been assigned to a regular territory in central Missouri. Mike had taken over this territory when one of the company's old-time salespersons retired. The territory had been a major producer of sales revenue in the central region for the past ten years.

After three months at Translo, Ann began to have serious doubts about Mike's selling ability, motivation, and experience with Translo products. Mike had not met his sales or his cost goals since joining the company. Ann was so busy with other work, that she had not been able to spend much time with Mike. She had looked at his sales numbers and wasn't impressed. Ann asked Barry Lynch, director of marketing, if he would make several sales calls with Mike and observe his sales techniques. After Barry and Mike spent a week together calling on customers, Barry reported back to Ann. Barry commented that Mike was poorly trained, didn't understand the technical specifications of Translo's products, and was having some interpersonal problems in the central Missouri office. These interpersonal problems seemed to stem from his inability to get along with the others in the office. Being single and located in a small town did not suit Mike's life style. The other salespeople in the office were married and many belonged to the same church and country club. Further, Barry believed that many deals were made in the locker room after a game of golf or tennis. Mike didn't participate in those

> sports and thus was left out of most of the informal conversation that eventually led to sales.
>
> During the next several months, Ann's responsibilities grew. She became deeply involved in preparing a five-year business plan that she would have to present to the board of directors and was instrumental in hiring a new director of finance. Because of these pressing activities, she had not been able to talk with Mike about what Barry had observed. What she did observe was that Mike was still not meeting his monthly sales quota.
>
> It just so happened that Ann's husband, John, was scheduled to make a business trip to central Missouri and Ann decided to go along with him for the long weekend. They left on Thursday afternoon and arrived that evening. Ann decided to relax and not call the company's central Missouri office, which was located in a nearby town. Friday afternoon she was relaxing by the motel's pool and happened to see Mike having a drink with a friend. She smiled, and he waved her over to meet his friend. After a brief conversation, Ann excused herself.
>
> When Ann returned to her office Monday morning, she saw a note from the office manager in central Missouri indicating that Mike had been absent all week with the flu and therefore had not been able to make any sales calls. Ann was furious. She picked up the phone and called Mike, seeking an explanation. Mike said that he had been sick earlier in the week and needed another day just to relax. He also told Ann that he didn't appreciate Barry making customer calls with him and acting as a watchdog. After a heated exchange, Ann said, "You're fired. Clean out your desk and leave by lunchtime. I'll inform the local manager."

Managing is a tough task and the difficulties that Ann had with Mike are typical. Ann is Mike's boss; but she had trouble getting him to do his work. The company expects Ann to get to know the people working for her well enough not only to maintain good day-to-day relationships, but also to obtain that extra effort when the going gets tough. What should Ann have done to boost Mike's performance? Managers face such decisions many times a day. The purpose of this book is to help you understand why problems like those facing Ann occur and to provide you with the means to resolve them.

What does Ann know? From her perspective, Ann knows only one thing for certain about Mike: his performance has been poor. Barry told her that he might have some interpersonal problems in the office and lacks selling skills, but that is only hearsay. Ann probably assumes that, because his performance is poor, his morale is low and that he lacks motivation. From Ann's viewpoint, trying to understand why Mike behaves as he does is like looking at the tip of an iceberg and trying to guess its size. Just as we can see only the one-ninth of an iceberg that is above water, Ann only knows certain things about Mike's behavior and how it affects Translo.

Consider the **organizational iceberg** in Figure 1-1 and relate it to Ann's situation. What should she know? As a manager, she should know something about the:

- goals of Translo, which are to make a profit, be a responsible member of each community in which it operates, show growth in sales of 15 percent a year, and become a leader in the energy field;
- technology of Translo, which includes computerized systems to handle the massive flow of paperwork, the oil rigs that drill for oil, the refineries that process oil, and the distribution systems that get the product to the consumer;
- structure of the company, which consists of the departments (human resources, engineering and construction, finance, marketing, sales, chemicals, legal) and the division of labor (president, vice-president, department manager, assistant department manager, and so on);
- skills and abilities required by employees to do their jobs, which include interpersonal, communications, technical, planning, and leading; and
- financial resources of Translo, which include current assets, liabilities, shareholders' equity, and the like.

Even with this knowledge about the company, Ann still does not know why Mike's performance is poor. She, like many managers, cannot see below the tip of the iceberg to the behavioral aspects of performance.

There are no easy or complete answers to why people and organizations do not always function smoothly. However, the study of **organizational behavior** provides a systematic way to attempt to understand the behavior of people in organizations. Because of the great diversity of people and organi-

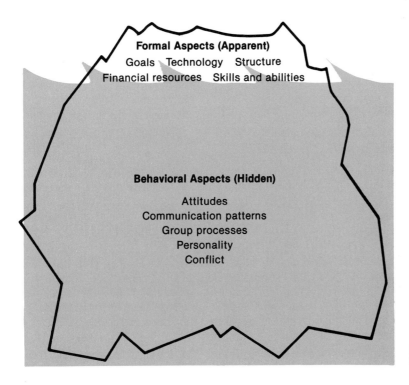

Formal Aspects (Apparent)
Goals   Technology   Structure
Financial resources   Skills and abilities

Behavioral Aspects (Hidden)

Attitudes
Communication patterns
Group processes
Personality
Conflict

FIGURE 1–1
Organizational Iceberg

zations, those engaged in the field of organizational behavior attempt to answer some intriguing questions, such as:

- What are the characteristics of successfully managed companies?
- What do managers do and how do they motivate employees?
- When do groups make better decisions than individuals?
- What kinds of people make the best leaders?
- How should an organization be structured to improve its effectiveness?
- What kinds of issues will people face during their careers and how can they resolve them?
- What are the major sources of stress in most organizations?
- What are the important factors in evaluating the work of others?
- How can people and organizations change?

Effective managers try to find answers to these and many similar questions. They also try to understand how their behavior affects others in the organization. In the chapters that follow, we present information that will help you to answer such questions and to become more aware of the importance of behavior in an organizational setting.

SUCCESSFULLY MANAGED COMPANIES

Good management is essential to the success of a company. In an attempt to find out what managers of successful companies do, Tom Peters and Bob Waterman studied 43 well-run companies, including International Business Machines (IBM), Procter & Gamble (P&G), Minnesota Mining and Manufacturing (3M), Texas Instruments (TI), Dana Corporation, and others. The results of their study were published in their book, *In Search of Excellence*, which by the summer of 1985 had already sold more than 5 million copies and had been translated into at least 15 different languages.[1]

Key Characteristics

Their study identified eight common characteristics, or principles, of these successfully managed companies.

- *A bias toward action.* Managers have a preference for doing something, rather than cycling a question through analysis and committee reports. At P&G, new product ideas must be condensed to one page or less.
- *Simple and lean form.* Small plants generally outperform large ones. Minnesota Mining executives believe that 200–300-person plants are the most effective. Hewlett-Packard and Digital Equipment managers say that there should be no more than 300–400. The key is small groups producing higher-quality goods or providing more personalized service, which are faster to innovate than larger groups. Small organizations also avoid excessive overhead and large numbers of staff people.
- *Staying close to the customer.* At P&G a toll-free 800 number is stamped on all products; each month, senior executives listen to customer complaints that have been taped with their permission. By lis-

tening to its customers, Milliken and Company, a large textile manufacturer, receives ideas for more than 50 percent of its product innovations.

- *Productivity improvement through people.* To increase productivity, people who do the actual work must be involved in decisions and exercise at least some control over the work. At the Edison plant of the Ford Motor Company, senior management put a button at each worker's station on an assembly line; an employee could push the button to shut down the line if he or she thought that the work up to that point or a part did not meet quality standards. People did push their buttons: they shut down the plant 30 times the first day and about 10 times a day thereafter. The average shutdown lasted only 10 seconds—just enough time to replace a faulty part, make a minor adjustment, tighten a bolt, and the like. Plant productivity increased, with the number of defects dropping from 17.1 per car to 0.8 per car. The total number of cars requiring rework fell by 97 percent.

- *Organizational autonomy to encourage entrepreneurship.* Managers are allowed and encouraged to be entrepreneurs and compete against each other. Minnesota Mining executives state that they always want the "second" product in a category to come from another competing 3M division. To encourage competition among divisions, divisional managers are given free hand to create new markets at companies like Johnson & Johnson, 3M, and Hewlett-Packard.

- *Stress one key business value.* Managers set one priority and try to do that one thing well: customer service at IBM, productivity improvement at Dana, new product development at Hewlett-Packard and 3M, and product quality at P&G. The company does not allow conflicting values to weaken its primary emphasis.

- *Emphasis on doing what they do best.* A successful company defines its strength—marketing, customer contact, new-product innovation, low-cost manufacturing—then builds on it. A retired Johnson & Johnson manager stated: "Never acquire a business you don't know how to run."

- *Simultaneous loose-tight controls.* If a few variables are tightly controlled (for example, costs and revenues), management may allow leeway in day-to-day operations. During the 1970s cost reduction was the name of the game. In an effort to drive costs down, many managers unintentionally gave too short shrift to service and quality. In the 1980s, the emphasis is on quality; it must come first.

Peters and Waterman claimed that companies that had recognized and acted on these eight characteristics performed better than those which had not used them. A follow-up study showed that some of the companies identified by Peters and Waterman (such as Atari, Levi Strauss, Texas Instruments, and Revlon) had started to lose money.[2] However, the original book's message and that of its sequel, *A Passion for Excellence*, maintain that successful companies have a competitive edge over other companies by paying more attention to people—employees and customers—and by sticking to the skills and values that they know best.[3]

Good Places to Work

A different group of researchers asked people to name characteristics that make a company a good place to work.[4] Based on the responses they received, the researchers identified 100 of the best companies to work for. A comparison of the lists of companies studied by Peters and Waterman and the other researchers indicated about a 20 percent overlap. Therefore what employees say about working for companies and the factors that managers believe lead to excellence are somewhat different. What did employees say? We can group their responses into four essential categories.

- *Management of human resources.* This included meaningful benefits and rewards, such as profit-sharing, stock options, and team rewards; job security, such as promotion from within and no layoffs; accurate and timely performance appraisals; and creative incentives for learning new skills.
- *Concern for others.* These companies stressed their social responsibilities, such as a concern for minorities and emphasis on integrity in community activities; and personal development, such as career counseling, educational opportunities, and the like.
- *Job climate.* This included flexible working hours, being called by their first names, direct access to top management, shared eating and parking facilities, and participation in decisions that affect their jobs.
- *Organizational design.* People like small, as opposed to large plants, want to work under pleasant working conditions, and have sufficient authority to make decisions without constantly checking with a supervisor.

A comparison of these two studies leads to two interesting conclusions. First, successful companies and companies that people would like to work for stress concern for the individual employee. Management should respect the dignity and inherent rights of the individual and maintain high moral and ethical standards in all relationships. This involves treating them as members of the team, allowing them some control over their own work, letting them know what the company is about, and acknowledging that they are an important source of ideas. Second, effective companies are managed by individuals who have clear values and visions for the company. Values are shared by employees and learned through the use of myths, rites, and ceremonies. For example, Domino's Pizza, the second-largest pizza chain after Pizza Hut, lives by its pledge to deliver a pizza within 30 minutes. Therefore one underlying principle is to never allow a store to run out of dough. When a store is almost out of dough, Don Vicek, the person in charge of distribution, tells his employees, "Charter a plane. Get it there!" Once when a store did run out of dough and had to be closed, the regional manager brought 1,000 black armbands and made his entire regional staff wear them. The message was quite clear.

BASIC CHARACTERISTICS OF MANAGERIAL WORK

Few of the thousands of books and articles written about managers tell us anything about what managers actually do.[5] They give us the impression that managers spend most of their time reading reports in their air-conditioned offices, trying to get to the airport to catch the 5:30 plane, entertaining important customers, and solving complicated problems. Studies of chief executives suggest that they seldom stop thinking about their jobs. Four nights out of five are spent working for the company. One night is spent at the office, another entertaining business associates. On the other two working nights, when the chief executive goes home, it is not to a place to rest but to a place that serves as a branch office for more work.

This management approach, while freeing some time at work for the executive, creates stress in most family situations. Moreover, tightly scheduled workdays, frequent travel, and simultaneous demands exert considerable pressures on managers. It is not uncommon for top managers to work 60 hours or longer each week. They have their coffee during meetings, and often devote lunchtime to informal meetings with other managers in the company's executive dining room. Should some free time occur, subordinates are eager to fill it with their questions, problems, and proposals.

One reason that managers work at such a fast pace is that managerial work is open-ended. Engineers can point to a bridge and know that the project is finished; computer programmers can make a system operational and know that their work on it is completed. However, the manager's job is fast-paced, continuous action. The manager is constantly responsible for the success or failure of the organization, and there are no guidelines that enable him or her to say, "My job is finished."

Managerial work has five basic characteristics: (1) hard work in a variety of activities; (2) nonroutine tasks; (3) face-to-face verbal communication; (4) involvement in communication networks; and (5) a blend of rights and duties.

Hard Work in a Variety of Activities

Many jobs require specialization and concentration. A machine operator may require 40 hours to machine a part; a computer programmer may need a month to design a system to handle the materials flow of the purchasing department; and a certified public accountant may need a month to audit the books of a large firm. But a manager's job is characterized by *variety*, *brevity*, and *fragmentation*. One study found that factory supervisors averaged 583 different job problems a day (about one every 48 seconds). As a result, supervisors have little time to plan.

A general manager's day might include processing mail, listening to a subordinate explain a consumer group's boycott of the company's product, attending a meeting with other community leaders to discuss how to handle the local water shortage, listening to another manager complain about the lack of office space, attending a ceremonial luncheon for an employee who is retiring after 45 years with the company, discussing the loss of an $8 million contract with the marketing manager, and discussing construction of another plant to make production more efficient. Constant interruptions and a variety of activities characterize the executive's day, and an effective manager must be able to shift gears quickly and frequently. According to one vice-president in charge of a finance division, "I change hats every ten minutes. I act as a tax specialist for a while, a manager for the next few minutes, then a banker, a personnel specialist, and so on."

A manager's actions are brief, and most activities take less than 10 minutes. Telephone calls average about 6 minutes (they are brief and to the point), unscheduled meetings about 12 minutes, and routine desk work (dictating letters, reading *The Wall Street Journal*, and so on) about 15 minutes. Few managers have time to do more than merely skim long reports and memos.

Managers engage in fragmented activities. They frequently leave meetings before the meetings are over and interrupt subordinates and others to discuss a problem. One study found that a manager worked undisturbed for as long as 23 minutes only 12 times in 35 days.

Preference for Nonroutine Tasks

Managers move toward the active elements in their work. They delegate to subordinates the more routine jobs, such as handling the mail or reviewing long reports. Managers constantly seek new and "hot" information, which is picked up from unscheduled meetings, telephone calls, gossip, and speculation, and are important parts of managers' sources of information. When they receive this type of information, they give it top priority.

Routine reports do not contain the latest information, so managers pay little, if any, serious attention to them. Although most managers have to write reports as part of their jobs, few managers take the time to read the reports of others. Top managers are especially concerned with what is happening today and what is likely to happen tomorrow.

Although managers prefer not to deal with routine tasks or information, this does not mean that they do not make appointments or that they miss appointments. Managers are well aware that an unspecified meeting time like "sometime next Friday" does not generate much interest. Only if a meeting time is stated can anyone make plans and a commitment to attend.

Managers work in a stimulus-response environment: they respond to the immediate situation. Mark Macklin, division manager of Wales Trucking, had to make fast decisions when an 18-wheeler spilled its cargo on an interstate highway. Was the driver okay? Was there personal or property damage? Which wrecking service was nearby? Was the cargo hazardous? Had the owner of the cargo been notified? Was the cargo insured? As soon as Mark handled that situation, another arose: his chief financial officer handed in her resignation to go into business for herself—effective immediately. Mark's immediate concern shifted to determining whether the books were up-to-date and correct and whether there was an assistant he could promote into this position.

Face-to-face Verbal Communication

Managers communicate in five ways: mail (documented communication), telephone calls (verbal communication), scheduled and unscheduled meetings (formal person-to-person communication), and tours (visual communication). Fundamental differences exist among these different means of communication.

Mail communication is characterized by formality, long delays in feedback, and little opportunity for give-and-take. Mail processing is a chore and is something to be done but not enjoyed. Managers can dispose of more than 30 pieces of mail per hour by just skimming over inconsequential matters like solicitations and acknowledgments. Nearly 90 percent of all mail communication does not deal with "live" action, so managers tend to avoid using it and ignore most of what they get.

Managers prefer verbal communication. As shown in Figure 1–2, 78 percent of all managerial time is spent using verbal communication: in meet-

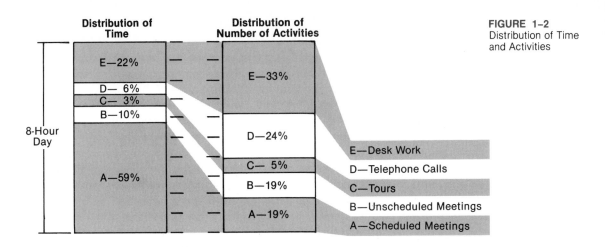

FIGURE 1–2
Distribution of Time and Activities

ings, on the telephone, and during tours. Telephone calls and unscheduled meetings are generally short, but together they account for nearly an hour and a half per day that an executive spends communicating verbally. Managers use the telephone and unscheduled meetings when the parties know each other and have to transmit information quickly. Through these forms of communication managers quickly give and receive a great deal of "live" information. When problems suddenly arise, unscheduled meetings can be called and telephone calls made to straighten things out.

Managers tend to hold scheduled meetings when a large amount of information needs to be transmitted, when information must be communicated to others who are not well-known to a manager, or when scheduling a meeting is the only way to bring together all the people who need the information.

Tours—walking through the building and chatting with employees—give managers a unique opportunity to get out of the office and talk informally with people. Managers use tours infrequently, but they are a good time to talk with individuals informally and to express personally their congratulations on a recent marriage, birth, graduation, or other achievements.

To summarize, managers like verbal communication. Informal telephone conversations and unscheduled meetings are important to maintain "live" action. Formal, scheduled meetings are used for special kinds of communication or for events that involve a large number of people, such as ceremonies, labor–management negotiations, and shareholder meetings. Communication is a manager's work. Managers do not do research, admit patients to the hospital, or write computer programs; they are transmitters and receivers of information—information that is essential to decision making.

Involvement in Communication Networks

Because managers prefer verbal communication, they are the center of communication networks that include subordinates, peers, superiors, and others outside the organization. Managers usually spend considerably more time with subordinates than with superiors (approximately one-third to one-half their time on the job). Studies of supervisors indicate that they spend only

10 percent of their time with superiors. The same appears to hold true for middle-level managers and top managers. Communication between first-line managers and their superiors is usually formal and includes routine written and verbal reports, such as status reports.

With whom do middle-level and top managers communicate? Much of their time is spent talking with other managers and people outside their departments and organizations. A manager must be in constant contact with managers of other departments about plans, facilities, schedules, customer problems, market opportunities, and people problems. Contacts outside the organization include those with trade associations, consultants, lawyers, underwriters, suppliers, government agencies, and consumer associations. Each of these groups provides special information to the manager. For example, the National Industrial Distributors Association keeps its members abreast of the latest legislation pending in Congress, union problems, and new product development.

Blend of Rights and Duties

What rights do managers have, and what duties do they perform? According to Peter F. Drucker,

> The manager has the task of creating a true whole that is larger than the sum of its parts. . . . One analogy is the conductor of a symphony orchestra, through whose effort, vision, and leadership, individual parts that are so much noise by themselves become the living whole of music. But the conductor has the composer's score; he is only the interpreter. The manager is both composer and conductor.[6]

Drucker portrays the manager as a person who brings order out of chaos. But there are times when managers are unable to control their activities. The telephone rings, the calendar pad is filled with a long list of meetings, subordinates drop in with a personal or organizational problem, and other unexpected problems arise.

Managers do have two important areas of freedom. First, they are able to make the decisions that initially define their long-term commitments. However, once they are committed, many of their activities will then be planned by others. For example, a manager can decide whether to join the board of directors of a local bank. Once the decision to do so is made, the manager is obligated to attend board meetings and spend other time on board business. Managers develop their own information channels and control the use of their time to a large extent through the key decisions they make.

Second, managers take advantage of their obligations. The retirement ceremony for an employee at Wales Trucking provides division manager Mark Macklin the opportunity to collect information from those in attendance. Also, during the short ceremony, Macklin can interject a few words about important company issues to those present. An effective manager seizes every opportunity to speak, to lobby for a cause, to short-circuit potential problems, and to kill stories in the rumor mill.

It should be clear by now that

■ managers spend most of their time communicating verbally;

■ the frequency of interaction with others is different for different managerial levels;

■ the importance of "hot" and "grapevine" information increases with the level of manager;

■ managerial work is hectic and fragmented; requiring the ability to shift continually from person to person and from problem to problem.

ACROSS CULTURES

What Do Managers Do in Other Countries?

The preceding sections focused on the work of American managers. Do these same characteristics apply to managers in other countries? In an attempt to identify the common work activities of chief executive officers in different countries, three researchers studied the activities of managers in Japan, Korea, and Hong Kong. The data in Table 1–1 compare the managerial activities of these managers and their U.S. counterparts.

Several interesting conclusions may be drawn from these data. First, most executives spend considerable time with others either in meetings or on tours and have very little time to themselves. Meetings, either scheduled or unscheduled, consume 70 percent of a manager's 8-hour day. Second, Japanese and Korean managers spend small amounts of time working in short segments, whereas American and Hong Kong managers spend considerably more time on activities of short duration. Japanese and Korean managers appear to be more deliberate in their work and devote a much higher percentage of their time to long discussions of issues. This does not imply that these managers are more effective than their U.S. and Hong Kong counterparts. Often Japanese and Korean managers discuss several topics during a meeting and try to reach consensus before breaking up. In both Korea and Japan, managers are very sensitive to rank and status, and often decisions cannot be made until the proper ritual and courtesies have been observed. The importance of group harmony that is rooted in Confucian laws in these countries requires managers to spend considerable time in social processes.[7]

TABLE 1–1   Distribution of Time and Activities For Managers in Different Countries

Category	Percent of Managers' Time			
	United States	Japan	Korea	Hong Kong
Desk Work	22%	24%	20%	10%
Telephone calls	6	1	2	11
Scheduled meetings	59	59	57	55
Unscheduled meetings	10	6	12	18
Tours	3	10	9	6
Duration of Activities				
Less than 9 minutes	49%	4%	10%	37%
Between 9–60 minutes	41	12	48	51
Longer than one hour	10	44	42	12

MANAGERIAL ROLES

According to Henry Mintzberg, there are ten different managerial roles. We define a **role** here as an organized set of behaviors. Figure 1–3 shows that these ten roles fall into three major groupings: interpersonal, informational, and decisional.[8]

Before we discuss each of these roles, let us consider these four points: (1) every manager's job consists of some combination of roles; (2) the roles played by managers often influence the five basic characteristics of managerial work; (3) the roles are described separately to aid in understanding them, whereas in practice they are highly integrated in a manager's job; and (4) the importance of these roles can vary considerably according to managerial level (first-line, middle-level, and top).

Interpersonal Roles

The three **interpersonal roles** arise directly from a manager's formal authority. The first interpersonal role is the *figurehead role*. The president who greets a touring dignitary, the mayor who gives a key to the city to a local hero, the supervisor who attends the wedding of a machine operator, the sales manager who takes an important customer to lunch—all are performing ceremonial duties that are important to the organization's success. While these duties may not appear to be important, they are expected of a manager. They demonstrate that management cares about its employees, customers, and others who deserve recognition.

The *leadership role* involves responsibility for directing and coordinating the activities of subordinates in order to accomplish organizational goals. Some aspects of the leadership role have to do with staffing, such as hiring, promoting, and firing. Other aspects concern motivating subordinates and ensuring to the greatest extent possible that the needs of the organization are consistent with the job-related needs of the employees. Still other aspects of the leadership role involve controlling the activities of subordinates and probing for problems that need managerial attention.

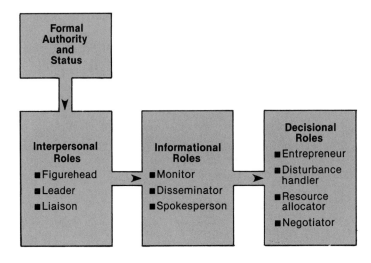

FIGURE 1–3
Managerial Roles

The *liaison role* involves dealing with people other than subordinates or supervisors—people such as clients, government officials, members of boards of directors, suppliers, and so on. In performing the liaison role, the manager gathers from others outside the organization information that can affect the organization's success. In effect, the liaison role helps to build the manager's information system and is closely related to the monitor informational role.

Informational Roles

Through these interpersonal roles, a manager builds a network of contacts, which enables the manager to receive and transmit vast amounts of information. A manager obtains and processes this information by playing three **informational roles**.

In the role of *monitor*, a manager is like a radar system, scanning the environment for information that may affect the department or organization's performance. Remember that a large part of the information received is verbal, often from gossip and hearsay. The role of monitor often enables the manager to be the best-informed person in his or her part of the organization.

In the *disseminator role*, the manager shares and distributes information to subordinates. Sometimes this information is passed along to subordinates as privileged information, meaning that—unless the manager passed it along—the subordinates would otherwise not have access to it. Passing information on to subordinates is often difficult and time consuming.

Finally as a *company spokesperson*, the manager transmits information to others in an official capacity. If the manager says it, the company says it.

Decisional Roles

The purpose of information is to help make decisions. As the person in charge of a department or an entire company, the manager can commit the organization to new courses of action. The **decisional roles** are perhaps more important than the interpersonal and informational roles because through them the manager actually commits the organization. A manager can play four different roles as decision maker.

As an *entrepreneur*, the manager seeks to improve the organization by initiating new projects or launching surveys to test new ideas. When Harry Cunningham became general vice-president for Kresge in 1957, he found a new direction for the chain: discounting. He developed the Kmart chain, and, before the first Kmart opened, he committed the company to $80 million in leases and merchandise for the original thirty-three stores. As the nation's premier discounter, he was able to change the direction of Kresge and the meaning of discount stores for the United States. As an entrepreneur, Cunningham was an initiator of change.

In the role of *disturbance handler*, managers respond to situations beyond their immediate control—situations such as a strike, a major supplier who goes bankrupt, or a supplier who reneges on a contract. Disturbances like these happen even to the best of managers because they cannot do much to anticipate and prevent them. Good managers learn how best to handle these disturbances when they do occur. Poor managers not only have these unforeseeable kinds of disturbances but also the preventable kinds that stare them in the face while waiting to occur.

As a *resource allocator*, a manager is responsible for deciding who will get which resources and how much they will get. These resources may include budgeted or extra funds, equipment, personnel, and access to the manager's time. A manager must continually make choices as to how resources will be allocated. Should money be spent for painting walls or new furniture? What proportion of the budget should be earmarked for advertising and what proportion for improving the existing product line? Should a second shift be added, or should the company pay overtime to handle new orders?

Closely linked to the resource allocator role is the *negotiator* role. As negotiators, managers bargain with others to obtain advantages for their department or company. For example, a purchasing manager negotiates with suppliers for lower costs and faster delivery times; a sales manager negotiates a price reduction to keep a major customer happy. These negotiations are an integral part of a manager's job because only the manager has the information needed to make decisions and the authority necessary to commit the organization to a course of action.

Summary of Roles

Ten managerial roles add up to one manager. A manager who does not perform all ten roles probably is not performing very well. Nevertheless, a manager may perform some roles more vigorously than others, depending on personal style, managerial level, type of organization, and career path.

Let us look briefly at how one top executive, Samuel Johnson, plays the decisional roles.

In Practice: Samuel Johnson of Johnson and Son, Inc.

Samuel Johnson is the chairman and chief executive officer of Johnson and Son, Inc., a $2 billion consumer products company. Founded in 1866 by Johnson's great-grandfather, the company has grown into one of the U.S.'s largest private corporations by churning out new product after new product in the floor wax market. But in the late 1970s, the company's new product development and growth stalled. The bureaucracy got bigger and poor strategic decisions were made. For example, top management made the mistake of moving away from what the company did best—packaging consumer goods—by acquiring 15 other companies, whose products ranged from scuba gear equipment to tent making. But what turned out to be "hot" markets turned into losses. Thanks to these strategic blunders, the company's growth into foreign markets also stagnated.

Johnson is determined to make his company leaner, more efficient and quicker to react to changes in the marketplace by intensifying competition in its markets. In 1982, he instituted a one-year wage freeze and with the help of some early retirement plans trimmed the number of employees by 3,500. These decisions were a marked contrast for Johnson Wax, one of the first companies to give employees paid vacations, pensions, and profit-sharing.

Even more important was his decision to reorganize the company in the summer of 1984. The purpose of the reorganization was to motivate managers, who had been traditionally preoccupied with only their function, such as marketing, finance, or manufacturing, to act as business managers in charge of one of the company's four major divisions—personal care (Agree Shampoo), home care (Pledge and other waxes), specialty chemicals, and insecticides (Raid). The new management structure is designed to put Johnson and Son on the leading edge of technology in these four product lines. Each of these product managers now has complete control over its own manufacturing, research and development, and marketing. With this new structure, if a personal care product is to be sold, the responsibility for that entire project is now in the hands of that product line manager. With the new structure in place, a manager's pay can now be more closely tied to performance. Since the reorganization, these divisions have added more new products, packaging designs, and promotional schemes than the company had done in the latter part of the 1970s.[9]

APPROACHES TO ORGANIZATIONAL BEHAVIOR

Now that we know some characteristics of successfully managed companies and what managers do, we can begin to understand *why* they do what they do. Furthermore, when we learn why employees do what *they* do, we can come to an understanding of the organizational behavior. We begin by looking to the behavioral sciences for help. The **behavioral sciences** represent a systematic body of knowledge drawn from sociology, psychology, and anthropology for the purpose of helping us understand why and how people behave as they do. We will apply several important concepts from the behavioral sciences to help us understand individual and group behaviors within organizations and how managerial actions can affect these behaviors. As we will discover, there are no simple solutions for organizational behavior issues and problems. Seldom is there one best answer or the ideal organization.

The key to understanding behavior in organizations is knowing what to look for and what to look at. We can begin by looking at an entire organization, or we can begin by looking at small parts of the organization, such as individuals, teams, groups, and departments. However, examining one part of an organization is not enough; eventually we must also know something about how that part relates to the other parts and to the whole. Tom Landry, coach of the Dallas Cowboys, says that to gain an understanding of a football team's performance, you need to give attention to each unit. For example, on the kick-off, how far did the receiving team return the ball? How many times did the team have the ball within its opponent's 30-yard line and fail to score? How many punts did the team block? Only by analyzing each unit's strengths and weaknesses can the coach get a feel for how well the entire team is functioning.

Traditional Approach

Originally it was thought that there was only one way to manage people because all organizations were the same, managerial tasks were identical, and all employee jobs were similar. This may have been true to some extent during the early part of this century, but today this approach is considered to be overly simplistic and, in fact, incorrect. The **traditional approach** to organizational behavior emphasized the development of principles that were appropriate to all organizations and managerial tasks.[10] These "universal principles" were generally prescriptive: there was only one way to manage organizations and employees. But that began to change with Frederick W. Taylor, Elton Mayo, F. J. Roethlisberger, and Douglas McGregor, who sought to develop concepts that would increase managers' understanding of behavior. Their work was the beginning of a more modern and realistic approach to human resources management.

TAYLOR   Frederick W. Taylor advocated the scientific management of factory production, using time-and-motion studies, standard parts, and standard processes, among other scientific and efficiency techniques. (Chapter 13 describes his approach in more detail.) Taylor's approach was to observe production operations in order to determine how they could be performed most efficiently.[11] He believed in a system of rewards and punishments geared to performance and output. Taylor also advocated setting up a system of management controls so that supervisors would have to deal only with the exceptional problem situation and not have to personally supervise the routine activities of subordinates.

MAYO AND ROETHLISBERGER   In the 1920s and 1930s, Elton Mayo and F. J. Roethlisberger of Harvard University applied their knowledge of sociology to industrial experiments at Western Electric Company's Hawthorne Plant.[12] (Chapter 9 discusses how the structure of the group affects its members' behavior.) Their work showed that an organization should be viewed as a social system; that the social setting played a more important role in influencing workers' behaviors than did management's rules and regulations. The results of their experiments emphasized that the worker is not a simple tool, but a complex personality interacting in a group situation that is often difficult for managers to understand. Mayo and Roethlisberger believed that, instead of trying to improve employee job performance according to Taylor's principles of scientific management, managers could improve performance by humanizing the work situation. In other words, managers should adopt participative leadership styles and pay attention to the social setting in which employees work. In the Preview Case, how much did Mike's lack of acceptance by his co-workers affect his performance?

MCGREGOR   In 1960, Douglas McGregor introduced a powerful perspective of the behavior of employees in organizations.[13] This perspective has been labeled Theory X and Theory Y. Before proceeding, take a few minutes and complete the questions in Table 1–2. The basic characteristics of both theories are summarized in Table 1–3.

Theory X implies an autocratic approach to managing people. According to Theory X, most people dislike work and will try to avoid it if possible. People are not willing to make a 100-percent effort because they are lazy. They have little ambition and will avoid responsibility if at all possible. They are self-centered, indifferent to organizational needs, and resistant to change. The ordinary rewards given by organizations are not enough to overcome employees' dislike for work, so the only way that management can get a high level of performance is to coerce, control, and threaten them. Although some managers may deny that they hold this view of people, their actions prove that they do—Theory X is their view of employees.

Theory Y implies a humanistic and supportive approach to managing people. According to Theory Y, people are not lazy. If they appear to be lazy, this behavior grew out of their experiences with organizations. If manage-

Table 1-2 **Management Practices Questionnaire**

Complete the following questionnaire. Indicate your agreement or disagreement with each of the eight statements by a check mark on the scale below each statement. Determine the appropriate score by noting the points for the response you made to each statement. For example, if your response to Question 1 was strongly agree you would give yourself five points; disagree is worth two points; and so on. Add the eight scores together.

1. The average human being prefers to be directed, wishes to avoid responsibility, and has relatively little ambition.

Strongly Agree (5)	Agree (4)	Undecided (3)	Disagree (2)	Strongly Disagree (1)

2. Most people can acquire leadership skills regardless of their particular inborn traits and abilities.

Strongly Agree (5)	Agree (4)	Undecided (3)	Disagree (2)	Strongly Disagree (1)

3. The use of rewards (for example, pay and promotion) and punishment (for example, failure to promote) is the best way to get subordinates to do their work.

Strongly Agree (5)	Agree (4)	Undecided (3)	Disagree (2)	Strongly Disagree (1)

4. In a work situation, if the subordinates can influence you, you lose some influence over them.

Strongly Agree (5)	Agree (4)	Undecided (3)	Disagree (2)	Strongly Disagree (1)

5. A good leader gives detailed and complete instructions to subordinates rather than giving them merely general directions and depending on their initiative to work out the details.

Strongly Agree (5)	Agree (4)	Undecided (3)	Disagree (2)	Strongly Disagree (1)

6. Individual goal setting offers advantages that cannot be obtained by group goal setting, because groups do not set high goals.

Strongly Agree (5)	Agree (4)	Undecided (3)	Disagree (2)	Strongly Disagree (1)

7. A superior should give subordinates only the information necessary for them to do their immediate tasks.

Strongly Agree (5)	Agree (4)	Undecided (3)	Disagree (2)	Strongly Disagree (1)

8. The superior's influence over subordinates in an organization is primarily economic.

Strongly Agree (5)	Agree (4)	Undecided (3)	Disagree (2)	Strongly Disagree (1)

☐ Total Score

Scoring Key: A score of greater than 32 points indicates a tendency to manage others according to the principles in Theory X. A score of less than 16 points indicates a tendency to manage others according to the principles in Theory Y. A score somewhere between 16 and 32 indicates flexibility in the management of others.

TABLE 1–3   McGregor's Theory X and Theory Y

Theory X	Theory Y
■ The typical person dislikes work and will avoid it if possible.	■ Work is as natural as play or rest.
■ The typical person lacks responsibility, has little ambition, and seeks security above all.	■ People are not inherently lazy. They have become that way as a result of experience.
■ Most people must be coerced, controlled, and threatened with punishment to get them to work.	■ People will exercise self-direction and self-control in the service of objectives to which they are committed.
	■ People have potential. Under proper conditions they learn to accept and seek responsibility. They have imagination, ingenuity, and creativity that can be applied to work.
With these assumptions the managerial role is to coerce and control employees.	With these assumptions the managerial role is to develop the potential in employees and help them release that potential toward common objectives.

Source: McGregor, D. *The Human Side of the Enterprise.* Copyright © 1960 by McGraw-Hill, Inc. Used with permission of McGraw-Hill Book Co.

ment will provide the proper environment to release the employees' potential, work will become as natural to them as play or rest. People will exercise self-direction and self-control to achieve objectives to which they have become committed. Therefore management's role is to provide an environment in which this potential can be released at work.[14]

McGregor argued that management had been ignoring the facts about people. Management had been following an outmoded set of assumptions about people because it adhered to Theory X, when the facts are that the behavior of people more nearly matches the set of assumptions in Theory Y. Most employees have at least some Theory Y potential for growth. Managers had failed to recognize this potential; consequently, their policies and practices failed to develop it. The result was that many people did not regard work as an opportunity for growth and fulfillment. Management needed to adopt a whole new theory, Theory Y, for working with people.

Systems Approach

One way to understand behavior is to assume that people do things for simple (uncomplicated) reasons. The tendency to think only in causal terms is an example of simple reasoning. For example, the automobile accident was "caused" by the carelessness of one of the drivers or by dangerous road conditions or by some other single factor that could be cited as the cause of a particular automobile accident. If we were to make a list—and it would be a long one—of single causes of automobile accidents, it would clearly show that many, if not all, of the items on the list could play some role in any one accident.

If the single-cause assumption is inadequate, an obvious substitute is the assumption that events are caused by many forces working in a complex interrelationship. In order to establish conditions that would reduce the frequency of automobile accidents, the primary factors associated with collisions *and* the interrelationships of these factors would have to be studied. The idea of a "system" assumes multiple causation and a complex interrelation of forces: everything is related to everything else. Organizations can be thought of as numerous systems, such as work flows, reward structures, communication networks, and role structures. All these systems, functioning together, constitute what we commonly refer to as an *organization*. The **systems approach**, which emphasizes the interrelatedness of parts and suggests the importance of interpreting an individual part only in the context of the whole, can lead to an understanding of organizational behavior.[15]

In order to be effective, managers do not need to know *all* that can be known about every relevant system. (If we did, we would never finish analyzing the first problem we encountered.) Instead, we establish who we are and our role, capabilities, and goals. We choose to analyze only the systems we want to control or understand and ignore other systems that involve conditions beyond our control.

Achieving the purpose of this book—to learn how to deal with behavior within organizations—entails learning about the individuals, groups, structures, and other factors that affect the behavior of people in organizations. Therefore we will describe and explain individual and group behavior, group interaction, and the role of groups within organizations—and their interrelationships.

Contingency Approach

The **contingency approach** to organizational behavior rejects the notion that universal principles can be applied to managing behavior in organizations. Its basis is the belief that there is no one set of rules that can be applied to all situations.[16] Further, no situation falls into one of a set of neatly defined classifications. Each situation must be characterized on its own and then managed accordingly. Principles are like proverbs—they give managers insight in a vague, general way. Principles have important functions, however, and the contingency approach uses principles when the situation calls for them.

Before reading further, examine and answer the questions in Table 1–4. If you answered maybe/sometimes to all the questions, you already have a good idea of the meaning of the contingency approach. For example, satisfied workers are not always more productive; the satisfaction they derive from their jobs can come primarily from the work group, co-workers, and the ability to form friendships at work, all of which have very little to do with performance. Bureaucratic organizations, such as McDonald's, Kmart, Burger King, Anheuser-Busch, and State Farm Insurance Company, are efficient because they perform routine tasks and their customers, suppliers, and regulatory bodies are relatively stable. Daily changes in McDonald's menu, for example, would make it a less efficient operation. Not all workers want challenging jobs. Many workers want jobs that provide good pay, require little thinking, provide security, and offer good fringe benefits (for example, vacation time, sick days, paid holidays, and life/medical insurance). These workers turn down promotions to jobs that would challenge them.

ADVANTAGES OF THE CONTINGENCY APPROACH   What are some advantages of using the contingency approach to understanding organizational behavior? First, rather than proposing that there is one best way to design organizations or departments, motivate employees, lead subordinates, conduct group meetings, and design reward and punishment systems, the contingen-

TABLE 1-4   Contingency Quiz

Instructions: Answer each of the following questions by checking yes, no, or maybe/sometimes.

	Yes	No	Maybe/Sometimes
1. Satisfied workers are more productive workers than dissatisfied workers.	___	___	___
2. Adding a piece-rate pay system to a job context where the employee is already intrinsically motivated to work will be best in the long run for management.	___	___	___
3. Bureaucracy is inefficient and is a bad way to organize.	___	___	___
4. Workers should participate in decisions that concern them.	___	___	___
5. Workers want challenging jobs.	___	___	___
6. Cohesive work groups are more productive than noncohesive work groups.	___	___	___
7. Organizational structures should be very flexible and readily changed to achieve maximum productivity.	___	___	___
8. Leaders should use styles that are person oriented rather than task oriented.	___	___	___
9. The behavior observed in an organization is the result of the total of all the personalities in it.	___	___	___
10. Cohesiveness among group members will result in better group decision making than will a lack of cohesiveness.	___	___	___

cy approach advocates a variety of management responses based on the characteristics of the specific situation. The key to becoming a successful manager is to diagnose the situation correctly.

According to the contingency approach, the nature of the organization's environment, its size, its technology, the character of its markets, its legal charter, its personnel, and other factors not only confront the organization with problems but simultaneously offer opportunities. Organizations do not respond to a problem by "solving" it; rather changes evolve as organizations respond both to the problem and the opportunity. Thus organizations should adapt to situations. The contingency approach holds that different kinds of structures, reward systems, and change strategies may be appropriate responses to different situations.

The second advantage of using the contingency approach stems from the belief that the environment of an organization is constantly changing. Managers must recognize and adapt to changes that are occurring both inside and outside of the organization. For instance, managers who assume that their market is stable will not be successful for very long. The Gillette Company offers an example of how a company adapted its marketing strategies to fit the market place.

In Practice: The Gillette Company: Marketing Razors in Europe

The international division of the Gillette Company operates 31 factories in 22 countries overseas and accounts for well over one third of the firm's total sales. Gillette has had considerable experience in developing marketing strategies that fit European life-styles. The company carefully analyzes and plans everything from choosing a product's name to its promotional strategy, as the company has done with its Trac II razors.

For the European market, Gillette decided on the brand name of G II for the razors known as Trac II in the U.S., after detailed research studies showed that in some Romance languages "trac" means fragile. Said a Gillette vice-president, "We wanted our target audience—men—to know that they could count on a good strong razor and not one that would easily break." Gillette verifies all brand translations for accuracy at the international division's London office.

In promoting the G II razor in Europe, Gillette has relied on print advertising, because many consumers do not have television. The promotion theme for G II features a sports analogy showing the importance of coordinating movements to reach a goal (in G II's case, the goal is a clean, close shave). The sports analogy is understood by Europeans and it is readily adaptable to print media. In all, Gillette has prepared more than 50 advertisements focusing on tennis players, boxers, and, of course, soccer players. These ads are adapted to individual cultures, pretested by market, and monitored for effectiveness.

The Trac II is promoted quite differently in the U.S., where television commercials are used extensively. The U.S. theme centers on the razor's construction. An animated sequence shows the first blade raising the whiskers on a man's face and the second blade shaving the whiskers closely.

While the G II razor has been quite popular in Europe, its success in other parts of the world, such as Latin America, the Middle East, and Africa, is more doubtful. Many consumers in these regions consider razors to be a luxury, and a number of countries restrict the import of razors by placing high tariffs or embargos on them.

Gillette is also facing difficulties in the marketing of some of its products in Europe. For example, it has been unable to stimulate demand for deodorants, because "the people of the European continent have a cultural resistance toward anything that impedes perspiration. They see it as unhealthy."[17]

NO ONE BEST WAY The fundamental concepts of the contingency approach are more difficult to grasp than the traditional principles of management. They do, however, facilitate a more thorough understanding of complex situations and increase the probability that managers will take action that is appropriate and yields the intended results. An old Chinese proverb perhaps best summarizes this advantage:

> Give a person a fish, and you feed that person for a day;
> Teach a person to fish, and you feed that person for life.

The contingency approach enables a manager to diagnose each situation so that he or she can manage it effectively. We want to teach you to fish, not simply to give you fish.

FUNDAMENTAL CONCEPTS OF ORGANIZATIONAL BEHAVIOR

One purpose of this book is to clarify the basic knowledge about the behavior of people in organizations. Students of physics or accounting learn certain basic, or fundamental, principles. The law of gravity is the same in Dallas, in Paris, and in Singapore; a hydrogen atom in New York is identical to a hydrogen atom in Los Angeles. An account receivable is carried on the books of a company in Seattle the same way it is on the books of a company in Atlanta; a cash transaction credit and debit are the same in Boston as they are in Phoenix. Such hard-and-fast rules do not exist for people and their behavior in organizations; nevertheless, four fundamental concepts can help us to understand people and managers and their behavior in most situations.

Basics of Human Behavior

One of the basic concepts of psychology is that people are different from each other. From the day of birth each person is unique, and experiences in life increase the differences among people. This means that managers can get the best performance from individual employees by treating them according to their individual differences.

Both internal and external factors shape a person's behavior on the job. Some of the internal factors that affect a person's behavior are learning ability, motivation, perception, values, and personality. (These factors are discussed in more detail in Part II.) Among the external factors that affect a person's behavior are the organization's reward system, organizational politics, group behavior, managerial leadership styles, and organizational structure. These factors are examined in Parts III, IV, V, and VI.

Situational Perspectives

For years behavioral scientists have stressed that individual behavior is a function of the interaction between the personal characteristics of the individual and the situation. In order to understand a person's behavior in a work-related situation, we must analyze the pressures that the situation places on the person. For example, what are the situational factors affecting Sam Johnson's reorganization of Johnson and Son, Inc.? Some of the most important ones were loss of market share to competitors, rising costs of manufacturing, slow introduction of new products into the market, and the inability to pinpoint authority and responsibility.

Specifying all the factors in a situation is complex and can be very time consuming. The *contingency approach* can be used to identify and diagnose only the significant factors involved. This is done by examining the components of the specific situation—organizational structure, peer group pressures, leadership, job-related stress, organizational politics—and selecting for analysis those that are significant.

Organizations as Social Systems

People in organizations have both psychological and social needs; they have needs for approval, status, and power; and they play many roles (interpersonal, informational, and decision-making). Individuals' behavior is influenced by their group. Sometimes managers can use groups to improve performance and also satisfy employees needs for belongingness. Consider how top managers at Society National Bank used groups to improve performance.

In Practice: Society National Bank

One hour each week, several teams meet at Society National Bank of Cleveland. The teams consist of 4 to 12 members each, plus a group leader. The bank's top management decided to create these "quality circles," as the teams are called, to help solve problems. Management believes that the program has improved communications throughout the bank, increased the total awareness of all employees, decreased turnover and absenteeism, and generally aided the development of human resources and customer relations.

The concept of quality circles is based on the premise that it is not *what* people can do that is important; rather, it is what they *want* to do. By developing the participative management program, the bank has seen improvement in the attitudes and behavior of people at all levels of the organization.

More than 130 officers and employees are currently involved in the bank's quality circle program. Each team receives 14 weeks training in group decision making, communications skills, and human relations skills. The team members then put their skills to use to solve work problems and improve bank performance. Some recent accomplishments are:

- Branch Team—reduced balancing time from 45 minutes to 20 minutes at the end of each business day.
- Domestic Collection Team—developed new ways of processing redemption coupons in-house for a savings of $45,000.
- Customer Service Team—reduced customer calls from 3 percent to 1 percent; and reduced the percentage of calls answered by recorded messages from 5 percent to 2 percent.

The executive vice president and chief financial officer of the bank concluded: "We are convinced that employees and managers who are involved in shaping how they do their work achieve a superior work output. Today's world requires people who will acknowledge that they are responsible for their efforts and respond accordingly.[18]

Interaction between Structure and Process

Accomplishing something in organizations involves knowing who to see and how to present an idea to that person. **Structure** refers to how people are grouped within an organization. Recall that Sam Johnson restructured Johnson and Son by grouping people into four product divisions. Each division now has the responsibility for making its own products competitive in the market. **Process** refers to how the sequence of activities in the organization are carried out. Decision making, leadership, communication, and conflict-resolution practices are processes in organizations. At Johnson and Son, Sam Johnson now requires each of his four product-division managers to exercise leadership and make decisions for their own products. The four product managers are now entrepreneurs, free to run the divisions as they see fit. On the other hand, at Society National Bank, decisions are made by groups. Therefore the process by which their decisions are made and carried out requires the participation of employees and managers in making joint decisions.

ORGANIZATIONAL BEHAVIOR: A FRAMEWORK

The framework for understanding the behavior of employees in organizations consists of five basic components: (1) individual processes; (2) interpersonal and group processes; (3) organizational processes; (4) the interaction of individual, group, and organizational processes; and (5) individual and organizational change processes. The relationships among these components, as well as the important dimensions of each, are shown in Figure 1–4. As we

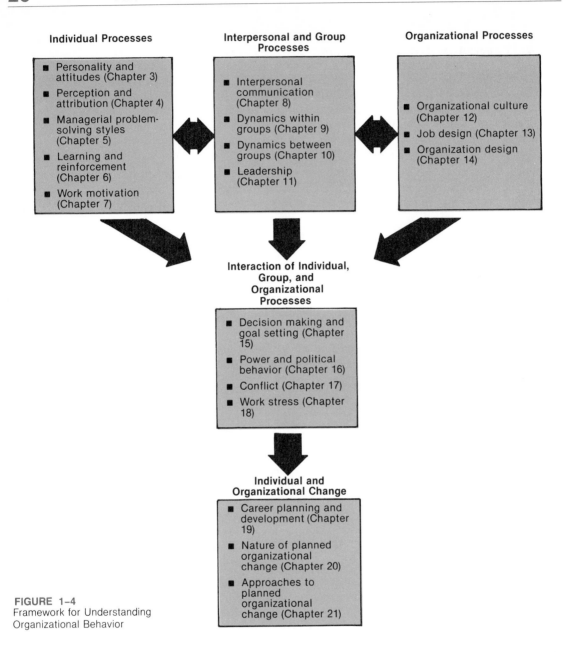

Individual Processes

- Personality and attitudes (Chapter 3)
- Perception and attribution (Chapter 4)
- Managerial problem-solving styles (Chapter 5)
- Learning and reinforcement (Chapter 6)
- Work motivation (Chapter 7)

Interpersonal and Group Processes

- Interpersonal communication (Chapter 8)
- Dynamics within groups (Chapter 9)
- Dynamics between groups (Chapter 10)
- Leadership (Chapter 11)

Organizational Processes

- Organizational culture (Chapter 12)
- Job design (Chapter 13)
- Organization design (Chapter 14)

Interaction of Individual, Group, and Organizational Processes

- Decision making and goal setting (Chapter 15)
- Power and political behavior (Chapter 16)
- Conflict (Chapter 17)
- Work stress (Chapter 18)

Individual and Organizational Change

- Career planning and development (Chapter 19)
- Nature of planned organizational change (Chapter 20)
- Approaches to planned organizational change (Chapter 21)

FIGURE 1–4
Framework for Understanding Organizational Behavior

analyze each one and its dimensions, we will begin to see a pattern emerge for understanding behavior in organizations.

The relationships among the components are much too dynamic to describe them by stating "laws." The variety of events that constantly occur affects the behavior of people in organizations and makes these relationships dynamic. For example, what happens when a company suddenly decides to restructure its organization and lay off people? In 1985, Superior Chemical Corporation announced that its specialty chemicals division, located in Lawson, would no longer report directly to the president, but that division would now be merged with the company's plastics division, located in Kerrville, North Carolina. To avoid duplication of jobs, people in the chemical division were given the opportunity of early retirement, the opportunity to move to Kerrville, or career counseling to help them find another job out-side of Superior. The behavior of managers and employees in the chemical division radically changed; it became *contingent* on decisions made by people in the plastics division more than 1,200 miles away. This example highlights three important factors involved in the contingency approach to organizational behavior: environment, behavior, and consequences.

First, the behavior of individuals in the Lawson office had for years been autonomous with respect to the people in the plastics division. Now the *environment* had changed. Business plans, sales calls, marketing re-ports, and international trade agreements had to be worked into the strate-gic business plan of the plastics division.

Second, the *behavior* of individuals in an environment depends on their alternatives. Those employees who had been with the company for 25 years or longer chose early retirement; those with key managerial positions trans-ferred to Kerrville and took up new assignments in the plastics division; and many were laid off by the company and started interviewing for other positions.

Third, the *consequences* of any behavior must be understood in that particular environment. Consequences are always contingent on behavior within the environment. At Superior, early retirement wasn't a feasible al-ternative for people in their mid-30's who were trying to raise children and make mortgage and car payments because of the low level of benefits pro-vided. Conversely, for those who had been with the company for 30 years and whose children had grown up and moved away, early retirement might be a feasible alternative. The consequence of taking early retirement might mean more time for leisure activities, or the possibility of starting another career in an entirely new field.

Individual Processes

Each person makes assumptions about the people with whom he or she works, supervises, or spends time in leisure activities. These assumptions, to some extent, influence a person's behavior toward others. Effective man-agers understand the psychological influences that affect their own behavior before attempting to influence the behavior of others. (Chapters 3–7 focus on factors that influence the behavior of individuals.)

Individual behavior is the foundation of organizational performance. Understanding individual behavior therefore is critical for effective manage-ment, as illustrated in the Preview Case. Each individual is a physiological system composed of a number of subsystems—digestive, nervous, circula-tory, and reproductive—and a psychological system composed of a number of subsystems—attitudes, perceptions, learning, personality, needs, feel-ings, and values. In this book, we concentrate on the individual's psychologi-cal system.

Because organizational effectiveness depends on individual perfor-mance, managers such as Ann Cannon and Sam Johnson must have more than a passing knowledge of the determinants on individual performance. In Chapter 3, we examine how personality and attitudes can affect an individ-ual's behavior on the job. An individual's capacity to learn depends on per-ception, which we discuss in Chapter 4. Because each person gives his or her own meaning to a situation, different individuals view the same situation differently. How do you think Mike perceived the situation when Ann saw him sitting with a friend by the motel pool? Do you think that Ann saw the situation similarly? One way in which a manager communicates his or her perceptions about the situation is the method used to make decisions. Chapter 5 focuses on ways in which managers gather information and make decisions about important organizational events.

Many managerial decisions are communicated to employees through an organization's reward system. Chapter 6 indicates ways that managers can use rewards to increase or decrease the behaviors of employees. Most managers agree that there are a number of ways to motivate others; motivation is extremely important because it is tied so closely to performance. Chapter 7 explains how behavior is stimulated, sustained, and stopped in organizations.

Interpersonal and Group Processes

People are inherently social; generally, it is not their nature to live or work alone. We are born into a group called a *family* and would likely not survive without membership in it. Almost all our time is spent interacting with others in groups and in interactions of our groups with other groups. We are educated in groups; we worship in groups; we play in groups. Our personal identity is derived from the way in which we are perceived and treated by other members of our groups. Thus skills in group functioning are vital to all managers. The time that managers spend in meetings takes up more than two-thirds of their working day. (See Figure 1–2.) Closely related is interpersonal communication (Chapter 8) which is also a key skill possessed by most successful managers.

Many of the goals of an organization can be achieved only with the coordination and cooperation of others. The history of organizations like GM, GE, IBM, Westinghouse, Kodak, and RCA is the history of organized groups that were created to provide mutual benefits, to find ways of improving the quality of life, and to satisfy the needs of their members and customers. The productivity resulting from effective group action makes the development of group skills one of the most essential aspects of managerial training. Furthermore, membership in productive and cohesive groups is essential to maintaining psychological health throughout a person's life.

Being an effective group member means understanding the dynamics of what happens in and between groups. Methods of increasing the group effectiveness are the topics covered in Chapters 9 and 10. Group members must be skillful in eliminating most barriers to the accomplishment of the group's goals, in solving problems, in maintaining productive interaction among group members, and in overcoming obstacles to developing a more effective group.

Management today needs leaders who have the ability to integrate employee goals with organizational goals. The ability of organizations to achieve their goals depends on the degree to which the leaders' ability and style enable them to control, influence, and act effectively. Chapter 11 examines how leaders influence others and choose a leadership style.

Organizational Processes

Individuals enter organizations to work and to pursue their own career goals. The process by which the individual learns of the organization's expectations is through the organization's culture (Chapter 12). Culture is the important set of assumptions and understandings that people share in the organization about how things really work in the company, that is, which policies, practices and norms are really important. Newcomers have to understand the underlying culture of the organization in order to be successful. Some companies use formal programs, whereas others simply rely on co-workers to socialize the newcomer about what to do and not do in the organization.

To work effectively, managers must have a clear understanding of their jobs and the organization's structure. Chapter 13 describes the process of job design by which managers specify jobs, methods and relationships among jobs at various levels. The technology utilized by the company has a tremendous impact on the design of managers' and employees' jobs.

Organization design (Chapter 14) refers to the overall structure of the organization. An organization chart presents an oversimplified view of authority, responsibility, and functions within an organization. Organizational structures are far more complex than that. Some of the factors that influence the design of an organization and some typical organization designs are the major features of this chapter. Sam Johnson's reorganization of Johnson and Son illustrates some of the basic considerations involved in the successful restructuring of an organization.

Interaction of Individual, Group, and Organizational Processes

The quality of decision making in an organization depends on selecting proper goals and identifying realistic means for achieving them (Chapter 15). Organizations rely not only on individuals but on groups as well to make timely decisions. Integration of individual and organizational processes, can lead to effective group decision making. Managers evaluate the performance of individuals and groups by using performance appraisal systems. The results of performance appraisals are used by managers to make decisions about who gets promoted, the size of pay raises, terminations, demotions, and transfers.

Not all behavior engaged in by managers is for the purpose of improving the performance of the firm. Power and political behavior (Chapter 16) are realities of organizational life. Managers use power to accomplish goals, and in many cases, to strengthen their own positions in the organization. A person's success or failure in using or reacting to power is largely determined by his or her understanding of power, knowing how and when to use it, and being able to predict its probable effects on others.

Conflicts between people and groups are common occurrences in many organizations (Chapter 17). As a result, people may compete against each other, or one group may compete against another. While competition among people or groups can have beneficial results, too much or the wrong kinds of conflict can produce negative results. Thus managing conflict is an important aspect of being a successful manager.

Stress is an important result of the interaction between the job and the individual. Whether stress has positive or negative effects depends on the individual's tolerance level. How people react to stress and how managers deal with stress—their own and their subordinates'—is important (Chapter 18). For example, a person who is never late for appointments, is very competitive, always feels rushed, and tries to do many things at once is prone to have high blood pressure, heart problems, and high levels of anxiety. Since managers have more control over the work environment than do their subordinates, it seems only natural that they have more opportunity to effectively contribute to how subordinates can cope with stress. Some individuals react to stress through increased motivation and commitment to finish the job. Others respond less positively by turning to outlets such as alcohol or drugs in an attempt to cope with stress.

Individual and Organizational Change

Most individuals look to an organization for opportunities to achieve satisfying work experiences throughout their careers. Chapter 19 emphasizes that a career consists of both attitudes and behaviors over a long period of time. How people react to organizational events, such as relocation, promotion, demotion, or firing, are related to their personality, career stage, and career alternatives. For example, a single person in her 20's, living in New York City, might react quite differently to relocation in a small rural town than a person who has school-age children and wants to avoid the complexity and problems of big-city life.

The management of change involves adapting an organization to the demands of the environment and modifying the actual behaviors of employees. If employees do not change their behaviors, the organization cannot change. A manager must consider many things when undertaking organizational change, including the types of pressures being exerted on the firm to change, the kinds of resistance to change that are likely to be encountered, and the person or persons who should implement change. A general model of organizational change is presented in Chapter 20, and four basic managerial strategies for achieving change are discussed in Chapter 21.

These strategies are:

- People approaches—using behavioral science techniques to involve employees in diagnosing organizational problems and planning actions to correct them.
- Technological approaches—changing the methods by which work is accomplished.
- Structural approaches—rearranging organizational authority, responsibility, and decision making.
- Task approaches—redesigning individuals' jobs.

SUMMARY

This chapter described the typical job characteristics of managers, some of the problems facing them, and how behavioral science techniques can improve managerial effectiveness. The five basic characteristics of managerial work are (1) hard work in a variety of activities; (2) a preference for nonroutine activities; (3) face-to-face verbal communication; (4) involvement in communication networks; and (5) a blend of rights and duties.

To accomplish their work, managers perform ten different roles, which can be grouped into three broad categories: interpersonal, informational, and decisional. Through the interpersonal roles of figurehead, leader, and liaison, managers exercise their formal authority within the system. The monitor, disseminator, and spokesperson roles enable managers to establish and maintain a network of personal contacts that are used to give and receive a wide range of information. Information is, of course, the basic input to the managers' decisional roles. As decision makers, managers are entrepreneurs, disturbance handlers, resource allocators, and negotiators.

Three approaches to the study of organizational behavior are the traditional approach, the systems approach, and the contingency approach. The contingency approach is not based on a fixed set of principles, although proven management principles are utilized when the situation calls for it. The contingency approach looks at the interrelationships within and among the various groups within an organization because each individual and group is dependent on others. The contingency approach is based on four fundamental concepts: (1) people are different; (2) behavior is a function of the personal characteristics of the individual, as well as the characteristics of the situation; (3) organizations are social systems; and (4) both structure and process variables influence employee behaviors.

The five major components of organizational behavior are (1) individual processes; (2) interpersonal and group processes; (3) organizational processes; (4) the interaction of individual, group, and organizational processes; and (5) individual and organizational change.

KEY WORDS AND CONCEPTS

Behavioral sciences
Contingency approach
Decisional roles
Informational roles
Interpersonal roles
Organizational behavior
Organizational iceberg

Process
Role
Structure
Systems approach
Theory X
Theory Y
Traditional approach

DISCUSSION QUESTIONS

1. How effective was Ann Cannon as Mike's manager? What are some of the dimensions you would choose for rating her performance as a manager?

2. Why are there differences between the characteristics of successfully managed companies and characteristics of companies you would like to work for? As a manager, how would you address these differences?

3. Why is a manager's job often described as hectic and fast paced?

4. Consider the various roles that the dean and the departmental chairperson of your college or university play. What are their similarities and differences?

5. Describe in your own words the model for this book. Apply it to your decision to attend the college or university of your choice.

6. What are the major differences among the traditional, systems, and contingency approaches to the study of organizational behavior?

7. What are the differences between Theory X and Theory Y managerial practices?

8. Apply the contingency approach to your study habits.

MANAGEMENT INCIDENTS AND CASES

Tony O'Reilly of Heinz: His Day has 57 Varieties

Through aggressive marketing, smart acquisitions, and fanatical attention to the bottom line, Tony O'Reilly has helped transform Heinz into one of the best performers in the food industry since he became Chief Executive Officer (CEO) in 1979. In 1984, Heinz was recognized by Merrill, Lynch, Pierce, Fenner & Smith as the best-run and best-structured of the major food companies. In 1984, Heinz earned a profit of $237.5 million on sales of $4 billion. O'Reilly still owns and manages several businesses in Ireland that range from newspapers to an oil exploration company. He has had several financial setbacks in Ireland primarily because the oil exploration company drilled several dry holes. To insure that this doesn't happen again, he is on the telephone almost daily with his Irish managers from Heinz's corporate headquarters in Pittsburgh. No key strategic decisions are made without his approval. Besides his business interests in Ireland, he is the founder and director of the Ireland Fund, which raises money to promote peaceful solutions to the troubles in Ireland.

His involvement in these activities makes for a grueling schedule. To make sure that all things get done, he makes a list each morning of what he absolutely must do. Sometimes the lists are quite long. For example, on one day he chaired a five-hour budget meeting at Heinz, caught a plane to Boston so that he could catch a flight to Ireland to speak at an Ireland Fund dinner the following day. After the speech, he caught a plane to New York City to attend a meeting of the Board of Directors for Mobil Oil Corporation. That evening, he flew to California for business and then back to Ireland to attend a funeral of some close friends who were killed in a plane accident.

O'Reilly's ability to do many things at once started during his college days. As a world class rugby player, he set a world record that still remains unbroken. On a rugby tour when players on his team would go out drinking and chase women, he would schedule meetings with senior executives at banks to learn about their problems. He believes that sports are analogous to running a business. "If you want to be better than anyone else, you better be as fit as them. And when you're fit and talented, it's determination that differentiates the good player from the great player."

His arrival at Heinz in 1979 sent shock waves running through the company. He started by putting in 14-hour days at what had been a 9-to-5 operation. To change Heinz, he shut down four factories, eliminated about one-third of Heinz's white-collar work force, and conceded defeat in the company's battle to compete with Campbell Soup Co. in the retail soup market. His acquisition of Weight Watchers International has more than offset the loss of sales to Campbell Soup. Since 1980, Weight Watchers classes and foods sales have more than tripled to more than $600 million yearly.

His management style is anything but traditional. He used to invite several hundred Heinz employees out to his eight-acre estate near Pittsburgh for Christmas Eve dinner and a football game called, "The Souper Bowl." The game's purpose was so employees could meet each other in an informal atmosphere. The games went on for years until they became too aggressive. O'Reilly still invites employees over, but now they play tamer sports, such as soccer or volleyball.

He has plans to expand Heinz's products into foreign markets such as Western Europe, China, and Japan. In 1985, Heinz plans to spend $25 million to launch its new instant baby food. According to him, "It's only next week's game that counts. The fans quickly forget last week's."[19]

Questions

1. What characteristics of managerial work did O'Reilly's day illustrate?
2. What roles did he play?

REFERENCES

1. Peters, T., and Waterman, R. *In Search of Excellence: Lessons from America's Best-Run Companies*. New York: Harper & Row, 1982.

2. Who's Excellent Now? *Business Week*, November 5, 1984, 76–88; Kinsley, M. Excellence by the Hour. *Fortune*, December 10, 1984, 225–232.

3. Peters, T., and Austin, N. *A Passion for Excellence*. Chicago: Random House, 1985. Also see Peters, T. and Austin, N. A Passion for Excellence. *Fortune*, May 13, 1985, 20–32.

4. Levering, R., Mokowitz, M., and Katz, M. *The 100 Best Companies to Work For in America*. Reading, Mass.: Addison-Wesley, 1984. For a different list of companies and criteria, see Sellers, P. America's Most Admired Corporations. *Fortune*, January 7, 1985, 11–30.

5. Most of these ideas are taken from Mintzberg, H. *The Nature of Managerial Work*. New York: Harper & Row, 1973. Also see Stewart, R. A Model for Understanding Managerial Jobs and Behavior. *Academy of Management Review*, 1982, 7, 7–14; Whitely, Wm. Managerial Work Behavior: An Integration of Results from Two Approaches. *Academy of Management Journal*, 1985, *28*, 344–362; Kotter, J. What Effective General Managers Really Do. *Harvard Business Review*, November-December 1982, 156–167; Gomez-Mejia, L., McCann, J., and Page, R. The Structure of Managerial Behaviors and Rewards. *Industrial Relations*, 1985, *24*,147–154.

6. Drucker, P. *Management: Tasks, Responsibilities and Problems*. New York: Harper & Row, 1973, 398.

7. Excerpted from Doktor, R., Lie, H., and Redding, S. A Day in the Life of a CEO—In Japan, South Korea, Hong Kong, and the United States. Paper presented at Second Pan-Pacific Conference, Seoul, Korea, May 1985.

8. Mintzberg, H. *The Nature of Managerial Work*.

9. Trying to Bring Out the Old Shine at Johnson Wax. *Business Week*, May 13, 1984, 138–145.

10. For further examples of these principles, see Hellriegel, D., and Slocum, J. *Management*, 4h ed., Reading, Mass.: Addison-Wesley, 1986, Chapter 2.

11. Taylor, F. *The Principles of Scientific Management*. New York: Harper and Brothers, 1911.

12. Mayo, E. *The Human Problems of an Industrial Civilization*. Cambridge, Mass.: *Harvard University Press*, 1933; Roethlisberger, F., and Dickson, W., *Management and the Worker*. Cambridge, Mass.: Harvard University Press, 1939; Sonnenfeld, J. Shedding Light on the Hawthorne Studies. *Journal of Occupational Behaviour*, 1985, *6*, 111–130.

13. McGregor, D. *The Human Side of Enterprise*, 2d ed. New York: McGraw-Hill, 1985.

14. Kiechel, W. How to Manage Your Boss. *Fortune*, September 17, 1984, 207–208.

15. Scott, W. *Organizations: Rational, Natural and Open Systems*. Englewood Cliffs, N.J.: Prentice-Hall, 1981.

16. Tosi, H., and Slocum, J. Contingency Theory: Some Suggested Directions. *Journal of Management*, 1984, *10*, 9–26.

17. Evans, J., and Berman, B. *Marketing*, 2d ed. New York: Macmillan, 1985, 640–641.

18. Abstracted from Quality Circles Solve Problems at Society National Bank. *American Banker*, May 6, 1983, 5, 10.

19. Abstracted from Symonds, W., and Wilson, A. Tony O'Reilly of Heinz: His Day Has 57 Varieties. *Business Week*, December 17, 1984, 72–73.

2 Learning about Organizational Behavior

LEARNING OBJECTIVES

When you have finished studying this chapter, you should be able to:

- State the three steps in the scientific approach.
- Identify the conditions for weak and poorly designed research projects.
- List the four research designs commonly used by managers.
- Describe ways that managers can gather data for a research project.
- State the ethical dilemma that could face managers when carrying out research.

OUTLINE

Preview Case

Performance Appraisal at Brooklyn Union Gas

Brooklyn Union Gas can trace its history back to the turn of the century. It provides gas services to customers in the borough of Brooklyn, New York. During the past few years, Brooklyn Union Gas has thought about redesigning its current performance appraisal system to meet the needs of its managers better. Recently, Harry Sutherland, Assistant Manager for Human Resources, met with Joseph Reisig, Director of Human Resource Planning, to discuss the company's need to redesign its system, what it should contain, and how to implement changes in it.

Joe and Harry believed that an effective performance appraisal system would accomplish three objectives. First, it should provide a structure for the growth and development of employees by examining both their potential and demonstrated work behavior. This would involve helping employees improve their current performance levels and guiding employees toward the maximum use of their abilities. Second, an effective performance appraisal system should provide people with clear feedback on how well they are doing. When employees receive such feedback, they are better able to make decisions about improving performance and what is adequate and acceptable behavior. An effective program would also provide methods for accurately measuring performance and helping managers give feedback to employees. Finally, a better performance appraisal system should assist managers in making long-range pay and promotion decisions, linking rewards (money, assignment of increased responsibility, autonomy) to actual performance more directly.

Thus Harry and Joe were faced with decisions about the kind of appraisal system to adopt, which managers should participate in these decisions, what materials should be presented to them, who should conduct training sessions, where the training sessions should be held, and how to evaluate the success of the new system.

The problems that Harry and Joe faced are not unlike those confronting many managers. The idea of training managers in the use of a new performance appraisal seems like a good one, but the questions raised in the Preview Case must be answered before any training starts. Unfortunately, managers often develop simplistic theories and approaches that are easy to understand, remember, and apply generally—but not very effective. Managers can no longer justify simplistic prescriptions for organizational problems (for example, "A satisfied worker is a productive worker"). This chapter will help you learn to solve managerial problems in organizational behavior by providing a framework for thinking about issues and applying the scientific approach to problem solving.

THE SCIENTIFIC APPROACH

Good management involves the ability to understand job-related problems and to make valid predictions about employee behavior. The key to this is understanding the **scientific approach,** a method for seeking out and analyz-

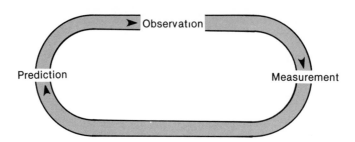

FIGURE 2–1.
The Scientific Approach

ing information in a systematic and unbiased manner. Figure 2–1 illustrates the three basic steps of the scientific approach: observation, measurement, and prediction. These steps are so basic that most people, without even realizing it, use them in their everyday living. The Dart Transportation Company is but one example of successful use of the scientific approach, in this instance to understand a costly employee turnover problem.

In Practice: Dart Transportation Company

Jim Steffel, president of Dart Transportation Company, was trying to figure out what was wrong. Jim has set a goal of $32 million in sales revenue in 1985. To reach this goal, Jim had to have 300 drivers in his fleet's operation. During 1984, driver turnover was nearly 75 percent. Jim knew that unless he and his assistant, Glen Pratter, could devise a plan to reduce turnover to 35 percent a year, it would be impossible to achieve the sales goal. Jim and Glen guessed that it cost the company $550 to recruit and train a driver who could handle the company's eighteen-wheelers. If the company could reduce turnover by 40 percent, that would also save the company a considerable amount of money.

Jim and Glen thought that they should first call the drivers who had quit the company and ask them why they had left. Was it for more money, shorter trips, more time at home, or what? While Glen was making these inquiries, Jim arranged for drivers, in groups of five or six, to stop by his office and chat about the problems they were having as drivers for Dart. Jim also arranged his busy schedule to spend time at major truck stops around the Chicago area where he could listen to what other truckers were saying about Dart and other companies. During these sessions, Jim would observe the drivers' responses to questions about pay, time off to go home, fuel charges, equipment malfunctions, and the length of time it took for the drivers to get paid. Jim and Glen also visited with several of the firm's largest customers and chatted with their shipping managers about Dart's drivers.

After several weeks of gathering these data, Jim and Glen felt that they had heard most of the drivers' complaints. To see if these complaints were real, Glen devised a measurement system to find out the actual number of times a driver got home, whether the drivers were able to drive about 10,000 miles a month, whether the drivers were paid on time, and whether the drivers were taking advantage of fuel and equipment purchases from company-run truck stops throughout the country. From these measurements Jim and Glen were able to identify those drivers who had profiles that matched those who left Dart and those who had stayed. This enabled Jim and Glen to predict the type of driver that would probably leave the firm. Those drivers who left Dart had (1) a higher number of injury accidents; (2) less total outside income; (3) delivered less loads; (4) made less money; and (5) ran more unloaded miles. In hiring new drivers, Jim and Glen now were able to focus more clearly on those factors that lead to high turnover than before their study.

This example illustrates the three basic steps of the scientific approach and some of its other important aspects. For example, Jim and Glen observed the drivers in several different situations rather than focusing on a single example of performance. If managers base conclusions about a person's performance solely on observations made at one time or in one particular situation, they may wrongly conclude that a worker is either a high or low performer. At Dart, for example, one employee might have been observed to be late for a customer pickup, but her reports were accurate and on time; the driver might have gotten to the customer late simply because she had a poor connection with the dispatcher and went to the wrong customer. The scientific approach encourages managers to study all the events that could affect an individual's performance. A thorough study—not just a one-shot observation or a study of a few isolated incidents—is needed. The scientific approach also requires managers to systematically test their assumptions. A careful testing of assumptions about an apparent problem may reveal that it does not exist or is less or more serious than initially assumed. The scientific approach guards against preconceptions or personal bias by requiring as complete an assessment of the problem or issue as resources permit.

Managerial applications of the scientific approach are not necessarily cold and clinical. Again, using an illustration of performance appraisal, employees being evaluated can receive feedback on their performances. Managers can encourage them to build on their strengths and give them advice on how to overcome their weaknesses. How employees react to this feedback becomes a part of an ongoing performance appraisal system.

PREPARATION OF RESEARCH DESIGNS

A **research design** is a plan, structure, and strategy of investigation developed to obtain answers to one or more questions.[1] The *plan* is the researcher's overall program for the research. It includes a list of everything the manager will do from the start until the final analysis of the data and submission of the report. The plan should identify the types of data to be collected, sample populations, research instruments, methods of analysis, tentative target completion dates, and the like. The *structure* is an outline that specifies the variables to be measured. Diagrams can be used to show the variables—and their assumed relationships—that are to be examined during the research. If we want to examine students' learning in a class, for example, the structure might indicate an assumed direct relationship between student evaluations of faculty performance and academic achievement. The *strategy* presents the methods to be used to validate the data, to achieve research objectives, and to resolve the problems that will be encountered in the research. In the classroom study, for example, strategic issues would probably focus on how to validly measure academic achievement and faculty performance. Other strategic questions might be: What happens if students do not sign their evaluation forms or if some students fail to fill out the forms completely? What statistical tests will be used to measure the degree of association between the two variables?

Purposes of Research Designs

A research design has two major purposes: to provide answers to questions; and to provide control for nonrelevant effects that could influence the results of the study. Researchers draw up research designs to obtain answers to questions as objectively, accurately, and economically as possible. The design determines what observations to make, how to make them, and how to analyze them. A *nonrelevant effect* is anything the manager has little control over but that could affect the results. In the classroom example, nonrelevant effects might include absence of half the class or return of an examination the day that instructor performance was evaluated.

Fundamentals of Research Designs

Rarely does a research design satisfy all the criteria associated with the scientific approach, but managers should strive to satisfy as many as possible in choosing their design.[2] The ultimate findings of a poorly conceived research design may be invalid or have limited applicability. The ultimate product of a well-conceived design is more likely to be valid and receive serious attention.

HYPOTHESIS   The design of a research project typically provides for the collection of data about a hypothesis in such a way that inferences of a causal relationship between an independent (causal) variable and a dependent (effect) variable can legitimately be drawn. A **hypothesis** is a statement about the relationship between two or more variables. It asserts that a particular characteristic or occurrence of one of the factors (the **independent variable**) determines the characteristic or occurrence of another factor (**dependent variable**). Hypotheses constructed by Jim and Glen at Dart Transportation include the following:

- Drivers who have working spouses are more likely to stay with Dart than those without working spouses.
- Truckers who drive more than 10,000 miles a month are more likely to stay with Dart than those scheduled to drive less than 10,000 miles a month.
- Drivers who have fewer injury accidents are more likely to stay with the firm than those who have many injury accidents.

Managers make a hypothesis and then investigate to determine whether the facts support or disprove it. A cause-and-effect relationship often is not easy to establish; yet managers informally pose hypotheses daily in making decisions. With this in mind, let us examine the basics of an experimental design.

EXPERIMENTAL DESIGN   Some types of hypotheses provide more convincing grounds for drawing causal inferences than do others. The concepts of causality and experimental designs are complex, and a thorough analysis of them is beyond the scope of this book. Therefore we will limit this discussion to points that are essential to an understanding of the requirements for an adequate research design.

In the Preview Case, Joe and Harry wanted to test the hypothesis that subordinates of managers who adopt the new performance appraisal system would perform better than those of managers who do not adopt the new system. In an experimental setting, Harry and Joe would arrange for one group of managers to attend performance appraisal training and for another group of managers not to attend this program. They would determine who would or would not attend the program by random selection or matching.

In *random selection,* each person has an equal chance of being selected. One way to obtain a random selection involves assigning each manager a number and then consulting a table of random numbers. Another way is to flip a coin for each manager: heads attend; tails do not. Random selection ensures that any experimenter preconceptions or biases do not influence the choices. Each manager would have the same chance as any other manager of being assigned to the program.

In *matching,* people first must be determined to be equal in all respects that are considered to be relevant to the experiment. In the performance appraisal example, all managers might have to be on the same managerial level, have been with the company for ten years, and be earning at least $35,000 a year. The managers who fit these requirements would then be divided into two groups (quite possibly by random selection).

Two groups are always used in an experiment.[3] The **experimental group**— in this example, managers receiving performance appraisal training—is exposed to the treatment, or independent variable. The **control group**—managers not taking the program—is not exposed to the treatment. Following completion of the training program Harry and Joe would compare job performance data on managers in the experimental and control groups. If the managers who adopted the new performance appraisal system had subordinates who performed better than those of the managers who did not take the training, Harry and Joe might have a basis for concluding that the new appraisal system had a positive impact on subordinates' productivity.

The use of a control group would permit them to rule out other causes for improvement in managerial job performance. Significant causes include:

- Natural maturing or development. Whether or not managers attended the program, day-to-day experiences that have nothing to do with that training could affect their performance.
- The influence of the measurement process itself. If managers felt that they were being studied, they might respond differently than if they felt that they were not being studied.
- Contemporaneous events other than the exposure of the managers to the program. Events that occurred during the training that were completely uncontrollable by the researcher might affect managers' performance.

Managers could increase their ability to give meaningful performance appraisals during the period of the training program whether or not they attended the sessions. However, if this maturing process could be assumed to be the same in the experimental and control groups, and if it could be assumed that the effect of the program was not specific to any given career stage of a manager, the effects of maturation could be ruled out when comparing the two groups.

If the managers felt like guinea pigs in the experiment, or if they felt that they were being tested and must make a good impression, the measurements obtained could distort the experimental results. (Variations in experimental designs can be used to take the effects of the measuring process into account but are too complex to discuss here.)

Contemporaneous events may affect the outcome of the experiment but cannot be controlled by the researcher. For example, while the managers were attending the program, a feature story in *Fortune* indicated that (according to a nationwide sample of chief executive officers) executives who were able to accurately assess the performance of others were in great demand by companies. The story, if read by most of the managers in the training program, might lead to an increased use of the new appraisal system by the managers regardless of the type of training program. Like maturational effects, however, if such an event affected the experimental group and the control group in the same way, this common effect would not be a cause of differences between them in terms of job performance.

The story about sugar and ants was told by Mark Twain. After reading it, name the independent and dependent variables.

In Practice: Sugar and Ants

I constructed four miniature houses of worship—a Mohammedan mosque, a Hindu temple, a Jewish synagogue, a Christian cathedral—and placed them in a row. I then marked 15 ants with red paint and turned them loose. They made several trips to and fro, glancing in at the places of worship but not entering.

I then turned loose 15 more painted blue; they acted just as the red ones had done. I now gilded 15 and turned them loose. No change in the result; the 45 traveled back and forth in a hurry persistently and continuously visiting each fane, but never entering. This satisfied me that these ants were without religious prejudices—just what I wished; for under no other conditions would my next and greater experiment be valuable. I now placed a small square of white paper within the door of each fane; and upon the mosque paper I put a pinch of putty, upon the temple paper a dab of tar, upon the synagogue paper a trifle of turpentine, and upon the cathedral paper a small cube of sugar.

First I liberated the red ants. They examined and rejected the putty, the tar, and the turpentine, then took to the sugar with zeal and apparent sincere conviction. I next liberated the blue ants and they did exactly as the red ones had done. The gilded ants followed. The preceding results were precisely repeated. This seemed to prove that ants destitute of religious prejudice will always prefer Christianity to any other creed.

However, to make sure, I removed the ants and put putty in the cathedral and sugar in the mosque. I now liberated the ants in a body, and they rushed tumultuously to the cathedral. I was very much touched and gratified, and went back in the room to write down the event; but when I came back the ants had all apostatized and gone over to the Mohammedan communion.

I saw that I had been too hasty in my conclusions, and naturally felt rebuked and humbled. With diminished confidence I went on with the test to the finish. I placed the sugar first in one house of worship, then in another, till I had tried them all.

With this result: whatever Church I put the sugar in, that was the one the ants straightway joined. This was true beyond a shadow of doubt, that in religious matters the ant is the opposite of man, for man cares for but one thing: to find the only true Church; whereas the ant hunts for the one with the sugar in it.

TYPES OF RESEARCH DESIGNS

There are many different types of research designs, and numerous textbooks have been written on the subject.[4] There is a growing recognition that managers and prospective managers need a basic knowledge of certain research methods in order to understand the contributions and limitations of research in organizational behavior. In addition, this discussion should temper the tendency to rush into cause-and-effect solutions to problems that frequently confront managers.

Managers should familiarize themselves with the similarities and differences among several research designs so that they can select the most efficient designs for the problem at hand. Managers should select the design that will do the most complete job, which depends on:

- The kinds of information the design provides.
- The purity of the data; that is, how confident the researcher can be about inferences based on the findings.
- The amount of time and money required and available to perform the research.
- The kinds of resources needed by the researcher and organization in order to use the design.

Instead of scientifically considering these and other issues, managers often select a research design, become comfortable with it, and then apply it in situations where its usefulness is limited. Unfortunately, prior habits, experiences, and biases often play a significant role in determining the manager's choice of research design. Instead of becoming solely interested in, say, laboratory experiments or field surveys, a manager should understand and appreciate basically the usefulness of all the available research designs.

The four most common types of research design are the case study, the field survey, the laboratory experiment, and the field experiment. They may be interrelated in many ways, and Figure 2-2 suggests one type of linear relationship. Although other feedback loops are possible (for example, field survey to case study, laboratory experiment to field survey, case study to laboratory experiment, and so on), the rationale for the sequence shown in Figure 2-2 is appealing because:

- A case study of an organization may identify one or more important variables that a researcher can then investigate by means of a field survey.

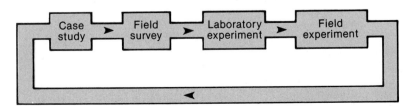

FIGURE 2-2.
A Linear Relationship of Research Designs

Source: Adaption of Figure 2–2 (p. 4) from *Organizational Experiments: Laboratory and Field Research* by William Evan. Copyright © 1971 by William Evan. Reprinted by permission of Harper & Row, Publishers, Inc.

- The major relationships uncovered in the field survey may leave un-answered questions concerning the dynamics and the cause-and-effect relationships among the important variables that can be pursued in a laboratory experiment.
- If the laboratory experiment yields a relationship of general significance to theory or practice, the researcher can then explore the importance of the relationship in a field experiment.

Case Study

In a **case study,** a researcher seeks detailed information about an individual or a group through a review of records, interviews and questionnaires, and observations.[5] The case study is a particularly useful method for stimulating insights into problems in relatively new areas where there is little experience to guide the researcher.

Three distinctive features of the case study make it an important tool for stimulating new insights. First, the researcher can adopt an attitude of alert receptivity, of seeking rather than testing. The factors being studied guide the researcher, who is not limited to the testing of existing hypotheses. Second, the case study is intense. The researcher attempts to obtain sufficient information to characterize and explain the unique aspects of the case being studied and other cases with which it shares common factors. Third, the case study relies on the researcher's ability to draw together many diverse bits of information into a unified interpretation.

If the researcher gives careful attention to these three key features, the case study can be an effective research technique for the analysis of organizational behavior. It is highly adaptable to many problems found in organizations; such as in obtaining the reactions of a newcomer to an established work group. A newcomer to a group tends to be sensitive to social customs and practices that members probably take for granted. For example, a six-person work group loses one member because of retirement, and a newcomer to the plant fills this vacancy. The social practices of the group (lunch breaks, kidding each other while working, and the bowling league) and its production standard (no more than 100 axles per day) must be communicated to this newcomer. In the analysis of the newcomer's reactions, the depth that can be attained through the case study is its major advantage.

The researcher must also consider the limitations of the case study. The method's most prominent disadvantage is that generalizing the results of one case study to other cases is not usually practical or logical. That is, only rarely can two cases be meaningfully compared in terms of essential characteristics (growth potential, number of employees, location, number of products made, levels of hierarchy, and technology used to manufacture the goods). Therefore case studies can rarely be repeated exactly or their findings applied validly to other settings.

A further disadvantage is that a case study does not usually lend itself to a systematic investigation of cause-and-effect relationships. Although a case study extending over time can offer the opportunity to determine changes, the range of variations observed in the case study may be too limited for practical cause-and-effect analysis. Case studies therefore may not yield definitive proof or rejection of a hypothesis; however, they frequently provide many clues and insights for further investigation.

Field Survey

In a **field survey,** data are collected through interviews or a questionnaire from a sample of people selected to represent the group under examination.[6] Using a sample avoids the expensive and time-consuming procedure of taking a census, or a complete accounting of every person in the group being studied.

The intent of a field survey is to gather information—to find out how people feel and think—and not to change or influence the respondents. You may be familiar with the ABC-Lou Harris poll. This field survey asks people to express their opinions about such topics as the economy, presidential decisions, and proposed legislation in Congress. Each person in the sample is asked the same series of questions. Their answers are combined in an organized way from which the researchers draw conclusions and state the results.

The field survey is not the best research design for obtaining some kinds of data; its use is limited to data about things that the respondents are consciously aware of. If people's unconscious motivations are important, an in-depth personal interview would be more productive.

A field survey generally requires a large number of people in its sample in order to draw valid conclusions. Of those initially selected to be sampled, many fail to respond: typically, only 20–30 percent of the people who receive a questionnaire fill it out. A single firm may have too few employees to provide an adequate sample (but too many for a 100-percent survey), and the case study then would be a better approach.

Problems with inferring cause-and-effect relationships also apply to the field study. For example, in an analysis of the relationships among job satisfaction, leadership styles, and performance, does job satisfaction lead to higher performance, and then do leaders change their personal style? Or is leadership related to job satisfaction, which is then associated with high performance? Because of the large number of variables that are usually involved in a field survey, questions concerning causal relationships among the variables remain unanswered.

Laboratory Experiment

Compared with the case study and the field survey, the laboratory experiment increases the ability of the researcher to establish cause-and-effect relationships among the variables. By conducting an experiment in an artificial setting, the researcher can create and control the exact conditions desired.

The essence of the **laboratory experiment** is to observe the effects of manipulating one or more independent variables on one or more dependent variables.[7] For example, an autocratic leader tells one group of three blindfolded subjects to build a tower as high as possible with Tinker Toys. A democratic leader asks another group of blindfolded subjects to perform the same task. The dependent variable is the height of the tower; the independent variable is leadership style.

There are several disadvantages of using the laboratory research design. For practical reasons, college students are the most common source of subjects in studies of organizational behavior. However, it is difficult to justify their use to represent actual managers involved in decision-making processes. Many students are young, transient, have not yet occupied positions of managerial responsibility, and do not depend on the successful completion of a task under laboratory conditions for their livelihood. Therefore to what populations and treatment variables can the laboratory results of experiments using students be generalized? Simulating many of the properties of organizational structure and process in the laboratory can be extremely difficult.

Another problem with the laboratory experiment is that much of the work undertaken in the laboratory deals with phenomena that cannot be reproduced in or applied to real-life situations. A firm could not readily restructure its organizational hierarchy to fit an ideal model. Even if it found and could hire the "perfect" personnel, the changeover would result in serious morale and productivity problems. Conversely, many behavioral problems in organizations cannot be isolated to permit their examination under laboratory conditions. Researchers thus tend to focus narrowly on problems that can be addressed in the laboratory setting. Nevertheless, laboratory experiments should be derived from studies in real-life situations, and results should be continually checked against them.

Field Experiment

A field experiment is an attempt to apply the laboratory method to ongoing real-life situations. The **field experiment** permits the researcher to manipulate one or more independent variables in an ongoing organization.[8] The researcher can study the changes in the dependent variables and can infer the direction of causality with some degree of confidence.

The subjects in a field experiment ordinarily know that they are under investigation, so the researcher must adopt procedures that will decrease the possibility that subjects will change their behavior simply because they are being observed. Compared with the laboratory researcher, the field researcher has less control over the situation, must assume that events affect both the experimental and the control groups equally, and must further assume that these events will not be a major determinant of the dependent variable.

In Practice: Assessing a Human Relations Program

John Fogarty and Joseph Wapner of the Standard Steel Corporation used a field experiment to assess the impact of a human relations training program on the behaviors of middle managers at this steel mill. The purpose of the research was to answer the question: Does the job-related behavior of executives enrolled in a human relations training program change? John and Joe hypothesized that managers who received the training would develop more sensitive attitudes to the needs of others, would more frequently structure their subordinates' work and show them consideration, and would be rated as more effective by their superiors than would managers who did not take part in the program. Forty-two managers were selected randomly from the same level in the organization. Half were randomly assigned to the experimental group that would undergo the human relations training, and the remaining half became the control group.

The independent variable was the human relations training program, which consisted of 90-minute training sessions given once a week for 28 consecutive weeks. It included printed materials on managerial styles, leadership, motivation, and communication, as well as lectures on group dynamics and time management. The dependent variables were the managers' attitudes toward themselves and others, their leadership behavior, and their performance.

The researchers measured leadership style and sensitivity to the needs of others by questionnaires. They measured performance by ratings from immediate supervisors on technical knowledge, drive and aggressiveness, reliability, cooperation, and organizing ability.

The results generally supported the hypothesis being tested.[9] Compared with members of the control group (those who did not receive the training), members of the experimental group (those who did receive the training) were rated more sensitive to the needs of others, more considerate of their subordinates, and significantly more effective. In fact, showing consideration to subordinates decreased for managers in the control group.

Comparison of Research Designs

Each of the four types of research design has both strong and weak points.[10] By selecting one, the researcher must often forego some of the advantages of the alternative. The following paragraphs compare and summarize a few aspects of the major designs.

REALISM   A major advantage of doing research in a natural setting, such as in a field experiment within an organization, is the ability to increase the level of realism. The researcher can be somewhat confident that the subjects (managers, workers, and administrators) are behaving under natural and ongoing conditions. This is an advantage over the laboratory setting, which typically involves artificial conditions; however, the researcher in the field loses the ability to manipulate the independent variable or variables as freely as in the laboratory.

SCOPE   Case studies and field surveys usually have a broad scope and incorporate many variables of interest to the researcher. Laboratory experiments, by their nature, are the most limited in scope, and a field experiment is often an expansion of a laboratory experiment.

PRECISION   Research attempts to measure accurately the variables under consideration, and research undertaken in the laboratory setting is usually more precise than research in the field. In the laboratory the use of multiple measures of the same variable or variables under controlled conditions allows the researcher to obtain more accurate information about the variables than do other strategies. The use of videotape, for example, permits the researcher to record an entire experiment and then study it at a later time, examining such things as styles of behavior, motives, and gestures.

CONTROL   Researchers hope to control the experimental situation so that events being observed will definitely be related to the causes hypothesized and not to some unknown unrelated events. The laboratory experiment allows researchers to reproduce a situation repeatedly, so that they do not have to rely on a single observation for their conclusions. By replicating a study, predictions about cause-and-effect relationships can be refined from "sometimes" to, say, "95 times out of 100." The laboratory experiment also avoids many factors present in the field over which the researcher has little control (personnel changes or employees forgetting to fill out the questionnaire, for example). However, the results obtained from ideal circumstances may not fit the real situation.

COST   Research designs differ in their relative costs and in the kinds of resources they require. Designs vary in initial setup costs, that is, in the time and resources needed to plan and initiate a study. They also vary in the cost per case for additional samples. For example, a laboratory experiment has relatively low setup costs, requires relatively few kinds of resources, and costs relatively little for additional subjects. The resources required can be found in most colleges. Because of high costs, field experiments and surveys tend to be carried out by large research organizations rather than by a researcher and a few assistants. These designs require a large number of subjects and computation facilities to analyze the data.

SUMMARY   All research designs have both strengths and weaknesses. Too much has been written about the reasons for one strategy being weak or one strategy being better than others: no one strategy is best in every case. It is far more important to study how each of the research designs differs from and is complementary to the others—to see what is gained and lost by choosing one strategy over the others. Rather than search for the ideal, effective managers select the research design that is best for their purposes and circumstances at the time, use all the strengths of that design, and limit or offset its weaknesses whenever possible.

DATA COLLECTION METHODS

Managers observe and gather data all day, every day. Some data they reject, some they store away, and some they act on. The problem with this ordinary method of data gathering, as opposed to scientific data gathering, is that day-to-day observations of behavior are frequently unreliable or biased by personal attitudes or values. Also, the sample of behaviors observed is often limited and does not truly represent typical behavior; hence it is not a good basis for generalizations. It is easy to understand why erroneous conclusions frequently are drawn from observations of human behavior.

The quality of research depends not only on the adequacy of the research design, but also on the adequacy of the data-collection methods used. The manager-researcher can collect data in a number of ways: by interviews, questionnaires, observation, nonreactive sources, or qualitative methods. The rules for using these data to make statements about the pertinent subject matter may be built into the data-collecting technique, or they may be developed as a supplement.

Interviews

The interview is one of the oldest and most often used methods for obtaining information. It relies on the willingness of people to communicate. Asking someone a direct question can save considerable time and money if the respondent is willing to talk and the answer is honest.[11]

An interview's quality depends heavily on the mutual trust and goodwill established between the interviewer and the respondent. A trained interviewer builds these relationships early in the interview, so that more of the data will be useful. One way to build trust is to assure the respondent that all answers will be confidential. In addition, an interviewer must be a good listener in order to hold the attention of the respondent.

On the other hand, the interview method of data collection has several major shortcomings. First, people may be unwilling to provide certain types of information readily in a face-to-face situation. Employees, for example, may be unwilling to express negative attitudes about a superior when the interviewer is from the personnel department. Getting employees to talk openly—even to an outsider—and answer questions about their jobs, other individuals, and the organization is a difficult task because trust is necessary for this to happen. Thus the importance of establishing trust cannot be overstated. The second shortcoming of the interview method is that interviews take time, and this costs money. Third, to achieve reliability, interviewers must be well-trained, and they must present questions in a way that ensures validity. Interviewers must eliminate personal biases, and their questions must be tested in advance of the actual interviews for hidden biases. Fourth, the questions asked by the interviewer place limitations on the answers that respondents will freely give.

Questionnaires

Questionnaires are sets of written items to which the subject is asked to respond. This is probably the most frequently used data-gathering device. A questionnaire may measure the respondent's attitudes, opinions, or demographic characteristics, or even two or all three of these variables.

Because of the wide variety of variables that questionnaires can measure, thousands of kinds of questionnaires are used to measure variables such as job satisfaction, need fulfillment, company satisfaction, job stress, leadership style, values, vocational interest, and so on.[12]

Developing a questionnaire is more of an art than a science. Such factors as the study's budget, the purpose of the study, the nature of the population to be sampled, and the like must be answered before a sound decision can be made about the use of a questionnaire. After carefully thinking through the reasons for using a questionnaire and deciding to use this method, researchers must construct the specific questionnaire that fits their purposes. To illustrate how the structure of questionnaire items can vary, consider the measurement of job satisfaction. At one end of the structure continuum, we could measure satisfaction by asking: "Are you satisfied with your job?" Each person would respond by checking either (a) *yes* or (b) *no,* the two alternatives provided to the subject. This would be an example of a highly structured question. A somewhat less structured question would be one that asks the person to indicate the extent to which he or she agrees with the statement: "I find my job quite satisfying," using the following response categories: (a) strongly agree, (b) agree, (c) neither agree nor disagree, (d) disagree, and (e) strongly disagree. An example of a totally unstructured question would be one that asks the person: "What do you like or dislike about your job?"

There are both advantages and disadvantages of using questionnaires to collect data. Among the advantages are that questionnaires

- provide a relatively inexpensive way to collect data;
- can be administered by relatively unskilled people;
- can be mailed to people or given to people in groups;
- provide the same stimulus to all people; and
- often can be answered anonymously, which may lead to a more open and truthful response than would be obtained, for example, during an interview.

In terms of disadvantages, the questionnaire may result in one or more of the following:

- Missing data may be a problem if people do not answer all the questions.
- A low response rate may make the results nongeneralizable.
- Questionnaires cannot be used with individuals who have major reading problems.
- Questionnaires do not permit the individual flexibility in answering and thus limits the amount of information people can give.

ACROSS CULTURES

Bargaining Behaviors of Managers from Ten Countries

Bargaining and negotiating are frequently used ways of reaching decisions in a variety of everyday events. Examples abound in family relations; in business between buyers and sellers; between countries which engage in bilateral negotiations concerning trade, armaments, and human rights; and among aggregations of countries (East-West; Arab-Israeli; Third World countries and others; Communist-Capitalist).

In all these cases, decisions must be made in a complex setting. A large part of this complexity is caused by the mixed motives people bring with them, and these guide their behaviors during the negotiations. Motivations of self-interest and competition in relation to the other party are nearly always coupled with motivations of joint-interest and cooperation with the other party. In most situations, there are no clear-cut rules of behavior or standards for decisions.

A sample of 791 executives from ten countries were surveyed by questionnaire. The questionnaire collected information on their attitudes toward risk versus risk avoidance, suspicion versus trust, and conciliation versus belligerence. It was translated from English to the relevant language by a native of each country. The translator eliminated questions that were meaningless or could not be translated adequately. The questionnaire was then translated into English by an independent translator (again a native of the country under consideration). The two translators then discussed any differences in the two English versions, either agreeing on necessary changes or eliminating the question. The questionnaire was then adapted for local usage and carefully checked by a third native of the country who was intimately familiar with the backgrounds of the executives in the sample. A small portion of the English version of the questionnaire used in this study is shown in Table 2–1.

TABLE 2–1   Questionnaire on Some Personal Attitudes and Opinions

Part I.   The items below are intended to determine what people think about a number of social questions. The best answer to each statement is *your personal opinion*. Many different points of view are covered; you may find yourself agreeing strongly with some of the statements, disagreeing just as strongly with others, and perhaps uncertain about others. Whether you agree or disagree with any statement, you can be sure that many other people feel the same way you do.

For each statement, circle with your pencil the number which best fits your reaction according to how much you agree or disagree with it. Please mark every one, using the following scale:

7:	I agree very much	3:	I disagree a little
6:	I agree pretty much	2:	I disagree pretty much
5:	I agree a little	1:	I disagree very much

If you are really completely neutral about an item, or if you are completely uncertain how you feel about an item, or if you don't understand it, mark *4*.

Item	Scale
1. When someone has been nasty to you, you should try to understand what's bothering him/her so that you can be helpful.	1 2 3 4 5 6 7
2. We should always help those who are in need, even if they are very unfriendly to us.	1 2 3 4 5 6 7
3. Doing something to please a person who doesn't like you can give you a lot of satisfaction.	1 2 3 4 5 6 7
4. It's a good idea to know the problems and worries of people around you, so that you can be helpful.	1 2 3 4 5 6 7
5. Even people who appear friendly to you may be unreliable because they are mainly concerned with their own interests.	1 2 3 4 5 6 7
6. When someone has said something to hurt you, it is not good to pay him back, even if the things you say about him are perfectly true.	1 2 3 4 5 6 7
7. We should try to get people from other countries to visit us and explain their points of view.	1 2 3 4 5 6 7
8. We should be completely frank in telling other people about our own shortcomings and mistakes.	1 2 3 4 5 6 7

Part II.   The next series of questions is about your likes and dislikes, preferences and habits in everyday life. There are no right or wrong answers to these questions; one answer can be just as good as some other answer.

For each question, circle with your pencil number 1, 2, or 3 for the answer that fits you best.

- ■ If your answer is *Yes*, circle number 3.
- ■ If you cannot decide, circle number 2.
- ■ If your answer is *No*, circle number 1.

Table 2-1 cont.	
Item	*Scale*
9. Would you like to drive a "hot-rod" in a race?	1 2 3
10. Do you like to bet money on athletic events?	1 2 3
11. Do you often feel impatient?	1 2 3
12. Would you be willing to take a chance by accepting a job you know little about?	1 2 3

Scoring for Questionnaire on Some Personal Attitudes and Opinions (Table 2–1)

Total
Points

I. *Conciliation versus belligerence*
Sum the point values you circled for Items 1, 2, 3, and 4. Scores can range from 28 (high conciliation) to 4 (high belligerence).   _____

II. *Risk taking versus risk avoidance*
Sum the point values you circled for Items 5, 6, 7, and 8. Scores can range from 28 (high risk taking) to 4 (high risk avoidance).   _____

III. *Trust versus suspicion*
Sum the point values you circled for Items 9, 10, 11 and 12. Scores can range from 12 (high trust) to 4 (high suspicion).   _____

Major differences were found to exist among countries. The executives from South Africa showed the greatest belligerence, whereas those from Spain and Greece showed the strongest tendencies toward conciliation. Similarly, Thai executives demonstrated the least amount of risk taking, while U.S. executives showed the greatest acceptance of risk taking. Only the U.S. executives scored relatively high on the trust dimension. The remaining executives all exhibited strong tendencies toward suspicion.

Source: Adapted from Harnett, D., and Cummings, L. *Bargaining Behavior: An International Study.* Houston: Dame, 1980.

Observation

We all observe the actions of others. On the basis of these observations, we infer others' motivations, feelings, and intentions. A major advantage of the observation method is that it focuses attention on the behavior of individuals rather than relying only on their verbal or written expressions. By looking at behavior, the observer can study the entire person or group. The total behavior of the person or group studied becomes the primary interest of the researcher.[13]

A major problem with the observation method is inherent in the observer. The researcher must digest the information derived from the observation and then make inferences from what he or she has observed. However, these inferences often are incorrect. Suppose, for example, that a person intensely dislikes college football because of its violence, the corruption in recruiting of athletes, and the emphasis on winning. This individual's previously formed personal biases may well invalidate any personal observations and inferences he or she might make after watching a game.

Utilization of a form on which the observer records specific conditions or acts reduces the effect of personal bias. Recall the situation at Dart Transportation Company and suppose that Jim and Glen had decided to observe Dart's drivers under actual working conditions. To help Jim and Glen avoid observing different driver behaviors and thus drawing different conclusions, they each could observe and record driver behaviors on an identical form while parked at a midwest truck depot. Data on Dart drivers could be obtained in the following observational categories:

- Condition of the truck   Clean ____ Dirty ____
- Condition of trailer   Clean ____; Dirty ____; Lights broken ____; Mud flaps on ____ or off ____.
- Length of stop   ____ minutes.
- Drivers chatted with   Other Dart drivers (if available) ____; Dart competitors ____; Others ____.
- Condition of drivers   Alert ____; Tired ____; Clean ____; Dirty ____.

When Jim and Glen returned to their office, they could compare their observations and discuss any differences in what they observed. If there were large differences, they could take a third person along with them for their next observation. These observations would be made at random times throughout the day for several days.

Nonreactive Measures

If we want to know something about someone, we might turn to nonreactive sources for our information instead of asking or observing that person directly.[14] Obtaining **nonreactive measures** does not require the cooperation of the person. Company records provide managers with valuable data on absenteeism, turnover, grievances, performance ratings, and demographics. In some cases these sources may yield more accurate data than that obtained by directly questioning the employee. Nonreactive measures have the advantage of being inconspicuous because they are generated without the producer's knowledge of their use. For example, radio dial settings can be used to determine the listener appeal of different radio stations. A Dallas automobile dealer estimates the popularity of different radio stations by having mechanics record the radio dial position on all cars brought in for service. The dealer then uses these data to select radio stations to carry his advertising. The wear on library books, particularly on the corners where the pages are turned, offers another example of a nonreactive measure librarians can use to learn the popularity of a book.

Qualitative Measures

Qualitative methods are measures used by researchers to describe and clarify the meaning of naturally occurring events in organizations. These methods are, by design, open-ended and interpretative. Qualitative data are rarely quantifiable; thus the researcher's interpretation and description are significant in a qualitative study.

Qualitative methods use the experience and intuition of the researcher to describe the organizational processes and structures that are being studied.[15] The type of data collected requires the qualitative researcher to become very close to the situation or problem studied. For example, a qualitative method used for years by anthropologists is known as the **ethnography**. Ethnography requires the researcher to study the organization for long periods of time as a participant observer. That is, the researcher becomes part of the situation being studied in order to feel what it is like for the people in that situation. The researcher thus becomes totally immersed in the situation. One researcher studying a big city police department actually went through police academy training and then accompanied police officers on their daily duties. Thus, he was able to provide vivid descriptions of what police work was really like; informally interview others, read important documents, and use nonreactive methods to gather other data.[16]

Criteria for Data Collection

Any data-collection method used to measure behavior must meet three important requirements: reliability, validity, and practicality.

RELIABILITY   The accuracy of measurement and the consistency of results determine **reliability**, which is one of the most important characteristics of any good data-collection method.[17] A bathroom scale would be worthless if every time you stepped on it you got a different reading. Similarly, a questionnaire would be useless if the scores obtained on successive administrations were not consistent. Consistently different performance scores by the same individual at different times reflects low reliability.

Control normally is the only prerequisite for high reliability. So long as the directions for a data-collection method are clear, the environment is comfortable, and ample time is given for the subject to respond, the method should be reliable. However, unexpected environmental interferences can threaten reliability. Furthermore, all data-collection methods, except those utilizing nonreactive sources, are affected to some degree by random changes in the subject, such as fatigue, distraction, or emotional strain. These conditions can also affect the researcher's reliability, especially in the observation method. Finally, changes in the setting, such as unexpected noises or sudden changes in weather, can also affect reliability of the data collected.

VALIDITY   Even a reliable data-collection method is not necessarily valid. **Validity** is the degree to which a test or questionnaire actually measures what it claims to measure.[18] Validity is an evaluation, not a fact and is usually expressed in broad terms such as high, moderate, or low, instead of precise quantities or numbers. A method can reliably measure the wrong variables. For example, a low score on a math test denies a job to a potential machine repairer. The test may have reliably measured the applicant's abstract math ability, but it may not be a valid measure of the applicant's actual manual skill at repairing machines.

The validity of many psychological tests used by firms in employee selection is being questioned. The Equal Employment Opportunity Commission insists that the use of tests that cannot be validated be discontinued. Tests that are not valid are worse than useless: they are misleading and dangerous. Often such tests have been used—either consciously or unwittingly—to discriminate against certain social or ethnic groups. Those who challenge the use of psychological tests in the selection process question not their reliability, but their validity.

PRACTICALITY   Do not underestimate the importance of **practicality,** the final requirement of a good data-collection method. Questionnaires, interviews, and other data-collection methods should be acceptable to both management and the employees who are asked to participate. Unions traditionally have raised questions about what management has the right to know. Therefore, where employees are unionized, the union must approve the data-collection method. The use of a planning committee consisting of representatives from each management level and the unions can ensure widespread acceptance because the researcher can consider the viewpoints of these groups in deciding on the data-collection method to be used. The method chosen should also involve easy accessibility by the participants and administration in order to save time and money and to minimize disruption of the organization's normal operations.

Let us look at how one large corporation, American Can Company, used a combination of data-collection methods to survey their employees. This effort also included a sound research design.

In Practice: American Can Company

American Can Company, a $4 billion diversified packaging and consumer products organization headquartered in Greenwich, Connecticut, has a human resources philosophy that emphasizes an exceptional working environment through individual responsibility and achievement. In 1979, it installed a flexible compensation program that covered 9,000 nonunionized, salaried employees. Flexible compensation allows each employee to build a benefits package tailored to personal needs. The company in turn, can attain greater cost efficiencies by providing high employee satisfaction for a given level of costs.

Early in 1979, the vice-president for human resources decided to explore whether a flexible compensation system would be applicable to the company. A task force designed a tentative, nonflexible core of benefits that represented the company's basic security obligations to employees. This nonflexible core featured a comprehensive medical plan, group term life insurance, disability income replacement, vacations, and a competitive pension plan.

During the middle of 1979, the flexible compensation plan was beginning to take shape, but many questions remained. How would the program work? Would the concept prove acceptable? Would employees really "play the game"? Could the process of signing up be handled efficiently for 9,000 employees scattered in more than 160 locations throughout the United States? What would the participation rates be for the options being offered? What changes could make the program more appealing and useful? What would it take to communicate an understanding of the flexible benefits coverage concept as well as the details of the benefit options?

To answer these questions, the company conducted a two-stage test. The first stage involved a study group of about 100 randomly selected employees from American Can's Consumer Towel and Tissue Division. In small group meetings, employees spent several days studying benefit design and costs, reviewing the existing program, and evaluating both the core coverage recommendation and the options developed by the task force. As a result, certain options were modified or eliminated, and the task force collected a number of ideas to make the communication and administration processes work more smoothly.

Stage two of the testing process was a trial run. The program was introduced to all 600 nonunionized employees in the Consumer Towel and Tissue Division. Materials describing the plan and methods of enrollment were distributed. Employees at this test division became the pilot group.

A written questionnaire quantified the pilot group's reaction to this trial run and compared these responses to those of the earlier, randomly selected group. Both groups were asked to rate the statement, "The overall value of the proposed benefits plan to me is greater than the present plan's overall value." The randomly selected, earlier group responded as follows:

41%	25%	22%	10%	2%
Strongly Agree	Agree	Undecided	Disagree	Strongly Disagree

This scale shows the responses of the pilot group:

73%	14%	9%	4%	0%
Strongly Agree	Agree	Undecided	Disagree	Strongly Disagree

Interviews conducted with employees at the Consumer Towel and Tissue Division determined employee reactions to the program in greater depth. Generally, the interviews confirmed the results of the questionnaire. Other indicators also pointed to a general acceptance of the flexible benefits concept.[19]

ETHICS IN RESEARCH

Researchers who obtain data from the general public, students, or company employees must deal with the problem of the ethical and legal obligations owed by the researcher to these subjects. Some obligations may be implicit in the conduct of any kind of relationship; others specifically apply to the research designs and data collection methods that we have discussed.[20]

One of the primary ethical requirements is maintaining the confidential nature of the relationship between the researcher and subjects. For example, a researcher testing the relationship between job satisfaction and performance must obtain the individual's performance data. The researcher determines that employees who are highly satisfied with the company and its policies perform better than employees who are not satisfied. Someone in the company wants to know which employees are in each group. However, the researcher should maintain the confidentiality of the data sources to protect the anonymity of the respondents.

Another ethical problem arises because certain types of research designs require a lack of knowledge on the part of the respondent that would be impaired under experimental conditions of complete candor. In marketing research, for example, subjects are often asked to evaluate two identical samples of a product that are presented in different packages. Obviously, the research would be largely worthless if the researcher informed the respondents prior to the evaluation that the contents of the packages were identical.

Similar practices are common in psychology, where researchers present false statements or attribute true statements to false sources to determine credibility influences. The code of ethics of the American Psychological Association states that, "Only when a problem is significant and can be investigated in no other way is the psychologist justified in giving misinformation to research subjects." Many researchers feel an ethical obligation to inform the subjects of any false information presented as soon as possible after terminating the research.

The U.S. Department of Health, Education and Welfare issued an extensive report intended to protect human subjects. One requirement is that a *committee* must conduct objective and independent reviews of research projects and activities involving the use of human subjects when federal funds are involved. At Pennsylvania State University, for example, the independent review committee is composed of various directors of research from the colleges within the university. Each member arrives at a decision based on professional judgment as to whether the research will place the participating subjects "at risk." If a majority of the review-committee members feel that the procedure employed will not put the subject at risk, the committee will approve the proposal. After this approval, each subject must sign an agreement of informed consent. The basic elements of informed consent include the following:

- A fair explanation of the procedures to be followed, including those that are experimental.
- A description of the study.
- A description of the benefits to be expected.
- An offer to answer any inquiries concerning the procedures.
- An announcement that the subject is free to withdraw consent and to discontinue participation in the activity at any time.

When the researchers have completed the research, they should make available an abstract of the report to all interested subjects who took part in the study.

Procedures such as these do not resolve all the possible ethical issues associated with organizational behavior research. However, they do suggest some of the positive steps that researchers should take to minimize risk to human subjects.

SUMMARY

The research methods that managers find useful in the study of organizational behavior are all based on the scientific method, which consists of systematic observation, measurement, and prediction. This approach involves testing a hypothesis, or a tentative statement that links one or more independent and dependent variables. The four most commonly used research designs to test hypotheses are case studies, field surveys, laboratory experiments, and field experiments. Each method has advantages and disadvantages. Case studies provide insights, but they cannot be used to prove or disprove anything. Field surveys, which are the most widely used research design, enable researchers to collect information about employees, but cause-and-effect relationships cannot be determined from them. Laboratory and field experimentation are superior for determining cause-and-effect relationships. Laboratory experiments offer the greatest control for the researcher but decrease the researcher's ability to generalize findings to other situations.

Most researchers in organizational behavior use one of four methods to collect data: interviews, questionnaires, observations, and nonreactive sources. The researcher must select the most effective method for answering the research question posed, and this method must be reliable, valid, and practical. The way data are collected is very important. Ethical practices, trust, and confidentiality are important considerations in organizational behavior research.

KEY WORDS AND CONCEPTS

Case study
Control group
Dependent variable
Ethnography
Experimental group
Field experiment
Field survey
Hypothesis
Independent variable

Laboratory experiment
Nonreactive measures
Practicality
Qualitative methods
Reliability
Research design
Scientific approach
Validity

DISCUSSION QUESTIONS

1. What are the purposes of a research design? What makes a good or poor research design?
2. Why should a researcher use both a control group and an experimental group?
3. What are the advantages and disadvantages of each of the following research designs: case study, field study, laboratory experiment, and field experiment?
4. What are some advantages and disadvantages of using qualitative research methods?
5. What are some potential ethical problems in conducting survey research?
6. Why is validity important for managers?

MANAGEMENT INCIDENTS AND CASES

State Health Department

Attitude-survey data that a State Health Department collected as part of its on-going attempt to stay in contact with its employees served as a basis for initiating and evaluating a training program. The program was designed to develop the manage- rial capabilities of program directors. The initial survey had found that program directors were by and large not involved in the decision-making process because division directors, their immediate supervisors, preferred a directive (Theory X) style of management. One of the consequences of this style was the relatively short supply of program directors who were promotable to more responsible positions.

A program was designed by a consulting firm to develop the division managers' ability to work with their program directors in less directive, more participative (Theory Y) ways. It was also anticipated that program directors would need training in how to accept and use their increased authority. The program provided for the division directors and the commissioner's office to meet as a group on a regular basis. During these sessions, they read *In Search of Excellence* by Peters and Waterman; *The 100 Best Companies To Work For in America* by Levering, Mokowitz and Katz; and other materials that stressed the benefits of participative management. Case studies and other training materials were provided and discussed during the sessions.

Two months after the completion of the training sessions, a second attitude survey was completed by all employees. The respondents remained anonymous, except for level in the managerial hierarchy. Thus it was possible to compare the responses of program and division directors to obtain group scores. The consultant presented the data from the second attitude survey to the division directors. She noted one result that she believed they should discuss. That result seemed to indicate that one of the objectives of the

program had not been achieved: the intended downward delegation of authority to program directors.

A number of questions on the survey instrument measured the amount of authority. Generally, the program directors indicated that their authority had declined since the first attitude survey. One particularly interesting question to which all the directors responded on both surveys was stated as follows:

> How much "say" do you think each of the following people usually has in deciding work objectives of the departmental program? Circle one in each line across. (See bottom of page.)

Figures 2–3 and 2–4 present the group means for responses to this question for the division directors (solid line) and program directors (dashed line). Plainly the program directors' perceptions of what had happened during the previous year were contrary to what was supposed to happen. As indicated by their responses, they believed that not only did they have less say in their programs, but that division directors had considerably more than before. And the division directors reported that they had considerably less and that program directors had more "say" in deciding work objectives.

The division directors were confused by the questionnaire results. How could it be, they asked the con-

	Usually has a great deal of say 1	Quite a bit of say 2	Some say 3	Just a little say 4	Usually has no say at all 5
Program Directors	1	2	3	4	5
Division Heads	1	2	3	4	5
Commissioner's Office	1	2	3	4	5

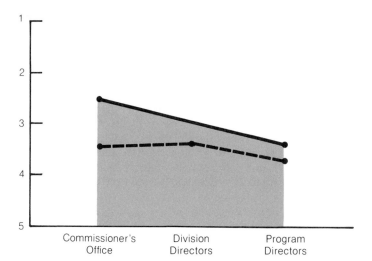

FIGURE 2–3.
Group Means for
Response of Division
and Program Directors
Prior to Training
Program

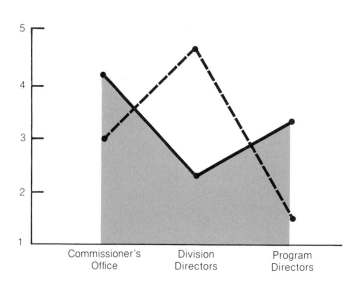

FIGURE 2–4.
Group Means for
Responses of Division
and Program Directors
after Training Programs

sultant, that despite our efforts they believe that we have more and they have less authority? Are the data reliable? Is there any other evidence to indicate that the program has backfired, at least as it was to affect program directors? What do we do now? Scrap it and start all over?[21]

Questions

1. What kind of a research design was used by the State Health Department to evaluate this program? What are the design's strengths and weaknesses?

2. What other kinds and sources of information would be useful in determining the validity of the attitude survey data?

References

1. Kerlinger, F. *Foundations of Behavioral Research*. New York: Holt, Rinehart and Winston, 1964; Cambell, J., Daft, R., and Hulin, C. *What to Study: Generating and Developing Research Questions*. Beverly Hills, Calif.: Sage, 1982.

2. McGrath, J., Martin J., and Kulka, R. *Judgment Calls in Research*. Beverly Hills, Calif.: Sage, 1982.

3. Campbell, D., and Stanley, J. *Experimental and Quasi-Experimental Designs for Research*. Chicago: Rand McNally, 1966.

4. A few of the better sources include Cook, T., and Campbell, D. The Design and Conduct of Quasi-Experiments and True Experiments in Field Settings. In M. Dunnette (Ed.) *Handbook of Industrial Psychology*. Chicago: Rand McNally, 1976, 223–326; Kenny, D. *Correlation and Causality*. New York: John Wiley Interscience, 1979; Hunter, J., Schmidt, F., and Jackson, G. *Meta-Analysis: Cumulating Research Findings Across Studies*. Beverly Hills, Calif: Sage, 1982.

5. Yin, R., and Heald, K. Using the Case Survey Method to Analyze Policy Studies. *Administrative Science Quarterly*, 1975, *20*, 371–381.

6. Stone, E. *Research Methods in Organizational Behavior*. Santa Monica, Calif.: Goodyear, 1978.

7. Ilgen, D. Laboratory Research: A Question of When, Not If. In E. Locke (Ed.) *Generalizing from Laboratory to Field Settings: Research Findings From Industrial-Organizational Psychology, Organizational Behavior, and Human Resource Management*. Lexington, Mass.: Lexington Books, 1986.

8. Pfeffer, J. Four Laws of Organizational Research. In A. Van de Ven and Wm. Joyce (Eds.) *Perspectives on Organization Design and Behavior*. New York: John Wiley Interscience, 1981, 409–418; Dipboye, R., and Flanagan, M. Research Settings in Industrial and Organizational Psychology. *American Psychologist*, 1979, *34*, 140–150.

9. Hand, H., and Slocum, J. A Longitudinal Study of the Effects of a Human Relations Training Program on Managerial Effectiveness. *Journal of Applied Psychology*, 1972, *56*, 412–417.

10. Glick, Wm., and Roberts, K. Hypothesized Interdependence, Assumed Independence. *Academy of Management Review*, 1984, *9*, 722–735.

11. Goodale, J. *The Fine Art of Interviewing*. Englewood Cliffs, N.J.: Prentice-Hall, 1982.

12. Shaw, M., and Wright, J. *Scales for the Measurement of Attitudes*. New York: McGraw-Hill, 1967.

13. Martinko, M., and Gardner, Wm. Beyond Structured Observation: Methodological Issues and New Directions. *Academy of Management Review*, 1985, *10*, 676–695.

14. Webb, E., Campbell, D., Schwartz, R., and Sechrest, L. *Unobtrusive Measures: Nonreactive Research in the Social Sciences*. Chicago: Rand-McNally, 1966.

15. Daft, R. Learning the Craft of Organizational Research. *Academy of Management Review*, 1983, *8*, 539–546; Glaser, B., and Strauss, A. *Discovery of Grounded Theory: Strategies for Qualitative Research*. Chicago: Aldine, 1967.

16. Van Maanen, J., Dobbs, J., and Faulkner, R. *Varieties of Qualitative Research*. Beverly Hills, Calif.: Sage, 1982; Staw, B. Repairs on the Road to Relevance and Rigor: Some Unexplored Issues in Publishing Organizational Research. In L. Cummings and P. Frost (Eds.) *Publishing in Organizational Sciences*. Homewood, Ill.: Richard D. Irwin, 1985, 96–107.

17. McCormick, E., and Ilgen, D. *Industrial and Organizational Psychology*, 8th ed. Englewood Cliffs, N.J.: Prentice-Hall, 1985.

18. Mitchell, T. An Evaluation of the Validity of Correlational Research Conducted in Organizations. *Academy of Management Review*, 1985, *10*, 192–205; Schwab, D. Construct Validity in Organizational Behavior. In B. Staw and L. Cummings (Eds.) *Research in Organizational Behavior*, vol. 2. Greenwich, Conn.: JAI Press, 1980, 3–44.

19. Adapted from Schlachtmeyer, A., and Bogart, R. Employee-Choice Benefits—Can Employees Handle It? *Compensation Review*, Fall 1979, 12–19.

20. Ethical Standards of Psychologists. *American Psychologist*, 1963, *18*, 56–60; Von Glinow, M., *et al*. Ethical Issues in Organizational Behavior. *Academy of Management Newsletter*, March 1985, 1–3.

21. Adapted from Gibson, J., Ivancevich, J., and Donnelly, J. *Organizations: Behavior, Structure and Processes*, 5th ed. Plano, Texas: Business Publications, Inc., 1985, 704–706.

PART II

INDIVIDUAL PROCESSES

3 Personality and Attitudes

LEARNING OBJECTIVES

When you have finished studying this chapter, you should be able to:

- Define what is meant by personality.
- Discuss the basic sources of personality differences.
- Explain the relationship between personality and behavior.
- Give some examples of personality dimensions that influence individual behavior.
- Define what is meant by attitudes and list the components of attitudes.
- Describe the general relationship between attitudes and behavior.
- Define what is meant by job satisfaction and explain why it is important.

OUTLINE

> **Preview Case**
>
> **The Grade**
>
> Taylor and Barker are university business students taking an introductory course in management. When their instructor returned the first examination, both students were disappointed to receive a D grade. Immediately following class, Taylor spoke to the professor. She was obviously distressed and upset. Her hands trembled noticeably, her face was flushed, and she appeared to be on the verge of tears. Speaking slowly and softly, almost in a whisper, she said, "I'm really sorry that I did so poorly—it was so stupid of me. I don't know how I could have done such a terrible job." Taylor returned to her dorm and spent most of the day alone. She wrote several long letters to members of her family and cut the rest of her classes.
>
> Barker's reaction to the grade was very different. She rushed out of the lecture room at the end of class and joked loudly with her boyfriend about the management course. She commented acidly about the value of the course and made fun of the professor's lectures and appearance. She said nothing about her grade to her boyfriend as they walked to their next class. In that class, Barker surprised her teacher by making a number of excellent comments during class discussion.

As illustrated in this Preview Case, different people faced with the same situation do not necessarily behave the same way. Some two thousand years ago the Greek philosopher Theophrastus asked, "Why is it that while all Greece lies under the same sky and all Greeks are educated alike, it has befallen us to have characters variously constituted?"[1] This question—Why are people different?—is as important today as it was in ancient Greece for understanding human behavior. The manager must understand and appreciate individual differences in order to understand the behavior of people in complex social settings such as organizations.[2] The behavior of an employee, for example, always involves a complex interaction of the person and the situation. That is, events in the external environment (including the presence and behavior of others) strongly influence the way people behave at any particular point in time; yet people always bring something of themselves to the situation. We often refer to this "something," which represents the unique qualities of the individual, as *personality*.

To fully understand an individual's behavior, we need to know many things about that person—past experiences, personality, attitudes, values, and so on—and have a great deal of information about the situation or context within which the individual is behaving. Part II of this book is devoted to "individual processes" within organizations. We focus first on the individual in order to develop an understanding of organizational behavior. We will begin, in this chapter, to discuss some **individual differences**, specifically personality and attitudes.

PERSONALITY: AN INTRODUCTION

No single definition of personality is accepted by all authorities. However, a key idea in the concept of personality is that it represents personal characteristics that account for consistent patterns of behavior.[3] People seek to understand these behavioral patterns in interactions with others. In fact, most people engage in an informal attempt to understand human behavior all of their lives. The study of personality represents a more formal, systematic attempt to do the same thing. Certainly in organizations, managers and employees need to understand the consistencies in others' behavior in a variety of situations.

A well-known personality theorist, Salvatore Maddi, has proposed the following definition of **personality**:

> Personality is a stable set of characteristics and tendencies that determine those commonalities and differences in the psychological behavior (thoughts, feelings, and actions) of people that have continuity in time and that may not be easily understood as the sole result of the social and biological pressures of the moment.[4]

This definition contains some important ideas. First, note that nothing in the definition suggests limiting the influence of personality to only certain behaviors, certain situations, or certain people. Personality theory is a **general theory of behavior**—an attempt to understand or describe the behavior of all people, all of the time.[5] In fact, some people feel that to attempt to define the concept of personality is to attempt to explain the very essence of what it means to be human.

Second, Maddi's phrase *commonalities and differences* suggests an important aspect of human behavior. An often quoted adage suggests that every person is in certain respects

- like all other people;
- like some other people; and
- like no other person.[6]

Theories of personality often make statements both about things that are common to all people and things that set people apart from each other. To attempt to understand the personality of an individual, then, is to attempt to understand what that individual has in common with others, as well as what makes that individual unique. For the manager, this means that each subordinate is unique and may or may not respond the same way to praise, reprimands, pay raises, and so on. This complexity is one of the things that makes managing people so challenging.

Finally, Maddi's definition refers to personality as being *stable* and having *continuity in time*. Most people intuitively recognize this stability. If a person's entire personality could change suddenly and dramatically, that individual's family and friends would be confronted with a stranger. People do not expect this to happen, but an individual's personality can change over time, and the definition presented here does not imply otherwise.

Personality development can occur to a certain extent throughout life, although the greatest changes occur in early childhood. Experience—that is, being exposed to new people and situations—*does* influence personality. People learn new ways of behaving and can vary their behavior from previously established patterns. For example, new employees can be influenced significantly by the demands of a work setting, and their personalities may change somewhat as a result of the socializing influence of the organization.

SOURCES OF PERSONALITY DIFFERENCES

What determines an individual's personality? This question has no single answer because too many variables contribute to the development of each individual's personality. However, the sources of personality differences can be grouped into several major categories such as heredity, culture, family, group membership, and life experiences. Examining these categories helps us to understand why individuals are different.

Heredity

A belief in a genetic basis for personality is deeply ingrained in many people's notions of personality. Expressions such as "She is just like her father," and "He gets those irritating qualities from your side of the family, dear," imply a genetic explanation for personality. Heredity determines physique, eye color, hair color, certain physiological characteristics of the muscle and nervous systems, and so on. The way others react to a person's appearance and physical capacities can affect the formation of that individual's personality. Genetic factors also influence personality in a more direct manner although the extent to which they do is the subject of much debate. The **nature–nurture controversy** in personality theory concerns the question of how much personality is influenced by genetics. The extreme *nature* (or nativism) position argues that personality is largely inherited. The *nurture* (or empiricism) position is that personality attributes are not inherited, but rather are determined by a person's experiences. Current thinking with regard to the nature–nurture debate can be summarized as follows:

- The degree to which personality is genetically or environmentally determined varies a great deal from one personality characteristic to another.
- To understand personality development, we must examine the interaction between heredity and environment, since each plays a part.
- Heredity sets limits on the range of development of characteristics; within this range, characteristics are determined by environmental forces.[7]

On balance, most experts consider that the environment plays a larger role in shaping personality than do inherited characteristics, as suggested by Figure 3–1.

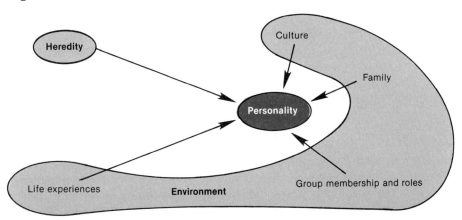

FIGURE 3–1.
Influences on Personality Development

Culture

Anthropologists working in different cultures have clearly demonstrated the important role that culture plays in personality formation.[8] Individuals born into a particular culture are exposed to existing values and norms concerning acceptable and appropriate behavior. Culture defines how the different roles necessary to life in that society are to be performed. For example, to varying degrees, people in all cultures commonly socialize children differently according to sex. Also, every society expects different behaviors from people of different age groups. However, each culture uniquely prescribes which behavioral responses are to be reinforced. For example, U.S. culture rewards people for being independent and competitive; Japanese culture rewards individuals for being cooperative and oriented toward group needs.

While culture determines, in part, broad patterns of behavioral similarity among people, extreme differences in behavior can exist among individuals within a culture. For example, the Protestant work ethic is usually associated with Western culture, but it is incorrect to assume that this value influences all individuals within this culture to the same degree. Thus managers must recognize that culture has an impact on the development of employees' personalities, but they must not assume that all individuals respond to the influence of their culture equally or that all cultures are homogeneous.

Family

The primary vehicle for socializing an individual into a particular culture is the person's immediate family. Both parents and siblings play important roles in personality development for most individuals. Members of the extended family—grandparents, aunts, uncles, cousins—if present in a person's life to any appreciable degree, also influence personality formation. Parents, in particular, influence their children's development in three important ways:

- Through their own behavior they present situations that elicit certain behavior in children.
- They serve as role models with which children often strongly identify.
- They selectively reward certain behaviors.[9]

In addition, the family situation also serves as an important source of personality differences among people. Situational influences include the socioeconomic level of the family, family size, birth order, race, family religion, geographical location, parents' educational level, and so on.[10] For example, a person raised in a poor family simply has different experiences and opportunities than a person raised in a rich family. Being an only child is different in some important respects from being raised with eight brothers and sisters.

Group Membership

The first group to which most individuals belong is the family. However, people also participate in a wide variety of groups during their lives, beginning with their childhood playmates and continuing through schoolmates, sports teams, social groups, and so on into adult work and social groups. The numerous roles and experiences resulting from varied group membership represent another important source of personality differences among people. While playmates and school groups early in life may have the strongest influences on personality formation, social and group experiences in later life continue to influence and shape personality to a certain extent. The impact that other people have on your personality continues throughout your life. A full understanding of a person's personality at any point in time requires an understanding of the groups—past and present—to which that person belongs.

Life Experiences

In addition to genetic, cultural, family, and group membership differences, each individual's life is unique in terms of events and experiences. These events and experiences can serve as important determinants of personality. For example, a student who cannot decide on a professional career, or who is equally drawn to several different vocations, happens to sit in an airplane next to a lawyer who is an engaging and persuasive advocate of the legal profession. Their discussion may set off a chain of events that expose the student to situations that lead to further personality shaping or even a change in academic program. Of course, life experiences and circumstances occur in the context of the other categories of influences presented. For example, family events such as divorce or child abuse have been shown to sometimes have a dramatic and negative impact on personality development in children.[11]

Interdependence of Influences

An individual's personality is the product both of inherited traits or tendencies and experiences. These experiences occur within the framework of the individual's biological, physical, and social environment—all of which are modified by the culture, family, and other group ties. All of these considerations must be balanced in determining influences on personality. The following description illustrates the complex interdependence of influences on personality, as well as the importance sometimes attached to an individual's personality.

In Practice: T. Boone Pickens

To many, he is a real-life J. R. Ewing, the ruthless but fascinating wheeler-dealer whom viewers of Dallas love to hate—and sometimes secretly admire. To his victims, mostly entrenched corporate executives, he is a dangerous upstart, a sneaky poker player, a veritable rattlesnake in the woodpile. To his fans, though, he is a modern David, a champion of the little guy who takes on the Goliaths of Big Oil and more often than not gives them a costly whupping. Whichever image he evokes T. (for Thomas) Boone Pickens, 56, has swept up like a twister out of Amarillo, Texas, to become one of the most famous and controversial businessmen in the U.S. today.

Pickens, the chairman of Mesa Petroleum (1984 sales: $413 million), an oil and gas producer with 650 employees, has gone eyeball to eyeball with the biggest, strongest and sometimes least loved of all U.S. firms, oil companies, and forced them to blink. Indeed, just the fear of Pickens has sent energy giants scrambling to merge with one another. Says Joseph Fogg III of the investment banking firm Morgan Stanley: "You would have to go back to the past century, to people like Jay Gould and Jim Fisk, to find someone who has had an equivalent impact on a major American industry." Those two financiers reshaped U.S. railroads by forcing the consolidation of many different lines. Today Pickens is performing much the same feat in the energy industry.

(. . .)

Pickens has made more than $800 million for Mesa and its partners in the past three years by all but rearranging the map of a key sector of corporate America. The consequences of his actions have been stunning. They have resulted in the end of Gulf Oil, Cities Service and others as independent companies. Pickens last year forced Gulf (1984 sales: $28.4 billion), the fifth largest U.S. oil company, to sell out to No. 4 Chevron ($29.2 billion) for $13.2 billion in the biggest merger in business history. The Pickens group's profit on that deal: $760 million. Earlier, it earned $31.5 million by driving Cities Service ($8.5 billion before its 1982 merger) into the arms of Occidental Petroleum.

(. . .)

The Texas oilman has reaped his vast payoffs through the mastery of the take-over battle, a colorful form of corporate warfare fought with dollars, stock and shareholder votes. The campaigns are as vivid as the terminology of their tactics. A takeover raider typically launches his attack by buying a significant percentage of a firm's stock and offering to pay other shareholders more than the current market level for their securities. The goal is to get enough shares—typically 51%—to win control of the company and the ability to run it. Management and the raider frequently get into open warfare through expensive mailings and full-page ads in newspapers in which they disparage their opponents and appeal to stockholders. Eventually shareowners have to decide whether they want to support the current management or the raider.

(. . .)

Pickens has contempt for what he calls the entrenched managers who run Big Oil. He views them as high-salaried hired hands who care more about maintaining their jobs than improving stock value for their shareholders. Says he: "Chief executives, who themselves own few shares of their companies, have no more feeling for the average stockholder than they do for baboons in Africa." Pickens calculates that, as a group, officers of the energy giants own just three-tenths of 1% of their firms' shares. (Pickens owns 2.2% of Mesa.) Since they have relatively small investments in their corporations, he argues, oil executives have tended to let stock prices languish. "It infuriates me," he says, "to see them invest their own money in Treasury bills rather than work to improve the value of their companies' stock. According to John S. Herold Inc., an appraiser of oil companies, shares of major energy firms are currently trading at about 45% of what the corporations would be worth if they were broken up and their assets sold separately.

(. . .)

Some of Pickens' hostility toward his gargantuan rivals stems from frustration. "Big Oil is a club," says he, "and they'll do everything to keep me out." That can sometimes seem to include snubbing him at social gatherings. The chairman of one oil giant, a former friend, now looks the other way when he runs into Pickens at industry meetings.

Oil industry executives are as tough on Pickens as he is on them. "He's only after the almighty buck," says G. C. Richardson, a retired executive of Cities Service. He's nothing but a pirate." Gulf Chairman James Lee accuses Pickens of "hit-and-run tactics." Says Chevron Chairman George Keller: "Pickens does not break any laws doing what he does. But he breaks tradition." Many oilmen are reluctant to discuss Pickens publicly for fear of drawing his attention to their companies. Says one executive: "They want to let sleeping dogs lie."

(. . .)

Like many independent oilmen, Pickens was born within sight of working wells. He grew up in Holdenville, Oklahoma (pop. 6,300), a cow town surrounded by pastures, where cattle graze alongside active oil pumps. An only child, Pickens was raised on a street of white clapboard houses and green lawns. The family is fond of tracing its ancestry back to the same part of England that produced a distant kinsman, Daniel Boone.

Pickens' father, Thomas Boone Pickens Sr., now 86 and living in Amarillo, was an inveterate gambler who made and lost a fortune buying and selling oil leases. He also wagered frequently on college football games. During the depths of the Great Depression, he drove around Holdenville in a dazzling Pierce-Arrow. Recalls Tommy Treadwell, a retired local banker: "Little T-Bone, as his father called him, was so embarrassed about that car that he insisted on being dropped two blocks from school whenever his father drove him there." Pickens' mother, by contrast, was a practical woman who never made snap decisions. During World War II, she ran Holdenville's gas-rationing program. "I was very fortunate in my gene mix," says Pickens. "The gambling instincts I inherited from my father were matched by my mother's gift for analysis." While in high school, Pickens moved with his family to Amarillo (pop. 170,000), the unofficial capital of the Texas Panhandle, which has remained his home.

(. . .)

The master takeover tactician combines down-home shrewdness with boardroom savvy. While his talk is rich in good-ole-boy phrases like "that dog won't hunt" or "it's better than a poke in the eye with a stick," Pickens is every inch the businessman. In place of the pointed boots and Stetson hats that many independent oilmen wear, he favors sober gray suits, button-down shirts and striped ties. He rarely smiles, but when he does, the grin spreads slowly, almost reluctantly, across his face. Says a friend: "He deals with everyone, from Senators to bank presidents, as if he's telling them fishing stories." Yet he can be flint hard. Told of a worker who had been laid off after having given 30 years to his company, Pickens snapped, "Given? Didn't he get paid?"

(. . .)

Pickens constantly portrays himself as the friend of the little guy. Crisscrossing the country in his jet, he addressed 87 audiences and 45,000 people last year. He now averages two speeches a week on the evils of Big Oil and the need for a shareholder uprising against bad management. He frequently tells audiences: "Blacks have learned to use their right to vote, and so will shareholders." Pickens is putting his ideas into a book that he is writing with San Francisco journalist Moira Johnston.[12]

PERSONALITY AND BEHAVIOR

Do the individual differences referred to as personality have any concrete, identifiable impact on individual behavior? Recall that a key idea, introduced earlier, in the concept of personality is that it represents characteristics of people that account for consistency in their behavior in various situations. Behavioral science research has isolated a number of personality dimensions, or traits, that can be linked convincingly to behavior. This section contains descriptions of several dimensions that are particularly important for interpersonal and organizational behavior.[13]

Locus of Control

The **locus of control** refers to the extent to which individuals believe that events that occur to them are basically under their control. Individuals who have a high *internal locus of control* believe that the events in their lives are primarily (but not necessarily exclusively) the result of their own behavior and actions. Individuals who have a high *external locus of control*, on the other hand, believe that life's events are primarily determined by chance, fate, or other people. Table 3-1 provides an example of questionnaire items used to measure locus of control beliefs. There is some evidence that *internals* have better control over their own behavior, are more active politically and socially, and more actively seek information and knowledge concerning their situation than do *externals*.

Other differences between internals and externals are significant in potentially explaining behavior in organizational settings. For example, in comparison with externals, internals make more attempts to influence or

---

TABLE 3-1   Example Items Used to Measure Locus of Control

Please state the extent of your agreement or disagreement with the following statements.
Internal Locus of Control:
  1. Whether or not I get to be a leader depends mostly on my ability.
  2. Whether or not I get into a car accident depends mostly on how good a driver I am.
  3. When I make plans, I am almost certain to make them work.
  4. How many friends I have depends on how nice a person I am.

External Locus of Control (Powerful others):
  5. I feel like what happens in my life is mostly determined by powerful people.
  6. Although I might have good ability, I will not be given leadership responsibility without appealing to those in positions of power.
  7. My life is chiefly controlled by powerful others.
  8. People like myself have very little chance of protecting our personal interests when they conflict with those of strong pressure groups.

External Locus of Control (Chance):
  9. To a great extent my life is controlled by accidental happenings.
 10. Often there is no chance of protecting my personal interest from bad luck happenings.
 11. When I get what I want, it's usually because I'm lucky.
 12. I have often found that what is going to happen will happen.

Source: Adapted from Levenson, H., and Miller, J. Multidimensional Locus of Control in Sociopolitical Activists of Conservative and Liberal Ideologies. *Journal of Personality and Social Psychology,* 1976, *33,* 199–208.

persuade others and are less amenable to influence from others. Internals may be more achievement oriented than externals. Some evidence shows that externals, compared with internals, prefer a more structured, directive style of supervision. Much research remains to be done, but real differences in behavior have been demonstrated across a wide range of people and settings; locus of control beliefs seem to represent a personality dimension of some importance for understanding human behavior. For example, Figure 3-2 illustrates the possible relationships among locus of control, task performance, and expectations about performance on future tasks.

The locus of control is a *continuous* personality dimension, as are the ones that follow. That is, people are not exclusively internals or externals. Imagine a continuum with "high internal" at one end and "high external" at the other: all people fall somewhere on that line with regard to their locus of control beliefs.

Introversion/Extraversion

The terms *introversion* and *extraversion* are often associated with the personality theory of Carl Gustav Jung, whose ideas are presented in Chapter 5. In everyday speech the labels *introvert* and *extravert* describe a person's sociability: Introverts are shy, retiring people, and extraverts are gregarious or outgoing. The terms have similar meanings when used to refer to a personality dimension. **Introversion** is a tendency of the mind to be directed inward and have a greater sensitivity to abstract ideas, personal feelings, and

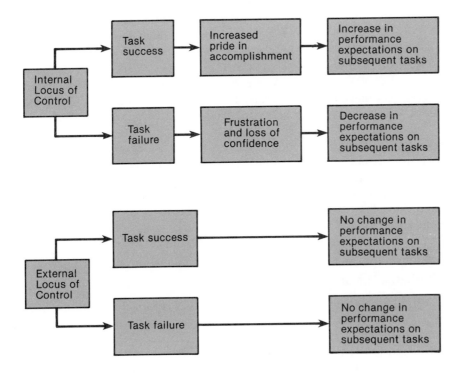

FIGURE 3-2.
Influence of Locus of Control on Performance Expectations

Source: Richard M. Steers. *Introduction to Organizational Behavior.* Copyright © 1981 Scott, Foresman and Company. Reprinted by permission.

so on. **Extraversion** is a more outward orientation of the mind directed toward other people, events, and objects.

In Jung's personality theory, both introversion and extraversion are present in each person as emotional orientations of the personality. Introversion orients the person toward the inner, subjective world, whereas extraversion orients the individual toward the external, objective world. One of these orientations usually dominates and exists in the conscious mind, and the other, subordinate orientation exists in the unconscious mind.

The research of Hans Eysenck has contributed much to the acceptance of introversion/extraversion as a personality dimension having important implications for social behavior. The work of Eysenck and others suggests that the extravert is best described as "sociable, lively, impulsive, seeking novelty and change, carefree, and emotionally expressive." The introvert, in contrast, is described behaviorally as "quiet, introspective, intellectual, well-ordered, emotionally unexpressive, and value oriented; prefers small groups of intimate friends; and plans well ahead."[14]

Most of us can probably think of individuals who tend to characterize the extremes of introversion and extraversion. However, individuals vary in the degree to which they are introverted, extraverted, or relatively balanced between the extremes. A wide distribution of introvert and extravert types occurs across educational level, gender, and occupation. As might be expected, extraverts seem to be disproportionately represented in the managerial occupations. Some research even suggests that extraversion is important to managerial success. Since the manager's role often involves identifying and solving problems with and through other individuals (Chapter 1), a certain degree of extraversion may be essential. However, an extremely extraverted orientation can result in individuals literally sacrificing themselves to external conditions and demands. Managers who become totally immersed in their jobs at the cost of their family and social lives are examples of this. Introverts, on the other hand, tend to interject a personal view between their perception of external demands and other outside factors and their work and decisions. As a result, the extreme introvert may choose courses of action that do not readily fit external situations. Either extreme can interfere with an individual's effectiveness in an organization.

One of the most striking implications of the introversion/extraversion personality dimension for organizational behavior involves task performance in different environments. Some evidence suggests that introverts perform better in an environment where there is little sensory stimulation, whereas extraverts perform better in an environment with greater sensory stimulation—more people, noise, change, and so on. Thus the extreme introvert might work best alone in a quiet office, while the extreme extravert may well prefer a noisy office with many people and clacking typewriters.

Authoritarianism and Dogmatism

The original research on **authoritarianism** was spurred by the events of World War II. It was designed to identify personality predispositions for susceptibility to fascistic or antidemocratic appeals. Over time, however, the concept broadened. The authoritarian personality is now described as one that rigidly adheres to conventional values, readily obeys recognized authority, exhibits a negative view of mankind, is concerned with power and toughness, and opposes the use of subjective feelings.

Dogmatism is a closely related term that essentially refers to the rigidity of a person's beliefs. The highly dogmatic individual regards the world as a threatening place, often regards legitimate authority as absolute, and accepts or rejects other people on the basis of their agreement or disagreement with accepted authority or doctrine. In short, the high dogmatic (HD) individual is close-minded, and the low dogmatic (LD) person is open-minded.

The implications of these personality dimensions for organizational behavior are less clear than the implications for locus of control and introversion/extraversion. However, there is some evidence that HDs depend more on authority figures in the organization and are more easily influenced by them. In addition, the authoritarian personality probably is subservient to authority figures and may even prefer a highly directive, structured leadership style from superiors. Also, there appears to be some relationship between the degree of dogmatism and interpersonal and group behavior. For example, HDs typically need more group structure than LDs to work effectively with others. This means that the performance of HDs on task forces, committee assignments, and so on may vary somewhat depending on how the group goes about doing its task. Some evidence also suggests that a high degree of dogmatism is related to a limited search for information in decision situations and, perhaps as a result, sometimes to poor managerial performance.

Self-Esteem

Self-esteem is defined as the evaluation an individual makes with regard to himself or herself. People have opinions of their own behavior, abilities, appearance, and worth. These general assessments or judgments of their worthiness as a person, while somewhat affected by situations, success or failure, and opinions of others, nevertheless are stable enough to be widely regarded as a basic characteristic or dimension of the personality. As such, self-esteem has some important relationships to behavior in organizational and other settings.[15] For example, self-esteem has been discovered to be related to initial vocational choice. Individuals with high self-esteem will take more risks in job selection, may be more attracted to high-status occupations, and are more likely to choose unconventional or nontraditional jobs than individuals with low self-esteem. A study of college students engaged in the job search process reported that levels of self-esteem predicted (1) interview evaluations received from organizational recruiters; (2) satisfaction with the job search; (3) the number of job offers received; (4) acceptance of a job before graduation; and (5) the length of stay in the job.[16]

Among school children, self-esteem has been found to be positively related to assertiveness, independence, and creativity. In addition, self-esteem is related to other important social and work behaviors.[17] Persons with low self-esteem have more difficulty in forming interpersonal attachments. High self-esteem persons often find it easier to give and receive affection and thus may make friends more easily in many settings. In organizations and other social settings, low self-esteem individuals are more easily influenced and high self-esteem individuals less easily influenced by the opinions of others.

At work, low self-esteem individuals will set lower goals for themselves, while employees high in self-esteem will tend to set higher goals. In a general sense, self-esteem is positively correlated with attempts to achieve or a willingness to expend effort in task accomplishment.

THE PERSON AND THE SITUATION

At this point in examining individual differences, it is important to again recognize that behavior always occurs within a particular situation or context. While individual differences, such as personality, are important in understanding behavior, every person's behavior is always a complex interaction of the person and the situation. Sometimes the demands of the situation may be so overwhelming that individual differences among people seem relatively unimportant. For example, if a room catches fire everyone in it may flee, yet the observation that everyone behaved in the same way certainly says nothing about important differences among the individuals involved. In other cases, individual differences may explain a larger portion of the variance in behavior. For example, the Preview Case describes two individuals who received the same *stimulus* from the environment (a grade of D on an examination), yet behaved very differently owing to important differences between them. The relative importance of situational versus personal determinants of behavior is an ongoing debate in the psychological sciences.[18] However, there is considerable evidence for both personality and situational determinants of behavior.[19] In order to understand behavior in complex social settings, such as organizations, we must have an *interactionist* perspective. That is, we must examine both the person and the situation within which the person is behaving in order to fully understand and explain the individual's behavior. The interactionist perspective is increasingly important for understanding organizational behavior.[20]

ATTITUDES: AN INTRODUCTION

Attitudes are defined as "relatively lasting organizations of feelings, beliefs, and behavior tendencies directed towards specific persons, groups, ideas, or objects."[21] As such, attitudes represent another type of *individual difference* that affects behavior in organizations. An individual's attitudes are a product of the person's background and various life experiences. As with personality, significant people in a person's life—parents, friends, members of social and work groups—strongly influence attitude formation.

We often speak of attitudes in everyday conversation as though they are a simple concept with clear relationships to individual behavior; in reality attitudes can be extremely complex. Some insight into this complexity is offered by social psychologists who often describe an attitude in terms of three components:

- An *affective* component or the feelings, sentiments, moods, and emotions about some person(s), idea, event, or object.
- A *cognitive* component or the beliefs, opinions, knowledge, or information held by the individual.
- A *behavioral* component or the intention and predisposition to act.[22]

These components do not exist or function separately; thus an attitude represents the *interplay* of a person's emotions, cognitions, and behavioral tendencies with regard to something—another person or group, an event, an idea, and so on—in the individual's social world. For example, suppose that you hold a very strong, negative attitude about the nuclear arms race. You are at a job interview with a large corporation and, during the course of the interview, discover that the company is a major supplier of nuclear weapons (a fact you were previously unaware of). You might feel a sudden intense dislike for the company's interviewer (the affective component). You might form a negative opinion of the interviewer based on your beliefs and knowledge regarding the kinds of people who would work for such a company (the cognitive component). You might be tempted to make an unkind remark to the interviewer or suddenly terminate the interview (the behavioral component). In this case your actual behavior will depend on a number of variables, including the strength of your attitude toward the arms race.

ATTITUDES AND BEHAVIOR

A fundamental question that continues to interest investigators is: To what extent do attitudes predict or cause behavior? For a long time, it was thought that individuals behaved in a manner consistent with the attitudes that they held. While there is little question that attitudes are related to behavior, it is now widely accepted that there is frequently not a simple, direct link between attitudes and behavior.[23] In the above example, the person being interviewed might have those negative feelings, opinions, and intentions described and yet choose not to behave negatively toward the interviewer because (1) the individual desperately needs a job; (2) the norms of courteous behavior are stronger than the person's desire to express a negative attitude; (3) the individual decides that the interviewer is an inappropriate target for the negative behavior; or (4) the individual acknowledges the possibility of incomplete information.

There has been considerable interest in measuring attitudes and then trying to predict subsequent behavior. It has been found that prediction of behavior from attitudes can be improved if three principles are observed:

- General attitudes best predict general behaviors.
- Specific attitudes best predict specific behaviors.
- The less the time that elapses between attitude measurement and behavior, the more consistent will be the relationship between attitude and behavior.[24]

For example, attitudes toward conservation in general would not be as good a predictor of whether someone will join the Sierra Club as would specific attitudes toward the Sierra Club. General attitudes toward religion would not be good predictors of specific behavior, such as giving to a certain church-related charity or observing a specific religious holiday, but may accurately predict general religious behavior, such as the overall level of involvement in church activities. Attitudes are learned and can change over time. Thus, as a rule of thumb, the longer the time between the measurement of an attitude and some behavior, the less likely it is that some relationship will be observed. This third principle is now well-known to political pollsters, and they are typically careful not to predict voting behavior too far in advance of an actual election. (Or they may be careful to add certain qualifiers to published polls, such as "If the election were held today. . . .")

A model of the attitude–behavior relationship has been presented by Ajzen and Fishbein.[25] In their **behavioral intentions model** Ajzen and Fishbein suggested that behavior is more predictable (and understandable) if we focus on a person's specific *intentions* to behave in a certain way rather than solely on his or her attitudes toward that behavior. The model is illustrated in Figure 3-3 and shows that intentions depend on both attitudes and norms regarding the behavior. A *norm* is defined as the individual's perception of social pressures to perform or not to perform the behavior in question. (The concept of norms will be explored more fully in Chapter 9.) If both attitudes and norms are positive with regard to the behavior, the intention to behave in a certain way will be high. If attitudes and norms conflict, their relative strength may determine the individual's intentions and subsequent behavior. The behavioral intentions model further suggests that both attitudes and norms are affected by beliefs that the individual holds regarding specific behaviors. In the case of attitudes, the important beliefs are thought to be concerned with the relationship between the behavior and its consequences (outcomes). (These beliefs, sometimes called *expectancies,* also play an important role in our understanding of motivation; see Chapter 7.) Beliefs regarding norms reflect an individual's perceptions of how others expect that person to act. The behavioral intentions model seems to explain why the relationship between attitudes and behavior can sometimes be strong and at other times be weak. The concept that attitudes have affective, cognitive, and behavioral components is not inconsistent with the behavioral intentions model: all three components can play a part in the attitude–behavior relationship.

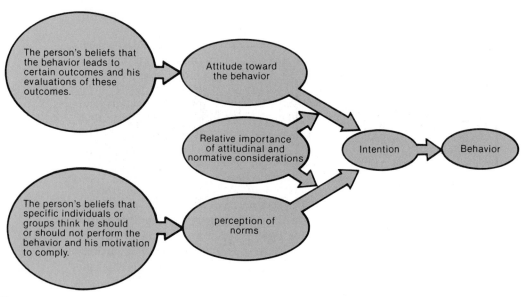

FIGURE 3–3.
The Ajzen–Fishbein Behavioral Intentions Model

ACROSS CULTURES

Changes in Japanese Work Attitudes

Some tiny cracks are appearing in Japan's celebrated work ethic. There are few numbers yet, and no traceable loss of productivity or erosion of quality. The evidence is mostly anecdotal, often as subtly Japanese as the tinkle of wind chimes in a garden. Workers rarely show up early anymore to warm the oil in their machines before their shifts start. Defying precedent, a young management trainee actually takes all of the 15 vacation days allotted to him. Growing hordes of young Japanese sometimes slip away early on Friday and crowd the ski slopes on weekends.

The shift in mood is perceptible enough to begin troubling employers as well as sociologists and others who ponder Japan's future. The country's most strategic natural resource may well be its devoted labor force, and any change in its attitude, no matter how slight, is cause for concern. Though competitors in the U.S. and Europe might welcome the trend, having its youth go flat would be a national disaster for Japan.

Blue-collar and white-collar workers alike embrace the new attitude, but it seems most noticeable, and most threatening, among recent college graduates, who will one day be running Japan's corporations. In March 1984 the Japan Recruitment Center, a private firm that collects information on hiring, published a survey of 7,800 male college grads about to enter the work force. The survey showed that the portion of those who describe themselves as oriented toward "home" rather than toward "company" continues to grow—72% this year vs. 66% when the center started the survey seven years ago.

Those findings square with employers' observations that younger workers are less committed to teamwork, more individualistic, and more detached from their jobs than their elders are. They don't even bring their problems, either personal or job related, to their superiors the way they used to, preferring to talk them over with family or friends.

A decade ago the Japanese language contained no idiom like the West's TGIF (Thank God It's Friday). Today many young office workers exchange salutations of "*Hana no kinyobi,*" which freely translated means "Friday's the greatest." They take longish Friday lunch hours and let their thoughts drift to the weekend social calendar. Sports and friends, not work and study, give meaning to life, young Japanese said in a recent government survey.

Some research suggests that Japan's younger workers are already more alienated from their jobs than workers in many Western countries. In a recent survey conducted by the Prime Minister's office, only 14% of young Japanese said they were satisfied with their workplace compared with 70% in the U.S. One big reason for that dislike of the job is the Japanese practice of assigning young managers to production or marketing or whatever, regardless of the employees' desires. Typically, Keisuke Nishimura, 27, complains that he'd like to move out of the labor section of Kirin Brewery, where he analyzes pay scales, into another department, but feels powerless to do anything about it.

The Aspen Institute for Humanistic Studies has recently examined how well jobs and worker values are matched in six countries: Britain, Israel, Japan, Sweden, the U.S., and West Germany. In defining values, it takes into account worker expectations for a living wage, additional material reward for good performance, and a sense of inner satisfaction

> from the job. Britain and Japan, the study found, show the greatest disparity between what workers hope for and what they actually get from their jobs.
>
> The Japanese work ethic will almost certainly not collapse, although it may sag enough to slow the country down. Japan's top management might do some things to prop it up, such as reconsidering the practice of assigning young managers without regard to their preferences. Short of a national emergency, however, Japan's young people seem unlikely to be transformed into what they call the "working devils" of a generation ago who astounded the world.[26]

WORK ATTITUDES: JOB SATISFACTION

In organizational behavior, perhaps the attitude that is of most interest is the general attitude toward work or toward a job—often called job satisfaction. In the most general sense, **job satisfaction** is "a pleasurable or positive emotional state resulting from the appraisal of one's job or job experiences."[27] This positive assessment or feeling seems to occur when work is congruent with the individual's needs and values. The kinds of needs that can be met in the work environment and the importance of these needs for understanding employee motivation and behavior will be explored in some detail in Chapter 7.

Although job satisfaction is often regarded as a unitary concept (that is, a person is satisfied with the job, or not), it is best considered as a collection of related job attitudes that can be divided into a variety of job aspects. For example, a popular measure of job satisfaction—the Job Description Index (JDI)—measures satisfaction in terms of five specific aspects of a person's job: pay, promotion, supervision, the work itself, and co-workers.[28] An employee can obviously be satisfied with some aspects of the job and, at the same time, be dissatisfied with others.

The sources of job satisfaction and dissatisfaction vary from person to person. Sources thought to be important for many employees include the challenge of the job, the degree of interest that the work holds for the person, the extent of physical activity, working conditions, rewards available from the organization, the nature of co-workers, and so on. Table 3-2 lists a number of work factors that research indicates are often related to levels of employee job satisfaction.

Of particular interest to managers and organizations are the consequences of job satisfaction. The difficulty of relating attitudes to behavior is pertinent here. For example, a common-sense notion suggests that job satisfaction should lead directly to better performance on a task. ("A happy worker is a good worker.") Yet, numerous studies have shown that a simple, direct linkage between job attitudes and job performance often does not exist.[29] Earlier, it was suggested that general attitudes best predict general classes of behaviors and specific attitudes are most strongly related to specific behaviors. These principles explain, at least in part, why expected relationships between job satisfaction and performance often are not present.[30] Overall job satisfaction, as a collection of numerous attitudes toward various aspects of the job, represents a very general attitude. Performance on a specific task cannot necessarily be predicted well by such a general attitude

TABLE 3-2   **Effects of Various Work Factors on Job Satisfaction**

Source	Effect
Work itself: Challenge	Mentally challenging work that the individual can successfully accomplish is satisfying.
Work itself: Physical demand	Tiring work is dissatisfying.
Work itself: Personal interest	Personally interesting work is satisfying.
Reward structure	Just and informative rewards for performance are satisfying.
Working conditions: Physical	Satisfaction depends on the match between working conditions and physical needs.
Working conditions: Goal attainment	Working conditions that facilitate goal attainment are satisfying.
Self	High self-esteem is conducive to job satisfaction.
Supervisors, co-workers, subordinates	Individuals will be satisfied with colleagues who help them attain rewards.
	Individuals will be satisfied with colleagues who see things the same way they do.
Company and management	Individuals will be satisfied with companies that have policies and procedures designed to help the individual attain rewards.
	Individuals will be dissatisfied with conflicting roles and/or ambiguous roles imposed by company and/or management.
Fringe benefits	Benefits do not have a strong influence on job satisfaction for most workers.

Source: Landy, F. J., and Trumbo, D. A. *Psychology of Work Behavior.* Homewood, Ill.: Dorsey, 1980, 410. Copyright 1980. Reprinted with permission.

measure, although it might well be predicted by very specific attitudes toward the task itself.

Although job satisfaction does not lead directly to good performance, there are a number of valid reasons why employee job satisfaction is very important for organizations. Levels of job satisfaction have been linked convincingly to absenteeism, turnover, and physical and mental health.[31] However, with regard to job satisfaction as well as other attitudes, the greatest understanding of attitude–behavior relationships probably comes from examining *specific* attitudes related to a behavior along with other variables that influence a person's *intention* to behave in a certain way.

SUMMARY

Personality represents the characteristics and traits of a person that account for consistent patterns of behavior across situations. Each individual is in some ways like other people and in some ways unique. Differences in personality stem from differences in heredity, culture, family, group memberships, and life experiences. There are a number of specific personality dimensions, such as locus of control, introversion/extraversion, and self-esteem, that have important implications for behavior in organizations. The study of personality and the understanding of interactions between the person and the situation are increasingly important for understanding organizational behavior.

Attitudes are organizations of feelings, beliefs, and behavior tendencies directed toward specific persons, groups, ideas, or objects. As such, they may be thought of as containing affective, cognitive, and behavioral components. The relationship between attitudes and behavior is not always straightforward although important relationships exist. The attitude-behavior relationship may be clearer if we can examine the individual's intentions to behave in a certain way. Job satisfaction—the general collection of attitudes an individual holds toward the job—is among the attitudes that are of greatest interest for organizational behavior.

KEY WORDS AND CONCEPTS

Attitudes
Authoritarianism
Behavioral intentions model
Dogmatism
Extraversion
General theory of behavior
Individual differences

Introversion
Job satisfaction
Locus of control
Nature–Nurture controversy
Personality
Self-esteem

DISCUSSION QUESTIONS

1. Discuss the basic factors that influence personality development.
2. Describe the opposing positions in the nature–nurture controversy over personality formation. What sources of influences on personality formation seem most important to you? Why?
3. Give some examples of how the family situation that an individual is born into might play an important role in determining adult personality characteristics.
4. Based on the profile presented in the chapter, write a brief description of the likely important influences on T. Boone Pickens' personality.
5. Describe the general relationship between personality and behavior.
6. Which of the personality dimensions discussed seems most important for managerial behavior? Why?
7. Which seems most important—personality characteristics or the situation—in determining behavior? Why?
8. What are the basic components of attitudes?
9. In your own words describe the Behavioral Intentions Model. Is this model a good representation of attitude–behavior relationships? Why or why not?
10. What is the meaning of job satisfaction? Why is it important?

MANAGEMENT INCIDENTS AND CASES

The Attitude Survey at Artisan[32]

In early summer 1985, twenty-nine year old Bill Meister was a little surprised at his "super-star" status. One year ago, in a crisis situation, he had taken over as president of the ten million dollar-a-year family-run company and successfully halted Artisan Industries' slide into bankruptcy. Outsiders, such as the banks and suppliers, had renewed confidence in the company and the em-

ployees now looked toward a chance at higher wages and job security.

Bill had looked forward to shaping up and heading an exciting, highly competent organization. He was greatly interested in the newest concepts of management, frequently commenting on the latest book or sending a copy of an article to his managers. The behavioral writing made a lot of sense to him and he was himself quite perceptive of behavioral processes in meetings or situations. The participative management systems and cooperative team environments were ones Bill wanted very much for Artisan.

However in his first year he had slowly begun to doubt that his managers and the workforce were ready. On a number of occasions he had observed his managers manipulating rather than cooperating, and the workers appeared neither skilled nor productive. The first-line supervisors lacked any current management training and had been of little use so far in his efforts. For example, when he discussed the workers' desires with the supervisors he was told they wanted a retirement program and higher pay, nothing else. Bill felt, however, this was really only what the supervisors themselves wanted.

Bill was ready to scale back his expectations if necessary and view improvement in the personnel systems as a very long term project. Rather than guess at what the employees saw and wanted, it made sense to carry out an attitude survey. From this he could sharpen his understanding of the employees and choose his actions more wisely.

Background

Artisan had been founded by Bill's father, a classical entrepreneur, in the early fifties. His father had done well against many setbacks to bring the company to its current size, but things had not gone well in recent years. He had fought against Bill's replacing him as president and several tense months resulted. Only outside pressure from the lenders resulted in Bill's ascension to the presidency.

In May 1984 when Bill Meister became president, Artisan was in critical condition. Sales had fallen off dramatically, there had been little profit for three years, the number of employees had fallen from 600 to 370, modern management did not exist in any area of the company, and there were few qualified managers. "When I took over, sales were running 50% off, we could not get a line of credit and we were on a cash basis only with our suppliers, inventory was still relatively high, Accounts Receivable were running over 120 days, manufacturing was without anyone in charge, and the company was sustaining a loss of approximately $10,000 per week. The general situation looked pretty hopeless."

But Bill had managed to turn things around and 1984 had ended with the best profit in years, $390,000. His major accomplishments had been improving the product line for saleability and implementing a price increase.

The company was one of four making up the wooden decorative products industry. Sales were seasonal, peaking with the Christmas period. Artisan's customers were some 13,000 retail shops which were serviced by outside sales representatives; and regional market shows were an important part of the marketing activity. The product-line consisted of over 1400 items and included almost anything for the consumer, from a tea-cart which was the largest item to a clothes-pin type desk paper clip which was the smallest.

Production was accomplished in two similar rural plants employing a total of about 300 people. Kiln-dry lumber entered at the back and progressed through six departments before finishing with staining, packing, and warehousing. Most jobs did not require high skill levels and wage rates were relatively low. Visitors to the plant considered the work-pace quite slow; the supervisors however did not. Orders were small, usually under 200 items, and made up of seven parts on the average. Thus runs were small, not at all like mass production.

Bill felt production efficiency was a major problem. In talks with machinery salesmen and other visitors to the plant over recent months, he had come to feel the machinery was generally inappropriate; but based on guesses about his competitors he felt his labor costs had to be reduced. Early attempts to work with the plant superintendent and the various supervisors to systematically improve output had met with no success. The supervisors had been unable to identify the needs for change in the plant or to develop the programs for bringing about improvement. To help the supervisors begin to improve their operations, a weekly production meeting had begun in June of 1984. At the meeting the supervisors were to examine the total dollar output and total labor cost for each plant for the past week, compare it to the labor percent goal set by Bill, and think about what could be done to improve operations for the coming week. Data on departmental performance was not available. During the first several meetings, a visiting consultant had to provide direction and ideas; the plant superintendent and his supervisors volunteered no ideas about what specifically limited the prior week's output. It was Bill's opinion that this kind of thinking and planning was not required under his father's management. The supervisors in general felt nothing was wrong in the plant and really seemed puzzled at the thought of doing anything except continuing what they had always done.

Recently an engineer from a competitor visited Artisan and dropped the following comments. He stated Artisan's workers were on average two-thirds as good as his. He added that this was the least directed operation he had ever seen, with the slowest pace and the lowest level of knowledge of this type of work. He noted they knew only the simple way of doing the job. Only one man in the company, for example, was able to count the board-feet of lumber, a skill possessed by the smallest cabi-

net shop and essential for any kind of usage control.

The Study

In May 1985 a business professor from a nearby university organized the study with Bill. It was based on a written questionnaire administered to all employees. The questionnaire was designed to (1) find out what employees wanted, for example more pay, retirement plans, more or less direction, etc., (2) gain insight into the probable impact of participative management moves, (3) establish benchmarks of employee satisfaction so that changes over time could be monitored, and (4) develop an objective profile of the workers.

The survey included questions developed specifically for this situation as well as a highly regarded attitude instrument, the Job Description Index. Although the wording was considered simple, many of the workers did not understand such words as "stimulating," "ambitious," or "fascinating," and it became necessary to read the entire questionnaire to them in small groups during an hour break period. The employees answered the questions very cooperatively and in good spirits.

The study provided some basic data such as that minorities accounted for 80% of the 300 employees; white females were the largest group at 40%. The workforce was 58% female, 57% white, and 39% over 45 years old. And as many people had been with the company under 2 years as had been with the company over 10 years—24%.

A portion of the data collected by the attitude survey is shown in Tables 3–3 and 3–4. In Table 3–4, the fifth of employees with the highest scores were labeled "satisfied" and compared with the fifth with the lowest scores, labeled "dissatisfied."

Questions

1. What are the employees like and what do they appear to want?

TABLE 3-3   Employees' Ranking for Things Wanted from Work

How important would improvement in the following things be to you?	Total Group Ranking
Longer coffee breaks	15
More holidays	8
Guaranteed work	2
Flexibility in hours or days off	10
More overtime opportunity	17
Better insurance	6
Better working conditions	4
Retirement plan	3
Higher pay	1
Education refund	16
Treated more as an individual	7
Better way to get complaints heard	5
Better equipment	4
More direction from supervisor	14
More opportunity to learn and improve self	4
More say in how my department does things	13
More opportunity to contribute to company success	9
Better decisions by top management	12
More information on what's going on	4
Be more in charge of own self	11

1 = Most Important

TABLE 3-4   Comparison of Satisfied and Unsatisfied Employees with Total Group

What is your opinion on the following statements? Do you agree or disagree? Please mark the appropriate box.	Total Group	Satis- fied	Unsat- isfied
1. My pay is fair for this kind of job.	2.26	2.6	1.9
2. My coworkers are good to work with.	4.14	4.6	3.4
3. My complaints or concerns are heard by management.	3.22	3.7	2.6
4. Things are getting better here.	3.45	4.5	2.3
5. The supervisors do a poor job.	2.35	2.1	2.6
6. I am fortunate to have this job.	3.95	4.6	3.4
7. Working conditions are bad here.	2.55	1.9	1.1
8. I benefit when the company succeeds.	3.11	3.5	2.5
9. I have all the chance I wish to improve myself.	3.19	4.1	2.4
10. The company is well run.	3.29	4.4	2.2
11. Communications are poor.	2.91	2.6	3.1
12. I don't get enough direction from my supervisor.	2.56	2.4	2.7
13. I enjoy my work.	4.13	4.8	3.4
14. I look for ways to improve the work I do.	4.21	4.7	4.0
15. I need more of a chance to manage myself.	3.11	3.0	3.5
16. I don't expect to be with the company long.	2.35	2.3	2.6
17. Morale is good here.	3.55	4.5	2.5
18. We all do only what it takes to get by.	2.19	1.8	2.2
19. I am concerned about layoffs and losing my job.	3.51	3.4	3.6
20. I like the way my supervisor treats me.	4.02	4.4	3.4
21. We need a suggestion system.	3.75	3.8	3.8
22. I want more opportunity for advancement.	3.86	3.8	3.9
23. My supervisor knows me and what I want from the job.	3.56	4.2	3.0
24. We are not expected to do a very good job.	2.01	2.1	2.0
25. There are too many rules.	2.58	2.2	2.9
26. I feel like part of a team at work.	3.82	4.3	3.1
27. The company and my supervisor seek my ideas.	3.06	3.6	2.4
28. I can influence department goals, methods and activities.	3.01	3.3	2.7

Answer format: 1 = Strongly disagree   4 = Agree
                 2 = Disagree   5 = Strongly agree
                 3 = No opinion

2. Is there a morale problem? Justify your answer.

3. What categories of items distinguish satisfied from dissatisfied employees?

4. What should Meister do to improve Artisan Industries?

REFERENCES

1. Quoted in Eysenck, H. J. *Personality, Genetics, and Behavior.* New York: Prager, 1982, 1.

2. For an excellent review supporting this point see Weiss, H. M., and Adler, S. Personality and Organizational Behavior. *Research in Organizational Behavior,* 1984, *6,* 1–50.

3. Pervin, L. A. *Personality: Theory and Research,* 4 ed., New York: Wiley, 1984, 4.

4. Maddi, S. R. *Personality Theories: A Comparative Analysis,* 4 ed. Homewood, Ill.: Dorsey, 1980, 10.

5. Hall, C. S., and Lindzey, G. *Theories of Personality,* 3 ed. New York: Wiley, 1978, 17–19.

6. Kluckholn, C., and Murray, H. A. (Eds.) *Personality in Nature, Society, and Culture.* New York: Knopf, 1948, 35.

7. Pervin, L. A. *Current Controversies and Issues in Personality,* 2 ed. New York: Wiley, 1984, 36–38.

8. Levine, R. A. *Culture, Behavior, and Personality.* Chicago: Aldine, 1973.

9. Pervin, *Personality: Theory and Research,* 10.

10. Hergenhahn, B. R. *An Introduction to Theories of Personality,* 2 ed. Englewood Cliffs, N.J.: Prentice Hall, 1984, 4.

11. Parke, R. D., and Asher, S. R. Social and Personality Development. *Annual Review of Psychology,* 1983, *34,* 465–509.

12. High Times for T. Boone Pickens. *Time,* March 4, 1985, 52–64. Copyright 1985 Time Inc. All rights reserved. Reprinted by permission from *Time.*

13. Descriptions of the following personality dimensions are based on Blass, T. (Ed.) *Personality Variables in Social Behavior.* Hillsdale, N.J.: Lawrence Erlbaum Associates, 1977; Jackson, D. N., and Paunonen, S. V. Personality Structure and Assessment. *Annual Review of Psychology,* 1980, *31,* 503–551; Lefcourt, H. M. *Locus of Control: Current Trends in Theory and Research,* 2 ed. Hillsdale, N.J.: Lawrence Erlbaum Associates, 1982; and Morris, L. W. *Extraversion and Introversion: An Interactional Perspective.* New York: Hemisphere, 1979.

14. Morris, *Extraversion and Introversion,* 8.

15. See, for example, Brochner, J., and Guare, J. Improving the Performance of Low Self-Esteem Individuals: An Attributional Approach. *Academy of Management Journal,* 1983, *26,* 642–656; Ellis, R. A., and Taylor, M. S. Role of Self-Esteem Within the Job Search Process. *Journal of Applied Psychology,* 1983, *68,* 632–640; Mossholder, K. W., Bedeian, A. G., and Armenakis, A. A. Group Process-Work Outcome Relationships: A Note on the Moderating Impacts of Self-Esteem. *Academy of Management Journal,* 1982, *25,* 575–585.

16. Ellis and Taylor, Role of Self-Esteem Within the Job Search Process.

17. Babladelis, G. *The Study of Personality: Issues and Resolutions.* New York: Holt, Rinehart and Winston, 1984, 171–176.

18. See, for example, Pervin, L. A. Personality: Current Controversies, Issues, and Directions. *Annual Review of Psychology,* 1985, *36,* 83–114.

19. Pervin, *Current Controversies and Issues in Personality,* 2–33.

20. Schneider, B. Interactional Psychology and Organizational Behavior. *Research in Organizational Behavior,* 1983, *5,* 1–31; Terborg, J. R. Interactional Psychology and Research on Human Behavior in Organizations. *Academy of Management Review,* 1981, *6,* 569–576.

21. Baron, R. A., and Byrne, D. *Social Psychology: Understanding Human Interaction,* 3 ed. Boston: Allyn & Bacon, 1981, 91.

22. See, for example, Neal, A. G. *Social Psychology: A Sociological Perspective.* Reading, Mass.: Addison-Wesley, 1983, 110–111; Penrod, S. *Social Psychology.* Englewood Cliffs, N.J.: Prentice-Hall, 1983, 294.

23. Cialdini, R. B., Petty, R. E., and Cacioppo, J. T. Attitude and Attitude Change. *Annual Review of Psychology,* 1981, *32,* 357–404; Cooper, J., and Croyle, R. T. Attitudes and Attitude Change. *Annual Review of Psychology,* 1984, *35,* 395–426.

24. Penrod, *Social Psychology,* 345–347.

25. Ajzen, I., and Fishbein, M. *Understanding Attitudes and Predicting Social Behavior.* Englewood Cliffs, N.J.: Prentice-Hall, 1980.

26. Reprinted with permission from Smith, L. Cracks in the Japanese Work Ethic. *Fortune,* May 14, 1984, 162–168. Copyright 1984 by Time Inc. All rights reserved.

27. Locke, E. A. Nature and Causes of Job Satisfaction. In M. D. Dunnette (Ed.) *Handbook of Industrial and Organiza-*

tional Psychology. Chicago: Rand McNally, 1976, 1300.

28. Smith, P. C., Kendall, L. M., and Hulin, C. L. *The Measurement of Satisfaction in Work and Retirement*. Chicago: Rand McNally, 1969.

29. Iaffaldano, M. T., and Muchinsky, P. M. Job Satisfaction and Job Performance: A Meta-Analysis. *Psychological Bulletin*, 1985, *97*, 251–273.

30. Fisher, C. D. On the Dubious Wisdom of Expecting Job Satisfaction to Correlate with Performance. *Academy of Management Review*, 1980, *5*, 607–612.

31. Schneider, B. Organizational Behavior. *Annual Review of Psychology*, 1985, *36*, 573–611; Staw, B. M. Organizational Behavior: A Review and Reformulation of the Field's Outcome Variables. *Annual Review of Psychology*, 1984, *35*, 627–666.

32. Case prepared by Professor Frank C. Barnes of the University of North Carolina at Charlotte and reprinted with permission.

4 Perception and Attribution

LEARNING OBJECTIVES

When you have finished studying this chapter, you should be able to:

- Describe the major elements in the perceptual process.
- Understand the internal and external factors that influence perceptual selection.
- Describe the concept of perceptual organization.
- Explain what determines how one person perceives another.
- Describe the various kinds of perceptual errors.
- Understand the process of attribution.
- Discuss how attribution influences behavior.

OUTLINE

ew Case

d What?

a supermarket when a girl about eight years old came running
corner. She looked back and screamed, "Stop! Stop! You're kill-
ou're killing my father!" I dropped my things and hurried in
on from which the girl had come. As I turned the corner I was
a grisly scene. A man was stretched out on the floor, and an-
top of him. The man on top must have been 6 feet, 6 inches
weighed 300 pounds. He looked only half-human. He had
the throat and was beating his head against the floor. There
rywhere. I ran for the store manager.
e the manager and I returned to the scene, the police were
t took quite a while to straighten things out, but here are
merged. The man on the floor was a diabetic who had suf-
reaction. As a result, he passed out and hit his head as he
s caused the cut (actually quite a minor one) that ac-
blood everywhere." The "man on top" had seen the dia-
d was trying to prevent him from injuring himself fur-
scious. He also had been loosening the man's collar.
returned, I would have sworn in court that I had seen a
erhaps is understandable. But I will never quite recover
I felt when I met the "murderer." This is the man, you will
ad seen a few moments before, in broad daylight, as a
creature. The man was not a stranger: he was my neighbor.
n dozens of times before and knew him by name. He is a
nan.

y illustrates rather dramatically the important role our perceptions play in understanding the world and also just how wrong these perceptions can sometimes be. People behave on the basis of what they perceive reality to be, not necessarily on the basis of what really *is*. As we receive
information, we assemble and incorporate it into a meaningful experience
unique to ourselves. We paint a picture of the "real" world that expresses our
personal view, and no two of us paint exactly the same picture. We are all
bound by the limits of our own perceptual world. This chapter continues the
exploration of *individual differences* begun in Chapter 3. Here, we will focus
on the important processes of *perception* and *attribution*.

PERCEPTION: AN INTRODUCTION

Perception is the selection and organization of environmental stimuli to provide meaningful experiences for the perceiver. As such, perception represents the psychological process whereby people extract information from
the environment and make sense of their world. Perception includes an
awareness of the world—events, people, objects, situations, and so on—and
involves searching for, obtaining, and processing information about that
world.[1]

The key words in the above definition of perception are *selection* and *organization*. Individuals selectively pay attention to some aspects of their environment and selectively ignore other aspects at any given time. For example, we may listen expectantly for our friend's footsteps in the hall, but ignore the sounds of people upstairs. In an office we ignore the bell announcing the arrival of the elevator, but we jump at the sound of the coffee cart's bell.

How we interpret what we perceive also varies considerably. A wave of the hand could be interpreted as a friendly gesture or as a threat, depending on the circumstances and the state of mind of the perceiver. Or, suppose you are introduced to someone you have never met before and she smiles at you. How you feel at the moment may determine whether you interpret the smile as indicating pleasure, shyness, or nervousness, or as masking boredom. Other people observing the introduction may all form different interpretations of the smile. Perceptions of any situation may differ from person to person both in terms of what will be selectively perceived and of how those things perceived will be interpreted.

As does personality, perceptual differences help to explain why people behave differently even though faced with the same situation. People often perceive the same things in different ways, and their behavioral responses depend, in part, on these perceptions. We will explore the basic nature of the perceptual process, external and internal factors that influence the perception of certain aspects of the environment, the ways that people organize perceptions to make sense of their world, the process of *person perception*, and various ways that the perceptual process can be in error.

BASIC ELEMENTS IN THE PERCEPTUAL PROCESS

Our perceptions are affected by the objects we perceive, our preconceptions about them, the ways in which we organize them, and the meanings we attach to them. Individual perceptual awareness varies. Some of us who have been in the dean's office only once can describe it in detail, whereas others barely remember anything about it.

Recognition of the difference between the perceptual world and the real world is important in understanding organizational behavior. The manager who is aware of this difference makes decisions with greater care and does not make complex and important decisions based on sketchy evidence.

Figure 4-1 summarizes the basic elements in the perceptual process from the initial observation to the final response, or behavior. Stimuli in the environment are observed through the five senses: taste, smell, hearing, sight, and touch.[2] All are important, but hearing, sight, and touch are the most important in the behavior of individuals in organizations. A selection process involving both external and internal factors filters sensory perceptions to determine which ones will receive the most attention. The individual then organizes those selected to be acted upon into meaningful patterns. A person's interpretation of sensory stimuli will lead to a response, either overt (actions) or covert (motivation, attitudes, feelings) or both. Each person selects and organizes sensory stimuli differently and thus has different interpretations and responses.

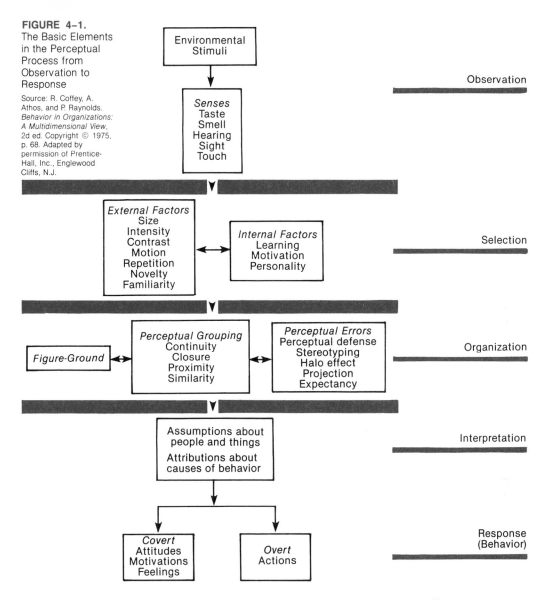

FIGURE 4–1.
The Basic Elements in the Perceptual Process from Observation to Response

Source: R. Coffey, A. Athos, and P. Raynolds. *Behavior in Organizations: A Multidimensional View,* 2d ed. Copyright © 1975, p. 68. Adapted by permission of Prentice-Hall, Inc., Englewood Cliffs, N.J.

The basic steps in the perceptual process shown in Figure 4-1 usually occur almost instantaneously. Rarely can separate steps between the observation and the response be distinguished.

PERCEPTUAL SELECTION

The phone is ringing, your roommate is watching television, a dog is barking outside, your kitten is batting at your shoelaces, your electric typewriter is making a strange noise, and you smell coffee brewing. Which of these stimuli will you ignore, and which will receive your attention? In general, people perceive things that promise to help satisfy their needs and that they have found rewarding in the past. They tend to ignore mildly disturbing things but will perceive very dangerous ones (for example, the house being on fire).

Perceptual selection is the process by which people filter out most stimuli so that they can deal with the more important ones. Perceptual selection depends on a number of factors, some of which are in the external environment and some of which are internal to the perceiver.

External Factors

As indicated in Figure 4-1, both external and internal factors affect perceptual selection. The external factors of perception are characteristics of the stimuli that influence the probability that they will be noticed. Some examples of these external factors may be stated as *principles* of perception:

- *Size*. The larger the size of an external factor, the more likely it is to be perceived.
- *Intensity*. The more intense an external factor, the more likely it is to be perceived (bright lights, loud noises, and the like). In addition, even the language of a memo from a boss to an employee can reflect the intensity principle. A memo that reads "Please stop by my office at your convenience" won't fill you with the sense of urgency that you would get from a memo that reads "Report to my office, *immediately*!"
- *Contrast*. External factors that stand out against the background or that are not what people expect are the most likely to be perceived. In addition, the contrast of objects with others or with their background may influence *how* they are perceived. Figure 4-2 illustrates this aspect of the contrast principle. Which of the solid center circles is larger? The one on the right appears to be larger, but it is not: the two circles are the same size. The solid circle on the right appears larger because its background—its frame of reference—is composed of much smaller circles. The solid circle on the left appears smaller because it is seen in contrast to larger surrounding circles.
- *Motion*. A moving factor is more likely to be perceived than a stationary factor. Soldiers in combat learn this principle very early.
- *Repetition*. A repeated factor is more likely to be perceived than a single factor. Marketing managers use this principle in trying to get the attention of prospective customers. An advertisement may repeat key ideas and the advertisement itself may be presented many times for greater effectiveness.
- *Novelty and familiarity*. Either a familiar or a novel factor in the environment can attract attention. People quickly notice an elephant walking along a city street. (Both novelty and size increase the probability of perception here.) You are most likely to perceive the face of a close friend among a group of people walking toward you.[3]

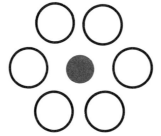

FIGURE 4–2.
Contrast Principle
of Perception

Any of these factors may be operating at any time to affect perception. They, in combination with certain aspects of the person doing the perceiving, determine whether any given stimuli are more or less likely to be noticed.

Internal Factors

The internal factors of perception are aspects of the perceiver that influence perceptual selection. Among other things, these internal factors include learning (Chapter 6), motivation (Chapter 7), and personality (Chapter 3).

As an example of the impact of internal factors on perception, an experiment was conducted with 23 executives enrolled in a company-sponsored training program. Six of these executives were in sales, five in production, four in accounting, and eight in other functional areas of the company. Researchers gave the participants in the training program a 10,000-word case history dealing with the organization and activities of another company. The assignment was to examine the case history and to determine the most important problem facing the firm. Five of the six sales executives felt that the major company problem was in the sales area. Four of the five production people said the problem was production related. Three of the four accounting people worked closely with sales; they all stated that sales was the most important problem. The researchers concluded that, although the case history called for looking at the problem from a companywide rather than a departmental perspective, most of the executives perceived the problem in terms of their own background.[4]

LEARNING As the above experiment indicates, perception is strongly influenced by past experiences and what has been learned as a result of those experiences. For example, imagine a real estate agent, an architect, and a lawyer all approaching a tall office building. These three individuals may notice distinctly different things about the building. The real estate agent may first perceive the general condition of the building and of the surrounding area, factors that would influence the building's price and salability. The architect may first notice the architectural style and the construction materials used in the building. The lawyer may only perceive that the size and placement of advertising on the building violates a zoning regulation. Each individual pays attention to different aspects of the same general stimulus because of his or her own background and training.[5]

An important part of an individual's experiences is determined by the culture into which he or she is born. Cultural differences can influence the perceptual process, as a recent study of time perception illustrates.

ACROSS CULTURES

Time Perception

Robert Levine is a professor of psychology at the California State University at Fresno. During a recent appointment as a visiting professor in Brazil, he observed something very interesting concerning his students' perceptions of time. What first attracted his attention was his Brazilian students' casual approach to arriving on time for class. It was not unusual for some students to arrive 30 minutes to a full hour late for a two-hour class. Even more mystifying, students didn't rush immediately from the class at its scheduled completion time, but rather would continue asking questions and drift away within 15–30 minutes after class was supposed to end. Levine contrasted this with his California students' behavior: "Back home in California, I never need to look at a clock to know when the class hour is ending. The shuffling of books is accompanied by strained expressions that say plaintively, 'I'm starving . . . I've got to go to the bathroom . . . I'm going to suffocate if you keep us one more second.'"

Intrigued by these differences in student behavior, Levine and his colleagues conducted a survey of student perceptions of time in several situations. For example, they asked students in both locations what they would consider as being late or early for a lunch date with a friend. The average Brazilian student defined lateness as 33½ minutes compared to 19 minutes for the average California student. California students, on average, considered 24 minutes to be early, while the average for Brazilian students was 54 minutes. There were also interesting differences regarding perceptions of people who were late for appointments. The tendency in the United States and Canada is to regard successful people as being prompt, but the Brazilian students surveyed tended to regard a person who is consistently late as being more successful than one who is always on time.

These marked differences in perceptions of time next led Levine and his colleagues to examine the "pace of life" in six countries on three continents: England, Indonesia, Italy, Japan, Taiwan, and the United States. In order to avoid language problems (concepts of time often do not translate well across languages) the researchers wanted to assess the pace of life using as little language as possible in the measures. Thus, they decided to compare (1) the accuracy of bank clocks; (2) the speed at which pedestrians walk; and (3) the length of time it takes to purchase a single stamp from the country's postal system. In each country the investigators took measurements in the nation's largest city and in a medium-sized one. Multiple measurements were made for each of the three categories. For example, 15 bank clocks were examined in each city; 100 pedestrians, walking alone, were timed in each city for how long it took to walk 100 feet.

The results of this study are presented in Table 4-1. The Japanese finished first in all three categories. Clock accuracy ranged from an average of about 30 seconds slow or fast in Japan to more than three minutes off

TABLE 4–1   The Pace of Life in Six Countries

	Accuracy of Bank Clocks	Walking Speed	Post Office Speed
Japan	1	1	1
United States	2	3	2
England	4	2	3
Italy	5	4	6
Taiwan	3	5	4
Indonesia	6	6	5

Source: Levine, R., and Wolff, E. Social Time: The Heartbeat of Culture. *Psychology Today,* March 1985, 35. Reprinted with permission.

Numbers (1 is the top value) indicate the comparative rankings of each country for each indicator of time sense.

the correct time in Indonesia. On average, Japanese walkers covered 100 feet in 20.7 seconds compared to 27.2 seconds for the slower-walking Indonesians. Italian postal clerks were the slowest, averaging 47 seconds, while Japanese postal clerks took an average of 25 seconds for the same transaction.

These results indicate a consistent relationship among clock accuracy, walking speed, and postal efficiency, suggesting that the pace of life differs across these cultures. Perceptions of time may be very different for individuals raised in these cultures. Levine states: "Appreciating cultural differences in time sense becomes increasingly important as modern communications put more and more people in daily contact. If we are to avoid misreading issues that involve time perceptions, we need to understand better our own cultural biases and those of others."[6]

Learning is an important factor in developing perceptual sets. A **perceptual set** is an expectation of a perception based on past experience with the same or similar stimuli. The powerful role that learning and past experience play in perception manifests itself in many ways. For example, in Figure 4-3 the young boy cannot be much taller than his mother; yet our eyes tell us that he is. Our eyes are relying on the depth and perspective cues supplied by the apparent shape of the room. These cues are based on our previous experiences with similar stimuli. What we cannot tell from the photograph is that things have been distorted to fool our eyes. The room is not an ordinary rectangle but an oddly shaped trapezoid. Neither windows nor floor tiles have squared corners; the walls, ceiling, and floor slope, and the boy is standing higher up and much closer to the camera than is his mother.

MOTIVATION   Motivation also plays an important role in determining what a person perceives. A hungry person is more sensitive to factors related to food, such as the odors of food cooking, than is a person who is not hungry. An individual's ability to follow a conversation in a noisy, crowded room depends to a large extent on motivation. This is the "cocktail party effect": a person who loses interest in what is being said tends to start picking up another conversation that might be more interesting.

FIGURE 4–3.
Perceptual Set
(Photo © Baron Wohlman)

A person motivated by a need for power will pay attention to environmental factors that seem to enhance power. Such "empire builders" in business seek to acquire large staffs because they believe this reflects power. They also seek to increase their departmental budgets, again perceiving size as an indication of power and never realizing that others might perceive their departments as being overstaffed and overbudgeted.[7]

PERSONALITY   Personality also has an interesting relationship to perception: personality is shaped, in part, by perceptions; in turn, personality affects what and how people perceive. What do you see in Figure 4-4? If you see an attractive, elegantly dressed woman, your perception concurs with the majority of first-time viewers. However, you may agree with a sizable minority and see a poor, ugly old woman. Which woman you see depends on your perceptual set, and personality more than learning determines this particular set.

Tests designed to examine the relationship between personality and perception frequently ask people to write stories about some picture, where the meaning of the picture is ambiguous. For example, researchers might ask subjects to write a short story about the picture shown in Figure 4-5 after looking at it for 10–15 seconds. Depending on individual personality, one of three factors may affect a person's perception of Figure 4-5: achievement, affiliation, or power. Individuals having dominant needs in one of the three areas will write a different type of story, even though each person looks at the same picture.[8]

Highly achievement-oriented people may see this man as an engineer who wants to win a competition and be awarded a contract to design a bridge. He is thinking of how happy he will be when he wins. He has been puzzled by how to make a long span strong enough, but decides to specify a new steel alloy of great strength. The man submits his entry, but he does not win and becomes very unhappy.

People who are highly socially oriented seek affiliation, and they may see the man as working late. He is worried that his wife will be annoyed with him for neglecting her and the children; she has been saying recently that he cares more about his work than about her and the family. He seems unable to

FIGURE 4–4.
Test of Personality-Determined Perceptual Set

FIGURE 4–5.
Personality Test
(Photo © Hellriegel, Slocum, Woodman)

satisfy both his boss and his wife, but he loves his wife and family very much and will do his best to finish up fast and get home.

Those highly motivated by power may see the man as a famous architect who wants to win a competition that will establish him as the best architect in the world. His chief rival has stolen his best ideas, and he is terrified of the disgrace of losing. But he comes up with a great new idea that absolutely bowls over the judges, and he wins.

PERCEPTUAL ORGANIZATION

Pioneer psychologist William James said, "to an infant the world is just a big, blooming, buzzing confusion." All infants are faced with the problem of making sense out of their perceptions. Gradually they learn to organize their perceptions, and these perceptual consistencies simplify their world.

Perceptual organization is the process by which people group environmental stimuli into recognizable patterns. In the perceptual process, once selection has occurred, organization takes over. The stimuli selected for attention are now seen as a whole. For example, all of us have a mental picture of an object with the following properties: wood, four legs, a seat, a back, armrests, and slats. This is our image of a chair. When we see an object that has all these properties, we recognize it as a chair. We have organized the incoming information into a meaningful whole.

There is still a great deal to learn about how the human mind assembles, organizes, and categorizes information, and the way that perceptual organization occurs continues to be the subject of much research interest.[9] How-

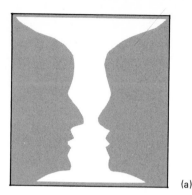

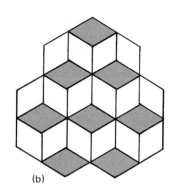

(a)   (b)

FIGURE 4–6.
Reversible Figure–Ground
Patterns

ever, certain factors in perceptual organization, such as *figure–ground* and *perceptual grouping* are considered to be important by many authorities.

Figure–Ground

The **figure–ground principle** states that people tend to perceive the factor they are most attentive to as standing out against a background. Figure 4-6 illustrates what can happen when there is no clear figure–ground pattern. These illusions are called *reversible figure–ground patterns*. In Figure 4-6(a) do you see a wine glass on a dark background or facing silhouettes on a white background? Do you see six or seven blocks in Figure 4-6(b)? Turning the page upside down may help you see seven blocks. Seeing both sets of blocks without turning the page upside down is difficult, because once we are locked into one way of organizing what we see, we often find it very hard to change that view. Life would be very difficult if we were constantly confronted with such figure–ground ambiguity. Often, however, the figure–ground principle is an important aid in understanding the world, as illustrated by the work situation in which Doris Graham was involved.

In Practice: Figure–Ground at Work

When Doris Graham started to work as secretary to Susan Green in the accounting department, the whole place and the people in it were a kind of amorphous blur in her mind. Slowly, it seemed, features of her new environment began to emerge. At first she was only really aware of chief accountant Susan Green's name and face and employment manager Dave Brigg's name and face. As she began taking dictation and typing, she began to realize that Mr. Portley was an important figure to Susan Green and, therefore, to her. Gina Kowalski seemed helpful and Bill Crandell nice, but she didn't really define them against the background of the rest of the accounting department at first. Then, after a couple of weeks or so, they began to emerge as people as well as important contacts in her job as secretary.

Here we see the figure–ground phenomenon at work. Certain "figures," Susan Green, Dave Briggs, Mr. Portley, Gina Kowalski, and Bill Crandell, emerge from the "ground" represented by the people and things that make up the rest of the accounting department and the company. Then, slowly, the entire department begins to emerge as a "figure" against the "ground" of the entire company.

Dave Briggs was the first person to emerge as a "figure." (She had memorized his name from the slip of paper given her at White Collar Employment Agency before she ever got out to the company.) He had made her feel comfortable and a little as if she belonged. But now, only several weeks later, because of lack of contact, he was fading into the general company "ground" as the accounting department became a more distinct entity. Here we see the phenomenon of figure–ground reversal, not unlike the visual eye trick which occurs when silhouetted designs can be seen to reverse themselves.

This reversal was also seen by Doris, back when she was identified by the rest of the office as attached to Ms. Green, and she herself identified with Susan Green more than she did with the others. As time went on, she and the rest of the office got to know one another better. Sometimes when she knew Ms. Green and Mr. Portley were going to be away from the office for a certain period of time, she would pass the information along to the gang and they could all relax a little. A mutual trust developed and the office group began to emerge as the figure, while Susan Green and Mr. Portley tended to become a part of the general company background.

Figure–ground, a phenomenon long known as a visual parlor stunt, is a useful means of organizing our perceptions. It is a helpful way to think about what we see and experience and why we happen to perceive some things the way we do.[10]

Perceptual Grouping

Perceptual grouping is the tendency to form individual stimuli into a meaningful pattern by means of continuity, closure, proximity, or similarity.

CONTINUITY *Continuity* is the tendency to perceive objects as continuous patterns. While continuity is often a useful organizing principle, it may have negative aspects as well. For example, inflexible or noncreative thinkers may be unable to perceive anything unique and instead always seek continuity. Inflexible managers may insist that employees follow set, step-by-step routines. They may not tolerate random activity, even though it may solve problems more imaginatively and proficiently, because it upsets their unbending need for continuity.

CLOSURE *Closure* is the tendency to complete an object so that it is perceived as a constant, overall form. It is the ability to perceive a whole object even though only part of the object is evident. Most people somehow perceive the 20 odd-shaped inkblots in Figure 4-7 as a dog. Obviously, someone who had never seen a dog would not be able to complete the closure.

PROXIMITY The *principle of proximity* states that a group of objects may be perceived as related because of their nearness to each other. Often people working together in a department are perceived as a unit because of their physical proximity. Suppose that four people on the third floor of a large office building quit their jobs. Even if they did so for four unrelated reasons, the personnel department may perceive it as a problem on the third floor and examine morale, pay, and working conditions there in an attempt to determine what is wrong.

FIGURE 4–7.
Closure

SIMILARITY   The *principle of similarity* states that the more alike objects are, the greater is the tendency to perceive them as a common group. Similarity is very important in most team sports. In football, for example, the quarterback must be able to spot an open receiver without a moment's hesitation. Many companies, especially those in buildings with open floor plans, color code the partitions and other accessories of each department to visually define separate functions and responsibilities. A company might require visitors to its plant to wear yellow hard hats and the floor supervisors white hard hats. The workers can then easily identify people who are unfamiliar with everyday precautions and routines when they are in the work area.

PERSON PERCEPTION

Of particular interest in organizational behavior is the process of *person* or *social* perception: how people perceive each other. While perceptions of situations, events, objects, and so on are important, individual differences in perceptions of others are critical for understanding behavior in complex social settings. As an example, suppose that you are introduced to a new employee. In order to get acquainted and to make her feel at home, you invite her to lunch. During lunch she begins to tell you her life history and spends a great deal of time describing her many accomplishments. Because her conversation is completely concerned with herself (she asks you no questions about yourself), you may form the impression that she is very self-centered. Later, you may come to see other aspects of her personality, but your perceptions may always be strongly colored by this first impression. **Person perception** is the process by which we attribute characteristics or traits to particular people.[11] As such, the process of person perception is closely related to the *attribution* process, which is discussed later in this chapter.

The factors influencing person perception are, in a general sense, the same as those factors that influence perceptual selection; that is, both external and internal factors affect person perception. However, it is particularly useful to categorize factors that influence how a person perceives another as:

- characteristics of the person being perceived;
- characteristics of the perceiver; and
- the situation or context within which the perception takes place.

Characteristics of the Person Perceived

In perceiving someone else, we process a variety of cues about the person: facial expressions, general appearance, skin color, posture, age, gender, voice quality, personality traits, behaviors, and so on. Some cues may contain important information about the person, but many do not. People seem to have *implicit personality theories* about which physical characteristics, personal traits, and specific behaviors are related to others.[12] At its best, the way that people group characteristics and traits helps them to organize their perceptions and hence to better understand their world. At its worst, implicit personality theories give rise to perceptual errors such as stereotyping.

Despite the obvious pitfalls of making assumptions about what a person is like based on physical characteristics or limited interaction with them, this is commonly done. For example, a recent report stated that some lawyers use consultants to help them pick prospective jurors based on their appearance, including certain facial characteristics.[13] Most competent authorities in the behavioral sciences would probably consider this nonsense, yet we cannot deny that our perceptions of others are influenced by their physical appearance. However, evidence clearly shows that our perceptions of others will be more accurate if we can avoid (1) generalizing from a single trait to a whole constellation of traits; (2) assuming that a single behavior will manifest itself in all situations; and (3) placing too much reliance on physical appearance.

Characteristics of the Perceiver

Listening to a friend describe the personality of a mutual acquaintance may tell us as much about our friend's personality as it does about the personality of the person being described.[14] Does this surprise you? Recall that perception is influenced by factors internal to the perceiver, including learning, motivation, and personality. Internal factors are particularly important in person perception. How we perceive another person is, in part, determined by our own personality traits, values, attitudes, current mood, past experiences, and so on. For example, it is generally considered more difficult to accurately perceive the personality of an individual raised in another culture. In part, this is because we interpret our perceptions of that person and his or her behavior in light of our own experiences, attitudes, and values. Often these do not give us an adequate basis to make accurate judgments about the personality and behavior of persons from a culture very different from our own.

The Situation

The situation or setting also influences how one person perceives another. While aspects of the situation may always influence person perception to a certain extent, the situation may be particularly important in understanding first impressions. For example, if you meet someone for the first time and she is with another person that you respect and admire, this may positively influence your assessment of her. On the other hand, if she is accompanied by a person you intensely dislike, you may form a negative impression. Of course, these initial perceptions (whether positive or negative) may change over time as you interact with the individual in a variety of settings and thus come to a more accurate understanding of the person. Nevertheless, *primacy effects*—the first information received—often continue to color our later perceptions of individuals.[15]

Perceptual Judgment

An important aspect of perceptual organization is the tendency for people to organize their perceptions as "wholes" in an attempt to more completely understand objects and events in their environment. This is particularly true in person perception. We gather limited bits of information about another person and, based on this knowledge, may supply other information in an attempt to understand the whole person. Characteristics that a person possesses are not perceived in isolation, but rather are seen as part of a whole. Sometimes this may have odd effects on perceptual judgment, as the following experiment illustrates. A stranger was introduced differently in each of five university classes, and after the visitor departed the students were asked to estimate his height.[16] The introduction used and the results obtained from each class are shown in Table 4-2. The visitor appears to grow taller as his status increases. In this case, the perceptual judgment of height has been influenced by surplus information about the person, which has nothing to do with physical stature.

PERCEPTUAL ERRORS

The perceptual process can result in errors in judgment or understanding in a number of ways, including perceptual defense, stereotyping, the halo effect, projection, and expectancy.[17]

TABLE 4-2   Perceptual Judgment

Class	Information	Visitor's Average Estimated Height
1	"Mr. Jones, a student from Cambridge"	5'9.9"
2	"Mr. Jones, demonstrator (teaching assistant) in psychology from Cambridge"	5'10.4"
3	"Mr. Jones, lecturer in psychology from Cambridge"	5'10.9"
4	"Dr. Jones, senior lecturer in psychology from Cambridge"	5'11.6"
5	"Professor Jones from Cambridge"	6'0.3"

Source: Adapted from Wilson, P. R. Perceptual Distortion of Height as a Function of Ascribed Academic Status. *Journal of Social Psychology,* 1968, *74,* 97–102.

Perceptual Defense

Once established, our way of viewing the world may become very resistant to change. A well-known folk song suggests that we hear what we want to hear and disregard the rest. **Perceptual defense** is the tendency for people to protect themselves against objects or situations that are perceptually threatening. The discussion of perceptual selection mentioned that people perceive things that are supportive and satisfying and tend to ignore disturbing things. Avoiding unpleasant stimuli often is more than escapism: it can be a sensible defensive device. People become psychologically deaf or blind to disturbing parts of their environment. For example, people who live near railroad tracks may not hear the trains. A woman does not love her husband less simply because he is aging physically, and she may even be unmindful of the changes that age has made in his appearance.

Stereotyping

Stereotyping is the tendency to assign attributes to someone solely on the basis of a category to which that person belongs. People expect someone identified as a doctor, president of a company, or minister to have certain positive attributes, even if they have met some who did not. A person categorized as a dropout, ex-con, or alcoholic is automatically perceived negatively. Even identifying someone by such broad categories as black, elderly, or female, which should not bring to mind any attributes beyond the obvious physical characteristics, can lead to misperceptions. The perceiver may dwell on certain expected characteristics and fail to recognize the characteristics that distinguish the person as an individual.

In Practice: **Stereotypes at Work**

Dave Briggs, employment manager, was working his way down through the pile of recently received application letters, when he came to a resume that caused him to emit a low whistle and reach for the telephone. Dialing quickly, Dave got Ed Yamamoto, chief engineer, on the phone. "Ed," enthused Dave, "I think I have the group leader for the bi-valve pump section." The bi-valve pump design section had been getting along without a direct supervisor since last February, when Hal Coombs had left the company. Herb Borgfeldt, senior man in the section, had twice refused the job, saying he was a designer, not a straw boss, and no one among the rest of the men in the section was experienced enough to take over as supervisor. The job really needed an expert pump designer, preferably with some supervisory experience.

"Graduated from Cal Tech, honors, three years with Livermore Radiation Lab, seven years with Cleveland Pump, last two and a half as supervisor of the bi-valve section. Let's see, two patents in own name, paper in 'Hydraulic Occlusion' at last year's SME meeting—" "Wow!" from Ed. "—and her letter says she wants to relocate here to be close to her mother, and since we are the only pump manufacturer in town, I can't see why we can't get her." "Wait one minute," Ed burst forth, "you said 'her'?" "Yeah," replied Dave, "Linda Herring. She apparently grew up here. Let's see, went to Horace Mann High School, where she was salutatorian and editor of the year book." "A woman!" snorted Ed. "Look, I'm no male chauvinist, you understand, but this is no job for a girl! There's lots of pressure. She'll be too emotional to run things, too illogical to think through design problems, too absorbed with details to see the big picture, too—" "W-a-i-t," protested Dave. "I'm not insisting you hire this engineer, but you did sound enthusiastic when I read her qualifications." "Well, *sure* who wouldn't be?" said Ed, "Cal Tech, supervisory experience, patents, papers, honors. But you hadn't told me he's a her!"[18]

In this situation, Ed is making the perceptual error of stereotyping. Ed is classifying Linda as a woman rather than as an engineer. In Ed's "cognitive map," *woman* seems to be associated with emotionalism, lack of logical thinking, focusing too much on details, and so on. Of course, a person might classify Linda (or Ed) as an engineer, and use this stereotype to make equally inaccurate and unfair assumptions about her personal characteristics. Here, we can clearly see a major danger of stereotyping: if Ed's reasoning prevails, a talented prospective employee may never be considered for employment on her own merits, with potential harm to both the individual and the organization.

Halo Effect

The **halo effect** is the process by which the perceiver evaluates all dimensions of another person solely according to one impression, either favorable or unfavorable. A *halo* blinds the perceiver to other attributes that should be evaluated in attaining a complete, accurate impression of the other person. The halo effect often plays a major role in employee performance rating. A manager may single out one trait and use it as the basis for judgment of all other performance measures. For example, an excellent attendance record may produce judgments of high productivity, quality work, and industriousness whether they are accurate or not.

Projection

Projection is the tendency for people to see their own traits in other people. That is, they project their own feelings, tendencies, or motives into their judgment of others. This may be especially true for undesirable traits that perceivers possess but fail to recognize in themselves. For example, a manager frightened by rumors of impending organizational changes may not only judge others to be more frightened than they are, but may also assess various policy decisions as more frightening than they really are. People whose personality traits include stinginess, obstinacy, and disorderliness tend to rate others higher on these traits than do people who do not have these personality traits.

Expectancy

Expectancy effects in the perceptual process are the extent to which prior expectations bias how events, objects, people, and so on are actually perceived. Sometimes the extent to which people perceive what they expect to perceive is amazing.[19] Your perceptions of a committee that you have been assigned to recently may be very different if you were told by your boss that the committee is an important one and will be staffed by talented people from several departments, as opposed to being told that the committee exists solely for "political reasons" and contains some real "deadwood" from other departments. The identical behavior by other members of the committee might be perceived in very different ways on your part under each of these sets of expectations. Earlier, we noted that past experiences and learning are very important to the perceptual process. As a result, people often approach situations expecting certain things to happen or other people to have certain attributes. These expectations may strongly influence their perceptions of reality. Another aspect of expectancy effects is the notion of the *self-fulfilling prophecy*. That is, expecting certain things to happen shapes the behavior of the perceiver in such a way that the probability that the expected will actually happen is increased.

ATTRIBUTION: PERCEIVING THE CAUSES OF BEHAVIOR

In the most general sense, **attribution** refers to the ways in which people come to understand the causes of others' (and their own) behavior.[20] Attribution, in fact, may be the central process in person perception. Harold Kelley, a well-known researcher in the area of attribution theory, made the following personal statement that eloquently captures both the importance and meaning of attribution.

> In the course of my interaction with other people, I often wonder why they act as they do. I may wonder how to interpret a compliment a student makes of a lecture I recently gave, why my friend is so critical of a certain common acquaintance, or why my colleague has not done his share of the work on our joint project. These are questions about the attribution of the other person's behavior—what causes it, what is responsible for it, to what is it to be attributed?[21]

The attributions that people make concerning the causes of behavior are important in understanding behavior in organizations. For example, a series of studies indicates that supervisors who attribute poor performance directly to the subordinates involved will tend to behave in a much more punitive fashion than will supervisors who attribute poor performance to circumstances beyond the control of the subordinates.[22] The relationship between attributions and behavior will become clearer as we examine the process of attribution.

The Attribution Process

The basic reason people make attributions is in an attempt to understand the behavior of other people and hence to make better sense of their environment.[23] A basic model of the attribution process is shown in Figure 4-8. People infer "causes" to the behavior they observe in others, and these interpretations often play a key role in determining their reactions to that behavior. As indicated in Figure 4-8, the perceived causes of behavior are a result of

FIGURE 4–8.
General Model of the Attribution Process

Source: Reproduced with permission, from Kelley, H. H., and Michela, J. L. Attribution Theory and Research. *Annual Review of Psychology, 31.* Copyright © 1980 by Annual Reviews, Inc.

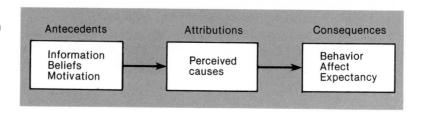

several antecedents: (1) the amount of information the perceiver has about the people and the situation, and how that information is organized by the perceiver; (2) the perceiver's beliefs (implicit personality theories, what other people might do in a similar situation, and so on); and (3) the motivation of the perceiver, including the importance to the perceiver of making an accurate assessment. Based on information, beliefs, and motives the perceiver often distinguishes between internal and external causes of behavior; that is, whether people did something because of a real desire or because of the pressure of circumstances. The assigned cause for the behavior—whether internal or external—helps the perceiver to attach meaning to the event, and is important for understanding the subsequent consequences for the perceiver. Among the consequences of this attribution process are the behavior of the perceiver in response to the behavior of others, the level of affect (how the perceiver feels about events, people, circumstances, and so on), and the effects on the perceiver's expectations of future events or behavior.

Internal versus External Causation of Behavior

Imagine the following scene in a busy department. Bill, the office manager, and Sam, section head for accounts receivable, are arguing loudly in Bill's private office. Even though they were careful to close the door before their discussion began, their argument has grown heated, and their voices have gotten louder and louder until all work has stopped and everyone else in the office is staring in discomfort and embarrassment at the closed door. After several minutes, Sam jerks open the door, yells a final, unflattering remark at Bill, slams the door, and stomps out of the department.

Individuals observing this scene are likely to wonder about what is going on and to make certain attributions in an attempt to understand why Sam behaved the way that he did. Attributions regarding Sam's behavior could be focused on internal causes: Sam gets mad easily because he has a bad temper; Sam behaved this way because he is immature and doesn't handle pressure well; or, Sam is not getting his work done and thus was called on the carpet by Bill. On the other hand, some observers might make external attributions: Sam behaved this way because Bill provoked him; or, Sam and Bill's behavior is caused by unreasonable work goals imposed on the department by the organization. Of course, many individuals may perceive more than a single cause for a complex social interaction such as this. Also, as should be clear by now, different members of the department are likely to make different interpretations of the events they have just witnessed.

A central question in understanding attribution concerns *how* perceivers determine whether the behavior of another person stems from internal (such things as personality traits, emotions, motives, or ability) or external (other people, the situation, or chance) causes. A widely accepted model proposed by Harold Kelley attempts to explain how people determine why others behave as they do.[24] This model is depicted in Figure 4-9. In making causal attributions, people focus on three major factors:

- *Consensus*—The extent to which others, faced with the same situation, behave in a manner similar to the person perceived.
- *Consistency*—The extent to which the person perceived behaves in the same manner on other occasions when faced with the same situation.
- *Distinctiveness*—The extent to which the person perceived acts in the same manner in different situations.[25]

As suggested by Figure 4-9, under conditions of high consensus, high consistency, and high distinctiveness, the perceiver will tend to attribute the behavior of the person perceived to external causes. However, when consensus and distinctiveness are low, the perceiver will tend to attribute the behavior of the person to internal causes. (Note that consistency is typically high under both attribution outcomes. When consistency is missing, observers will have trouble making any causal attributions at all.)

In the example of the argument between Bill and Sam, observers would be likely to attribute causation to Sam if others typically did not have simi-

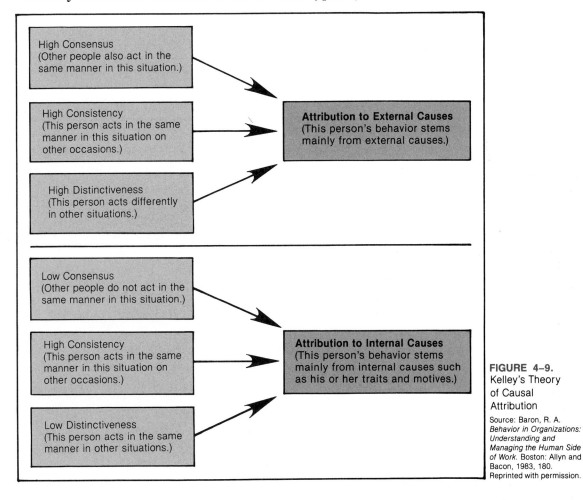

FIGURE 4–9.
Kelley's Theory of Causal Attribution

Source: Baron, R. A. *Behavior in Organizations: Understanding and Managing the Human Side of Work.* Boston: Allyn and Bacon, 1983, 180. Reprinted with permission.

lar arguments with Bill (low consensus), and Sam often has similar arguments with others in a variety of work situations (low distinctiveness). On the other hand, if other individuals frequently have run-ins with Bill (high consensus) and Sam seldom has arguments in other situations with his fellow employees (high distinctiveness), then observers may attribute Sam's reaction to external causes (in this case, Bill). You may want to reread this paragraph while examining each portion of Figure 4-9 to ensure that the differences leading to either external or internal attributions of behavior are clear.

It is well worth noting, with regard to internal versus external causes of behavior, that observers often make what is known as the **fundamental attribution error**. This attribution error is described as the tendency to *underestimate* the impact of situational or external causes of behavior and to *overestimate* the impact of personal or internal causes of behavior when seeking to understand why people behave the way they do.[26] In organizations this may mean that employees will often tend to assign blame for conflict (Chapter 17), political behavior (Chapter 16), or resistance to change (Chapter 20) to the individuals involved, and not recognize the contributions made by the dynamics of the situation.

Attributions of Success and Failure

In terms of task performance in organizations, the attributions that people make regarding success and failure are very important. For example, supervisors may make decisions about rewards and punishments depending on their perceptions of *why* subordinates have succeeded or failed in performing some task. In general, individuals often attribute their own (and others') success or failure to four causal factors: ability, effort, task difficulty, or luck. For example:

- I succeeded (or failed) because I had the skills to do the job (or because I did not have the skills to do the job). Such statements are ability attributions.
- I succeeded (or failed) because I worked hard (or because I did not work hard). Such statements are effort attributions.
- I succeeded (or failed) because it was easy (or because it was too hard). Such statements are attributions about task difficulty.
- I succeeded (or failed) because I was lucky (or unlucky). Such statements are attributions about luck or the circumstances surrounding the task.[27]

Attributions of ability and effort are internal causes and task difficulty and luck are perceived causes external to the person. These attributions (particularly the attributions an individual makes about his or her own success or failure) are influenced by the personality differences of self-esteem and locus of control beliefs described in Chapter 3.

You will probably not be surprised to learn that there is a strong tendency for people to attribute their success with a task to internal factors (ability or effort) and to attribute their failures to external factors (task difficulty or luck). This tendency is known as a **self-serving bias**. The tendency of employees to accept responsibility for good performance but to deny responsibility for poor performance can present a major challenge for managers and supervisors during performance appraisal sessions.[28] A self-serving bias can create problems in other ways also; for example, by preventing an individual from accurately assessing his or her own performance, abilities, or efforts on a task, or by making it more difficult for a group of managers to accurately examine why some course of action they selected has failed.

SUMMARY

Perception is the psychological process whereby people select information from the environment and organize it to make sense of their world. Two major components of the perceptual process are selection and organization. Perceptual selection represents the screening mechanism whereby people filter out less important information in order to focus on more important environmental cues. Perceptual selection is influenced both by external factors in the environment and factors internal to the perceiver. Perceptual organization represents the process by which people assemble, organize, and categorize information from the environment. This organization process groups environmental stimuli into recognizable patterns (wholes) that allow the person to interpret what is perceived.

How people perceive each other is particularly important for understanding behavior in organizations. Person perception is a function of characteristics of the person perceived, characteristics of the perceiver, and the situation within which the perception takes place. Unfortunately, the perceptual process can result in errors of judgment or understanding in a number of ways, including denying the reality of disturbing information, assigning attributes to someone solely on the basis of some category or group they belong to, and so on.

Attribution deals with the perceived causes of behavior. People infer causes for the behavior of others and their perceptions of why behavior is occurring have an important influence on their own subsequent behavioral responses and feelings. Whether behavior is internally caused by the "true" nature of the person or is externally caused by circumstances represents an important attribution that people make about the behavior of others. Individuals also make attributions concerning task success and failure that have important implications for behavior in organizations.

KEY WORDS AND CONCEPTS

Attribution   Perceptual organization
Expectancy   Perceptual selection
Figure–ground principle   Perceptual set
Fundamental attribution error   Person perception
Halo effect   Projection
Perception   Self-serving bias
Perceptual defense   Stereotyping
Perceptual grouping

DISCUSSION QUESTIONS

1. What are the basic elements in the perceptual process?

2. Give examples of how different people might interpret the same incident differently. Why might they do this?

3. From your own experience, which of the perceptual errors discussed seems most common? Give an example of a situation when this error was present.

4. What perceptual tendencies of managers could create special problems in their evaluation of subordinates' job performance?

5. Are there any benefits to using stereotypes? What are the dangers?

6. Describe how a person determines whether someone else's behavior represents what he or she is truly like or simply reflects the circumstances of the situation.

7. From your own experience, give an example of attributions made following either success or failure on some task. How common is the self-serving bias? Will this bias always be present? Why or why not?

8. What are the consequences of attributing the behavior of others to various causes that, in fact, are not truly causes?

MANAGEMENT INCIDENTS AND CASES

The Internship

"Well Ken, it's been a pleasure, and if I can ever do anything for you, feel free to give me a call." These words were spoken by Don Ahearn, Industrial Relations Manager at ARC Corporation, to Ken Barrett, student intern, as they shook hands on the final day of Ken's internship project. As he drove away from ARC's plant in Boston, Massachusetts, Ken could not help thinking about Mr. Ahearn's parting remark. Although the internship may have been a pleasure for Mr. Ahearn, Ken thought the most enjoyable part about it was getting it over with.

It all began in September. As a Junior at Babson College in Wellesley, Massachusetts, Ken had enrolled in "Problems in Organizational Behavior (POB)," a course coordinated by Dr. Ned Berry. POB was a field placement course, in which Dr. Berry placed students in a management internship position for the semester, and they would report back to him weekly with progress reports. For a final grade in the course, each student had to submit (1) a report of their particular project, counting 30%, (2) an organizational setting analysis, of the impact of physical facilities on employee attitudes and behavior in each student's host organization, counting 40%, (3) an oral presentation to class members at the end of the semester, counting 15%, and (4) a grade submitted by the host organization, counting 15%. Dr. Berry produced a list of participating organizations and a brief description of the projects required at each. ARC Corporation listed their project as "research concerning the implementation of an automated personnel system." Since Ken was majoring in Management and considering personnel management as a possible career choice, he requested placement at ARC. Ken received the placement, wrote a letter of introduction to Mr. Don Ahearn, and scheduled an appointment to meet with Mr. Ahearn one week later.

In that following week, Dr. Berry kept his students busy. Since each student was now placed in a host organization and was scheduled to meet with his/her contact person at the organization within two weeks, Dr. Berry used class periods to prepare the students for the internship experience. Through discussion and role-playing, Dr. Berry stressed the importance of setting project parameters at the initial interview. He felt it would benefit both the host company and the student to know exactly what to expect from each other, in terms of time spent with the company, work space provided, student expense reimbursement, support systems, such as student use of copy machines and secretarial service and, most importantly what specific project outcomes were expected from the student by the end of the semester. He also stressed the fact that each student was on his/her own in setting the project parameters. Dr. Berry was available as an advisor, but each student was responsible for seeing his/her own project through.

Ken was anxious to begin work on his project, but did have one concern which he discussed with Dr. Berry. Although Ken had a good understanding of the BASIC computer programming language, he was not an expert in computer programming in any way. He hoped that his project did not involve actual computer programming. Although Dr. Berry had only spoken with Mr. Ahearn over the phone, and like Ken had only sketchy details about the project, he felt sure from his conversation with Mr. Ahearn that the project was primarily a research project, and that Ken would not be involved in computer programming. Ken was relieved, and looked forward to his appointment at ARC the following week.

The next Monday morning, Ken found ARC located in an old manufacturing facility in an industrial section of Boston. He met Mr. Ahearn in his basement office and began the interview by asking for a more detailed description of the project. Mr. Ahearn looked puzzled and replied, "Oh Ken, there is no project." He went on to explain that he had an idea of automating the Personnel Department to cut down on the time he spent meeting the heavy reporting demands of the Office of Federal Contract Compliance Programs (OFCCP) and similar government agencies. He wanted Ken to do some research on automated personnel systems. Ken thought this was fine, but pressed Mr. Ahearn for

more details on what he wanted the automated personnel system to do, whether or not he would integrate payroll functions into the system, and how much he wanted to pay for the system.

Throughout the next hour Mr. Ahearn remained vague and did not really address Ken's questions. Consequently, the entire time was spent attempting to define the project, and Ken had little time to discuss other parameters. Ken did mention that a requirement of the internship was to conduct an organizational setting analysis, which would require Ken to distribute a questionnaire to thirty or so ARC employees. Mr. Ahearn said that was fine but asked to see the questionnaire before it was distributed to employees. At the end of the hour, Ken left disappointed. He had had no time to discuss parameters and still had only a vague idea of what he was to do. Since Mr. Ahearn would be out of town, Ken's next appointment with him was set for three weeks later.

During this first meeting, however, Ken did learn some things about ARC. They processed sheet aluminum for construction and were a division of a large Fortune 500 diversified communications firm. ARC employed roughly 700 people, 450 of which were hourly production workers. Personnel records were currently maintained on a Kardex file system. Although Mr. Ahearn made passing mention of a computer already used by ARC in payroll, Ken did not see it, and Mr. Ahearn did not seem interested in talking much about it.

Not sure where to begin, and knowing nothing about automated personnel systems, Ken decided to begin in the college library. He found some articles dealing indirectly with automated data processing in the personnel setting; there seemed little written on the subject. After this research, he called four computer firms to gather information and possibly arrange interviews. All four of the computer firms assured Ken that there was no such thing as an automated personnel system. However, they did state that a distributed processor could certainly be tailored to personnel operations.

At this point in each conversation, two problems developed. First, when the sales representatives asked Ken for details on the applications of the system, he was unable to give details, as he did not know them himself. Second, the computer firms were generally not very enthusiastic about spending much time speaking with a college student "doing research," as this would probably not lead to a sale. To complicate matters, Don Ahearn had asked Ken not to use the name ARC Corporation in any of his inquiries, for reasons Mr. Ahearn did not disclose. Only one computer firm, Sonex Equipment, offered to speak with Ken in person, and only if Ken would bring a letter of introduction from "whatever firm you're doing work for." Although disheartened, Ken called Mr. Ahearn and obtained the letter. Ken spent two hours with the sales representative at Sonex, and left with a great deal of information on a distributed processor priced at $24,000.

At his next appointment with Don Ahearn, Ken planned to present the information he had received at Sonex, and get Mr. Ahearn's reaction to it. However, when he appeared for his appointment, Mr. Ahearn led Ken into a vacant office, brought in a large box, and placed it on the desk. Mr. Ahearn told Ken "There's a computer in the box. Why don't you set it up and play around with it for awhile, so you'll know what we already have available." He explained to Ken that not much had been done with the computer since ARC purchased it, although he had purchased a pre-recorded Blackjack program and had played it at home a few times with his kids. Before opening the box, Ken explained about his interview with Sonex, and handed Mr. Ahearn the sales material Ken

had received while there. Mr. Ahearn said, "Oh," placed the sales material on the desk, and went back to his office. Ken was disappointed that Mr. Ahearn did not take the time to look at the material, but proceeded to open the box on the desk. Ken did not know that Mr. Ahearn already had a computer.

The contents of the box turned out to be a small personal computer, consisting of a CRT display, keyboard/processor, and cassette tape recorder used for data storage. Included was a beginner's instruction manual for programming the computer in BASIC. Ken recalled seeing such systems advertised for about $600.

Since Mr. Ahearn did not seem interested in discussing Ken's research at Sonex, Ken set the computer up and "played around with it" for about two hours. When he went to find Mr. Ahearn around noon, which was Ken's scheduled time to leave, Mr. Ahearn had already left the building for lunch. Ken left a note with Mr. Ahearn's secretary, which read:

> Mr. Ahearn: I will be back next week at this same time. If that's not a good time for you, give me a call at home at 555-1234. Also, I will bring a copy of my organizational setting analysis questionnaire for you to look at. If you like it, maybe you could give me that plant tour you promised, and we could distribute the questionnaire to twenty or so people. Sincerely, Ken.

In the following week, Ken wrote his questionnaire and first presented it to Dr. Berry, who remarked, "It is one of the better surveys I've seen." With that, Ken brought his questionnaire to ARC the following week. Since Don had meetings scheduled all day, he only had a moment to speak to Ken, and put the questionnaire in his "IN" basket. They had a short conversation about ARC's personal computer, and Mr. Ahearn asked Ken, "Do you think we could put an automated personnel system on it?" Ken explained briefly some of the limitations of the BASIC language, but since Mr. Ahearn was on his way to a meeting, there was not much time to talk. Ken spent the next several hours looking through the computer manual, and left. His next appointment with Mr. Ahearn was two weeks later.

During those next two weeks, Ken did some thinking about the project. He felt he had accomplished nothing and the semester was half over. Since he sensed that ARC was really not interested in a large computer system, but more interested in their personal computer, he thought he should change the direction of the project to center on the personal computer. Ken was beginning to feel that the outside research work was only "busy work," so he decided to present Mr. Ahearn with an alternative project. He would suggest that he discontinue the outside research and concentrate on writing a "simulation" program for the personal computer. Although Ken did not think the personal computer was appropriate for such heavy commercial applications, Mr. Ahearn did, and Ken thought the best way to illustrate the computer's limitations might be to make it work and demonstrate how much time was involved in the process. He would offer the "simulation program" alternative to Mr. Ahearn at their next meeting. Ken also resolved to get Mr. Ahearn's approval on the organizational setting analysis questionnaire, so he could get started on that.

When Ken visited ARC for his next appointment, Mr. Ahearn's secretary informed him that Mr. Ahearn had left on a business trip two days ago and had left no message. She suggested that Ken give Mr. Ahearn a call the following Friday to schedule another appointment.

When Ken called on Friday, neither person mentioned the business trip, but Ken did set up another ap-

pointment. He also took the opportunity to ask Mr. Ahearn if he had looked over the questionnaire. Mr. Ahearn said yes, so Ken asked him what he thought of it. Mr. Ahearn replied, "I find it unacceptable," Ken pressed for elaboration, but Mr. Ahearn was vague, replying, "You know we have three unions here, and the situation is volatile. I can't have you asking my people some of these questions." This surprised Ken because, although he did know that Mr. Ahearn dealt with three unions, he also remembered Mr. Ahearn bragging about how "great" relations were with all three unions. Ken told Mr. Ahearn that they would need to discuss it at their next meeting, and Mr. Ahearn agreed. In the interim, Ken reviewed his questionnaire to try and determine which questions might be objectionable to ARC. He could pinpoint none. He hoped that Mr. Ahearn did not object to more than five or six of the thirty-one questions, as the questionnaire worked best when taken as a whole. Dropping or modifying more than a few questions would render the questionnaire far less useful.

At the next meeting, Ken was shocked to find that Mr. Ahearn had objected to sixteen of the thirty-one questions, and said frankly that he did not like any of the remaining questions either. In a mocking tone of voice he read some of the questions back to Ken, and asked what they were supposed to measure. Although Ken attempted to explain, he could see he was getting nowhere. He then told Mr. Ahearn that the organizational setting analysis was required of all interns, and that if he could not distribute a questionnaire, he would have to conduct interviews. They both agreed that interviews were too time consuming, but Mr. Ahearn still did not want to distribute a questionnaire, and Ken still could not get a clear reason why. Mr. Ahearn remarked that ARC had conducted an extensive attitude survey two years ago, and offered to get the results for Ken, saying, "Maybe you can look at those results and do something with them." At a loss for what to do next, Ken agreed to look at the results. Mr. Ahearn said he would leave the results with his secretary so Ken could pick them up on the following Friday. They spent the remaining time discussing the simulation program, for which Mr. Ahearn was very enthusiastic.

When Ken went to ARC the following Friday to pick up the results, Mr. Ahearn's secretary said that Mr. Ahearn had left nothing with her. Mr. Ahearn had left several days ago on business.

Not knowing what to do next, Ken turned to Dr. Berry. During their weekly meetings, Ken had kept Dr. Berry informed of the problems he had been having at ARC, and the professor had offered suggestions of possible solutions. However, at this point Dr. Berry offered Ken the option of doing some outside research work in lieu of the organizational setting analysis. Dr. Berry said, "This is bound to prove more valuable than continued fighting over the questionnaire." Since Ken's classmates were still required to do the analysis, this again felt a little like defeat, but Ken gladly agreed.

When, at a subsequent meeting, Ken did obtain the results of the study, they turned out to be the text of a speech the company president had made to the workers, summarizing some of the firm's problems. Ken was glad he had taken Dr. Berry's option, as the speech was very "sterile," and provided no information for analyzing the organizational setting.

In the next several weeks, Ken worked on his computer simulation program. Since he was not an expert programmer, the program took about twenty-two total hours to write, test, and enter on the ARC personal computer. The finished program was roughly four hundred steps long, and held a sample of twenty employee files. Ken was pleased, as he felt the program ran

well and really did simulate what could be (and could not be) done with the personal computer. He scheduled an appointment with Mr. Ahearn to show him the program. Since Mr. Ahearn had been busy at meetings during Ken's last few appointments, he had not seen much of what Ken had been doing. Mr. Ahearn informed Ken that he had invited his boss, the Personnel Manager, to see the presentation with him.

In addition to the simulation program, Ken prepared a six page report on what qualities he felt ARC should look for in a computer for the Personnel Department. Since he knew that Mr. Ahearn and his department did not know much about computers, he thought an informational report of this type would be most helpful. Based on the criteria set forth in the report, Ken concluded with a recommendation that the small personal computer not be used in the Personnel Department. Since Ken felt that Mr. Ahearn really did want to use the existing computer, he hesitated before making this recommendation, but based on the criteria set up in his report, there was no choice but to recommend that the existing system not be used.

The presentation with Ahearn and the Personnel Manager went very well, athough it consisted only of Ken letting both men run through the simulation program, and answering a few questions about it. Neither asked to see his report or recommendations, so Ken did not make a point to go into it. The Personnel Manager remarked, at the end of the demonstration, "That's an excellent program, Ken. It looks like you put a lot of work into it." Mr. Ahearn agreed. At this point Mr. Ahearn shook hands with Ken, and made the remark appearing at the beginning of the case. Ken handed him the report and simulation tape, and his internship was over.

One week later, Dr. Berry received the grade determined for Ken by ARC, a "B –." Ken was disappointed, and wondered what he had done wrong, and what exactly he had learned from the whole experience.[29]

Questions

1. Make a list of the possible differences in the way the internship was perceived by Ken and by Mr. Ahearn.
2. To what things might Ken attribute Mr. Ahearn's behavior?
3. To what things would you expect Ken to attribute his "failure?"
4. What were the major problems faced by Ken during his internship project? Why did these problems arise?
5. If you were given Ken's internship, what would you have done to improve the situation?

REFERENCES

1. Bartley, S. H. *Introduction to Perception.* New York: Harper & Row, 1980; Dember, W. N., and Warm, J. S. *Psychology of Perception,* 2d ed. New York: Holt, Rinehart and Winston, 1979; Schiff, W. *Perception: An Applied Approach.* Boston: Houghton Mifflin, 1980.
2. For a good overview of the role of the senses in the perceptual process, see Heil, J. *Perception and Cognition.* Berkeley: University of California Press, 1983, 3–29.
3. Baron, R. A. *Behavior in Organizations: Understanding and Managing the Human Side of Work.* Boston: Allyn and Bacon, 1983, 163; Coon, D. *Introduction to Psychology: Exploration and Application.* St. Paul, Minn.: West, 1977, 104–127.
4. Dearborn, D., and Simon, H. Selective Perception: A Note on the Departmental Identifications of Executives. *Sociometry,* 1958, *21,* 140–144.
5. Baron, *Behavior in Organizations,* 162.
6. Based on Levine, R., and Wolff, E. Social Time: The Heartbeat of Culture. *Psychology Today,* March 1985, 28–35.
7. Zaleznik, A. Power and Politics in Organizational Life. *Harvard Business Review,* March 1970, 47–60.
8. McClelland, D., Atkinson, J., Clark, R., and Lowell, E. *The Achievement Motive.*

New York: Appleton-Century-Crofts, 1953.
9. See, for example, Beck, J. (Ed.) *Organization and Representation in Perception.* Hillsdale, N.J.: Lawrence Erlbaum Associates, 1982; Kolers, P. A. Perception and Representation. *Annual Review of Psychology,* 1983, *34,* 129–166.
10. Senger, J. Seeing Eye to Eye: Practical Problems of Perception. *Personnel Journal,* October 1974, 746. Copyright 1974. Reprinted with the permission of *Personnel Journal,* Costa Mesa, California; all rights reserved.
11. Schiff, *Perception: An Applied Approach,* 397.
12. Cook, M. *Perceiving Others: The Psychology of Interpersonal Perception.* London: Methuen, 1979.
13. Greene, R. Jury Tempering. *Forbes,* November 5, 1984, 214–218.
14. Hampson, S. E. Personality Traits: In the Eye of the Beholder or the Personality of the Perceived? In M. Cook (Ed.) *Issues in Person Perception.* London: Methuen, 1984, 28–47.
15. Penrod, S. *Social Psychology.* Englewood Cliffs, N.J.: Prentice-Hall, 1983, 176–177.
16. Wilson, P. R. Perceptual Distortion of Height as a Function of Ascribed Academic Status. *Journal of Social Psychology,* 1968, *74,* 97–102.
17. Descriptions of these and other perceptual errors can be found in Cook, *Issues in Person Perception;* Schneider, D. J., Hastorf, A. H., and Ellsworth, P. C. *Person Perception,* 2d ed. Reading, Mass.: Addison-Wesley, 1979.
18. Senger, Seeing Eye to Eye: Practical Problems of Perception, 750. Copyright 1974. Reprinted with the permission of *Personnel Journal,* Costa Mesa, California; all rights reserved.
19. Babladelis, G. *The Study of Personality.* New York: Holt, Rinehart and Winston, 1984, 75–76.
20. Baron, R. A., and Byrne, D. *Social Psychology: Understanding Human Interaction.* Boston: Allyn and Bacon, 1981, 58; Jaspars, J., Fincham, F. D., and Hewstone, M. *Attribution Theory and Research: Conceptual, Developmental and Social Dimensions.* London: Academic Press, 1983.
21. Kelley, H. H. Attribution in Social Interaction. In Jones, E. E., Kanouse, D. E., Kelley, H. H., Nisbett, R. E., Valins, S., and Weiner, B. *Attribution: Perceiving the Causes of Behavior.* Morristown, N.J.: General Learning Press, 1972, 1.
22. Mitchell, T. R., Green, S. G., and Wood, R. E. An Attributional Model of Leadership

and the Poor Performing Subordinate. *Research in Organizational Behavior*, 1981, *3*, 197–234.

23. Harvey, J. H., and Weary, G. Current Issues in Attribution Theory and Research. *Annual Review of Psychology*, 1984, *35*, 428.

24. Kelley, H. H. The Process of Causal Attribution. *American Psychologist*, 1973, *28*, 107–128.

25. Good explanations of Kelley's model may be found in Baron, *Behavior in Organizations*, 179–181; Penrod, *Social Psychology*, 187–188.

26. Harvey and Weary, Current Issues in Attribution Theory and Research, 431–432.

27. Babladelis, *The Study of Personality*, 76.

28. Sims, H. P., and Gioia, D. A. Performance Failure: Executive Response to Self-Serving Bias. *Business Horizons*, January–February, 1984, 64–71.

29. Case prepared by Professors Neal Thornberry and Joseph Weintraub of Babson College with the help of student Carl Brooks based on his experiences as a student intern, and reprinted with permission. Copyright © 1981.

5 Managerial Problem-Solving Styles

LEARNING OBJECTIVES

When you have finished studying this chapter, you should be able to:

- State two methods that managers use to gather data.
- State two methods that managers use to evaluate information.
- Describe Jung's model of problem-solving types.
- Identify your own problem-solving style.
- List the strengths and weaknesses of the four managerial problem-solving styles.
- Identify the jobs that are most closely linked with each problem-solving style.

OUTLINE

Preview Case

Behind the Wheels with Lee Iacocca

Few executives have a better feel for the importance of communication and vision—and the danger of letting piles of data paralyze decision making—than Lee Iacocca. The son of Italian immigrants, Iacocca has become the business version of Rocky. An engineering graduate from Lehigh University, he worked his way up to the presidency of Ford Motor Company.

Despite the enormous popularity of the Ford Falcon in 1960, Iacocca began to develop ideas for making a car that would be more popular and make Ford tons of money. While designing this car, he couldn't wait to get to work. He and others at Ford were continually playing with new ideas and trying out models on test tracks. Iacocca and his managers described themselves as artists, attempting to produce one of the finest masterpieces that the auto world had ever seen. This new car had to have three features: great style, reliable performance, and a low price. In terms of styling, Iacocca wanted something along the lines of the first Continental Mark, a quiet, understated car of the 1930s with a long front hood that conveyed the appearance of class and performance. Iacocca had the styling department produce more than 18 different clay models before deciding on the design.

Iacocca never looked at the cost. Forgetting about the "bean counters," on March 6, 1964, the first Mustang rolled off the assembly line. During the Falcon's first year, Ford had sold 417,174. Iacocca's goal was to outsell the Falcon. He did, by more than 1,600 cars. In the first two years, the Mustang generated profits of $1.1 billion for Ford.

Because of the success of the Mustang, Iacocca was promoted to vice-president of the corporate car and truck group. He was in charge of planning, production, and marketing of all cars and trucks in the Ford and Lincoln–Mercury Divisions. After serving in this position for less than five years, he became president of the Ford Motor Company in 1970.

Because of philosophical differences with Henry Ford II, he was fired on July 13, 1978, after serving as Ford's president for eight years and a Ford employee for 32 years. On November 2, 1978, he became president of Chrysler. The *Detroit Free Press* carried the headlines: "Chrysler Losses Are Worst Ever" and "Lee Iacocca Joins Chrysler."

Upon joining Chrysler, Iacocca found a state of confusion. There were 35 vice-presidents, each with his own turf. To remedy the situation, he eventually fired all but two of them. There was no committee setup, no formal organizational chart, no system of meetings to get people together—and people in the engineering department were not talking to those in manufacturing. Iacocca soon found out that Chrysler had no system of financial control. No one understood the basics of financial planning, and he couldn't find out anything. According to Iacocca, this was the biggest jolt in his business career. When he joined Chrysler, he said that he already knew about the lousy cars, low morale and aging factories. But he didn't have any idea that he couldn't get hold of the right numbers so he could begin to identify and attack the right problems.

After only three months at Chrysler, the gasoline crisis of 1979 started. Chrysler's biggest sellers had been vans and RVs and, when the price of gasoline doubled, Chrysler's financial picture turned bleak. Within six months, the small-car share of the U.S. market rose from 43 percent to 58 percent, and Chrysler's total market share dropped to less than 8 percent.

His strategy was to survive. Plants were closed and in April, 1980, 15,500 salaried workers were laid off. These moves saved $500 million. The new K-car was designed to be less than 176 inches long, so Chrysler could fit more of them on a freight car. During 1979 and 1980, Lee held meetings with more than 100 potential investors but, as the economy in general worsened, so did Chrysler's problems. The only way out was the government. Iacocca said, "Believe me, the last thing I wanted to do was turn to the government. Ideologically, I've always been a free enterpriser, a believer in the survival of the fittest. Once the decision was made to ask the government for a bailout, I went at it with all flags flying."

Iacocca knew that his bailout proposal would be controversial. His argument before Congress was quite simple: "You guys (Congress) have a choice. Do you want to pay the $2.7 billion now, or do you want to guarantee loans of half that amount with a good chance of getting it all back?" (The U.S. Treasury Department had estimated that if Chrysler collapsed, it could cost the country $2.7 billion during the first year alone in unemployment and welfare payments.) In order to sell Congress, Iacocca was flying to Washington, D.C., a couple of times a week, agreed to take a salary of $1, threw out the executive stock-option plan, cut managers' salaries by 10 percent, and told the union, "I've got thousands of jobs at $17 per hour, but none at $20 per hour. You'd better come to your senses." After convincing his own managers and the union, he spent most of his time working with banks. At the end of this process, there were 10,000 individual documents to sign. It cost Chrysler $2 million just to print all the documents.

The K-car was not an immediate success. There were still some problems, but in 1982 the economy turned around, and car sales rose. In 1982, Chrysler made a profit of $925 million, the largest in its history. Then Iacocca made the biggest decision of his life: to pay back the entire loan. A check was drawn for $813,487,500, but the government couldn't accept it. Because of red tape, it took the government more than a month to figure out how to handle it.

After paying off the loan, he had to convince the public that Chrysler meant business. He was told by Chrysler's public relations firm that the best way to get the message across was to feature him. In one TV commercial Iacocca walks through one of the Chrysler plants and says, "Quality, hard work and commitment, the stuff America is made of. Our goal: to be the best. What else is there? If you can find a better built car, buy it."

His name has been mentioned as a possible 1988 U.S. presidential candidate. But Iacocca maintains that he does not have the temperament for politics; that he's far too impatient, and candid. Iacocca says, "If a guy's giving me a lot of baloney, I tell him to buzz off because he's wrong. Somehow I don't think the presidency works that way."[1]

Would you like to work for Lee Iacocca? What is his managerial style? This chapter will help you understand why you reacted as you did to Iacocca's managerial style.

Chapter 4 indicated that most behavior is based on perceptions. If a manager's behavior is based on erroneous perceptions of others, of the situation, or both, the manager will not be effective. Consider the following conversation between a vice-president for operations and a senior manager of a consulting firm:

> VP OPERATIONS: What do you think we can do to increase our third- and fourth-quarter profits?
>
> CONSULTANT: That's a good question. Our firm has been thinking about it for the last week. We recommend that you systematically review your current asset position and develop a forecast of industrial trends that may have an impact on your business. After analyzing your asset base and estimating your market share, we can develop a projected long term marketing. . . .
>
> VP OPERATIONS: (Impatiently reaching for his wallet, taking out two $100 bills, and interrupting the consultant) Hey, do you see these two babies? You know, dead presidents. Money talks. How can I get more of them in the third and fourth quarters of this year?

This conversation satisfied neither the vice-president of operations nor the consultant. The consultant was trying to present a theoretical viewpoint. Unfortunately, the vice-president of operations wanted the consultant to deal with the real problem: money. The vice-president of operations viewed the consultant as being too unrealistic and wasting his time.

Anyone who has ever been involved in such a situation knows how frustrating and nonproductive it can be. Since effective communication and decision making are keys to developing and maintaining successful relationships, managers should become aware of their style and know how to anticipate and avoid such strained relationships. This chapter will examine different problem solving styles and the behavioral clues that help managers identify the types of people they deal with and their own style.

PSYCHOLOGICAL FUNCTIONS IN PROBLEM SOLVING

Psychologist Carl Gustav Jung defined four psychological functions that are involved in information gathering and evaluation: sensation, intuition, thinking, and feeling.[2] People who have the same primary orientation tend to exhibit similar behaviors. While a primary orientation dominates an individual's behavior, each may also have a secondary style for "fine tuning" his or her basic approach to perceiving and making judgments about the world.[3] According to Jung, individuals gather information either by sensation or intuition, but not by both simultaneously. These two functions represent ex-

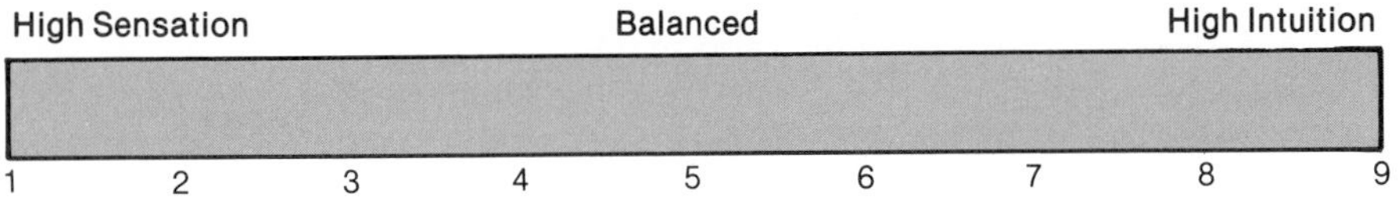

High Sensation   Balanced   High Intuition

```
┌──────────────────────────────────────────────────────────────────┐
│                                                                    │
└──────────────────────────────────────────────────────────────────┘
 1        2        3        4        5        6        7        8        9
```

FIGURE 5–1. Continuum of Information-gathering Orientations

High Thinking   Balanced   High Feeling

```
┌──────────────────────────────────────────────────────────────────┐
│                                                                    │
└──────────────────────────────────────────────────────────────────┘
 1        2        3        4        5        6        7        8        9
```

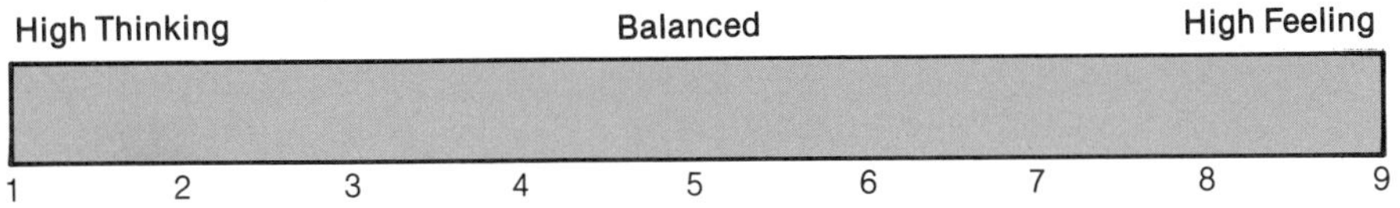

FIGURE 5–2. Continuum of Information-evaluating Orientations

treme orientations, or opposite ways of gathering information, and can be thought of as the extremes of a continuum, as shown in Figure 5-1.

Similarly, the thinking and feeling functions represent extreme orientations in evaluating information. As shown in Figure 5-2, thinking and feeling are also opposite ends of a continuum.

According to Jung, only one of the four functions is dominant in each individual. However, the dominant function is normally backed up by one (and only one) of the functions from the other set of paired opposites. For example, the thinking function may be supported by the sensation function, or vice versa. The sensation–thinking combination characterizes best the people in today's Western industrialized societies. As a result, intuition and feeling are the functions most likely to be disregarded, undeveloped, or repressed. However, Jung also believed that the developing individual tends to move toward a balance, or integration, of the four psychological functions.

We will first consider each of the four psychological functions as a dominant type and then consider the two information-gathering orientations (sensation and intuition) in combination with the two information-evaluating orientations (thinking and feeling) as they relate to managerial styles.

Sensation versus Intuition in Gathering Information

Individuals perceive or gather information differently according to whether sensation or intuition dominates. The paragraphs following Table 5-1 describe behavioral patterns and general characteristics of people with sensation and intuition type information-gathering styles. Seventy-five percent of the general population reports a preference for gathering information through sensation while 25 percent indicates a preference for intuition.[4] However, people do not belong to one clearly defined category or the other; the classification merely provides a good starting point for understanding ourselves and the expectations others have of us.[5]

SENSATION TYPE PERSON   The **sensation type person** wants facts, trusts facts, and remembers facts. Such a person believes in experience and relies on the past to learn how to approach current problems. When interviewing someone for a job, a sensation type person wants to know what experience

TABLE 5-1   Behavioral Style Clues for a Sensation Type and an Intuitive Type Person

Style Characteristic	Sensation Type	Intuitive Type
Emphasis	Action, getting things done, seeing results of efforts quickly	Ideas, concepts, theories, innovation, long-range thinking
Time orientation	Present	Future
Sources of satisfaction	Quick results, making things happen, feedback on efforts, being in charge	World of possibilities; problem-solving oriented, but not terribly interested in implementing solutions
Strengths	Pragmatic, assertive, directional, results oriented, objective, bases opinions on what is actually seen, competitive, confident	Original, imaginative, creative, idealistic, intellectually tenacious, ideological
Weaknesses (If style is overextended)	Lacks long-range perspective, seeks status; acts first, then thinks; lacks trust in others; domineering; arrogant	Unrealistic, fantasy bound, scattered, devious, out of touch, dogmatic, impractical
Typical occupations	Construction worker, pilot, banker, investor, professional athlete, salesperson, model, physician, land developer	Scientist, researcher, artist, professor, writer, corporate planner, entrepreneur

the applicant has had; the applicant's experience is important to the interviewer because it provides this type of person with a basis for a sound decision. The sensation type person uses words such as *actual, down-to-earth, realistic, practical, utility,* and *past experience* when making a presentation to others. In terms of a problem-solving style, the sensation type person tends to

- dislike new problems unless there are standard ways to solve them;
- enjoy using skills already acquired more than learning new ones;
- work steadily, with a realistic idea of how long a task will take;
- work all the way through a task or problem to reach a conclusion;
- be impatient when details get complicated; and
- distrust creative inspirations and usually does not get inspired.

The sensation type person dislikes dealing with unstructured problems, because they contain considerable uncertainty and usually require the individual to exercise some degree of judgment in deciding on a course of action and how to implement it. Such a person may experience considerable anxiety in making decisions in hazy areas because their consequences are not clear-cut. The sensation type person is mentally oriented to physical reality, external facts, and concrete experiences and is not inclined toward personal reflection or introspection into experiences or the self.

Sensation type people emphasize action, urgency, and bottom-line results. Through an assertive, quick-paced, and "let's do it now" approach to life and work, they dissipate anxiety through action and learn by doing, not by imagining or thinking. Sensation type people enjoy the thrill of the chase or the fast payoff.

INTUITIVE TYPE PERSON The routine and structured job that is enjoyed and performed well by a sensation type manager probably would be disliked and poorly performed by an intuitive type manager. An **intuitive type** person likes to solve new problems, dislikes doing the same things over and over again, jumps to conclusions, becomes impatient with routine details, and dislikes taking time for precision. Whereas the sensation type person tends to perceive the external environment in terms of details and parts, the intuitive type person tends to perceive the whole, or totality, of the external environment—as it is and as it might change—and lives in anticipation. When conducting a job interview, the intuitive type person is not likely to place too much emphasis on what the applicant has done in the past, but rather on the applicant's imagination, ability to hypothesize about the future, the growth possibilities of the organization, and how the applicant would go about solving a problem.

The language of the intuitive type person is filled with metaphors and imagery. Words such as *possible, fascinating, ingenious,* and *imaginative* are used to describe people and things. Such a person often daydreams, enjoys fantasy, and may be described by the sensation type person as someone who has his or head in the clouds. Because the intuitive type person's head is in the clouds, he or she may be subject to greater errors of fact than the sensation type person. A person once described an intuitive manager as one "who can see around corners." In terms of a problem-solving style, the intuitive type person tends to

- keep the total picture or overall problem continually in mind as the problem-solving process develops;
- show a tendency, willingness, and openness to continuously redefine the problem;
- rely on hunches and nonverbal cues;
- almost simultaneously consider a variety of alternatives and options;
- jump around or back and forth among the usual sequence of steps in the problem-solving process and may even suddenly want to reassess whether the "true" problem has even been identified; and
- quickly consider and discard alternatives.

Unlike the sensation type person, the intuitive type person feels suffocated by stable conditions and seeks out and creates new possibilities. Such a person is often a venture capitalist, politician, speculator, entrepreneur, or stockbroker. This type of person often initiates and promotes new enterprises, services, concepts, and other innovations in both the public and private sectors, skipping from one activity to the next and perhaps completing none. Jung described the intuitive type person as one who plants a field and then is off to something new before the crop is even beginning to break ground. Instead of staying around to see the vision come to fruition, the individual is off looking for new fields to plow.

Intuitive type people are imaginative and futuristic, and they enjoy mind-testing games like the Rubik's Cube, chess, and bridge. Technical details often slip past them. They become impatient with people who do not see the immediate value of their ideas. Although they may appear to be daydreaming, they are probably forming concepts and integrating experiences to determine the reasons behind things.

Feeling versus Thinking in Evaluating Information

Information evaluation involves making a judgment based on the information gathered. Jung believed that people rely on two basic functions when making a judgment: thinking and feeling. Those who use the impersonal basis are called *thinking* by Jung. Those who use the personal basis are called *feeling*. Some people are more comfortable with making impersonal, objective judgments and are uncomfortable with making personal, subjective judgments. Others are more comfortable with subjective judgments and less comfortable with objective judgments. Both ways of making judgments are necessary and useful. Table 5–2 summarizes the characteristics typically associated with these functions. Again, no one can be classified totally as belonging to one category or the other, in terms of evaluating information. Seventy percent of the U.S. population use thinking when evaluating information, while only 30 percent tend to emphasize feeling.

FEELING TYPE PERSON A **feeling type person** is aware of other people and their feelings, likes harmony, needs occasional praise, dislikes telling people unpleasant things, tends to be sympathetic, and relates well to most people.

TABLE 5–2 **Behavioral Style Clues for a Feeling Type and a Thinking Type Person**

Style Characteristic	Thinking Type	Feeling Type
Emphasis	Logic, organization, analysis, systematic inquiry	Human interaction, feelings, emotions
Time orientation	Past, present, future	Past
Sources of satisfaction	Seeing a problem through to implementing a solution, anything well organized or methodically thought out	"Reading between the lines," social interpersonal contact
Strengths	Effective communicator, deliberative, prudent, weighs alternatives, stabilizing, objective, rational, analytical	Spontaneous, persuasive, empathic, grasps traditional values, probing, introspective, draws out feelings of others, loyal
Weaknesses (if style is overextended)	Verbose, indecisive, overly cautious, overanalytical, unemotional, nondynamic, controlled and controlling, overly serious, rigid	Impulsive, manipulative, overpersonalizing, sentimental, postponing, guilt-ridden, stirs up conflict, subjective
Typical occupations	Lawyer, engineer, teacher, computer programmer, accountant	Entertainer, salesperson, writer, teacher, public relations specialist, nurse, social worker, psychiatrist, psychologist, secretary, retail businessperson

Feeling type managers would probably conform to a high degree and accommodate themselves to other people. They tend to make decisions that result in approval from others (peers, subordinates, and superiors). In problem-solving style, feeling type people tend to

- enjoy pleasing people, even in ways that others consider unimportant;
- dislike dealing with problems that require them to tell people unpleasant things;
- be responsive and sympathetic to other people's problems;
- heavily emphasize the human aspects in dealing with organizational problems; and
- see problems of inefficiency and ineffectiveness as caused by interpersonal and other human difficulties.

Feeling type people emphasize emotional and personal factors in decision making. They usually avoid problems that are likely to result in disagreements. When avoidance or smoothing over of differences is not possible, they often change their positions to those that are more acceptable to others. The establishment and maintenance of friendly relations may be more important to them than achievement, effectiveness, and decision making. Feeling type managers may have a difficult time suspending or discharging subordinates for inadequate performance, even when the problem is widely recognized by others, including the employees' peers.

In other words, feeling type people are emotional and spontaneous, the Erma Bombecks who are known for their love of people. They base their decisions on feelings, whether buying a car or choosing a friend, and they can be self-indulgent.

They choose words that reflect a personal tone, such as *subjective values, intimacy,* and *extenuating circumstances.* The ready use of words such as these tends to make the feeling type person good at persuasion or negotiating. He or she makes choices in the context of the personal impact of the decisions on other people.

THINKING TYPE PERSON   At the other extreme, the thinking type person has a preference for impersonal principles and is not comfortable unless there is a logical or analytical basis for a decision. Such a person is generally unemotional and uninterested in other people's feelings. The activities and decisions of this type of individual are usually controlled by intellectual processes based on external data and generally accepted ideas and values; problems and their solutions are fitted into standardized formulas. When making decisions, the person's application of impersonal formulas may result in the loss of all personal considerations, even his or her own welfare. For the sake of some principle, a thinking type person may neglect health, finances, family, or other interests that other people would normally regard as important.

Thinking type people are organized and structured, and they doggedly pursue facts. They seldom leap to conclusions but prefer to consider carefully all options before making a decision. They are conservative, both in dress and risk taking. They are the Oliver Wendell Holmeses of the world in their painstaking research and accuracy. On the negative side, thinking type people can get bogged down in analyzing situations over and over again. At worst, they can be perceived by others to be rigid, dogmatic, and boring.

When dominant, the thinking function is often productive because it results in the discovery of new facts, concepts, or models based on seemingly unrelated empirical data. In terms of a problem-solving style, thinking type people are likely to

- make a plan and look for a method to solve the problem;
- be extremely conscious of and concerned with their approach to a problem;
- define carefully the specific constraints in the problem;
- proceed by increasingly refining their analysis; and
- search for and obtain additional information in a very orderly manner.

ACROSS CULTURES

Do Problem-Solving Styles Vary According to Culture?

The answer to this question is yes. According to several studies comparing business students from Japan and the United States, culture influences the way students think about problems. The Japanese preference for planning and precision over spontaneity and openness is reflected in several ways.

Japanese business students prefer their business experiences to be more planned and structured than their U.S. counterparts. That is, the emphasis is on specific assignments to be handed in on certain dates as opposed to more broadly assigned topics with no specific completion dates. These same students preferred multiple-choice exams two-to-one over essay tests that usually have no single "right" answer. Japanese students prefer to follow an analytical or rational approach to problem solving, whereas U.S. students like to improvise along the way as needed to solve the problem. Similarly, U.S. students prefer abstract concepts and theories whereas Japanese students express a preference for well-established laws and truths. The laws are mainly found in mathematics, physics, and computer science. Interestingly enough, the abstract concepts North Americans use in explaining organizational behavior—concepts such as leadership, morale, and decision making—are not so well-defined in the Japanese language. In fact, there isn't a well-defined concept of "decision making" in Japan, despite the vast literature in the United States that has been translated into Japanese. Finally, Japanese students are less responsive to emotional appeals (40 percent to 25 percent) than their U.S. counterparts.

Source: Adapted from Torrence, P., and Sato, S., Differences in Japanese and United States Styles of Thinking. *Creative and Adult Quarterly,* Autumn 1979, 145–151; Doktor, R. A Cognitive Approach to Culturally Appropriate HRD Programs. *Training and Development Journal,* October 1982, 32–36; Nakamura, H. *Ways of Thinking of Eastern Peoples.* Honolulu: East-West Center Press, 1964

There is considerable similarity among the thinking type person's problem-solving style, the major elements in the scientific method, and what U.S. society characterizes as rational problem solving. Educational institutions emphasize development of the thinking function. This characteristic is obviously important in an advanced industrialized society, but the assumed superiority of the thinking over the feeling function has been overemphasized.

The discussion to this point has focused on each of the four dominant psychological functions used by people to gather and evaluate information. Each style has a different orientation and tends to lead to decisions in a different way. Based on the information presented in the Preview Case, what are the dominant psychological functions of Lee Iacocca? Under normal conditions, Iacocca exhibits the characteristics of a thinking–intuitive manager.

MANAGERIAL PROBLEM-SOLVING PROFILES

Figure 5-3 shows a model of managerial problem solving based on the four psychological functions. The vertical axis represents the thinking–feeling continuum. The horizontal axis represents the sensation–intuition continuum. Most of us can and do use both types of information gathering and evaluation in our daily lives but usually have a preference for one way of gathering information and one way of evaluating information.

Much about a person's problem-solving style can be learned from his or her brief written description of an ideal organization. Take ten minutes and write your own description. Then compare it with the highlights culled from those of thousands of executives, as presented in the following sections, to identify your own problem-solving style.

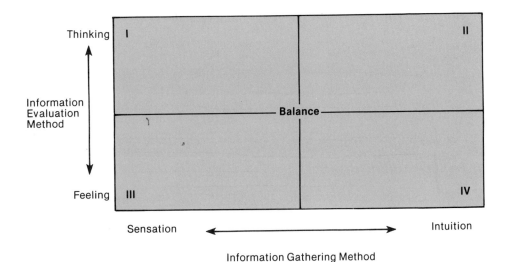

FIGURE 5–3.
Managerial Problem-Solving Styles Model

This section describes the managerial styles of **sensation-thinker** (ST), **intuitive-thinker** (NT), **sensation-feeler** (SF), and **intuitive-feeler** (NF) according to managers' written descriptions of the ideal organization. The strengths and weaknesses of each style will also be illustrated.[6]

Sensation-Thinkers

Managers who are STs will establish effective managerial rules and regulations to create a stable organization. They are decisive and make excellent decisions that involve precise interpretations of facts and figures. These managers persevere, work steadily with realistic ideas of how long a task will take, seldom make errors of fact, and can be counted on to follow through on commitments. Before they make a decision, they weigh the costs and benefits and try to see the practical effect of the decision. They tend to be on time and their work on schedule—they keep a system running. They like to clarify, settle, and conclude situations and problems and may be frustrated until they make a decision. Others with whom they work know where they stand on the issues.

These managers are applied thinkers and want their organizations to be run on facts. They are able to absorb, remember, manipulate, and manage a large number of details, objects, or facts. They are dependable leaders who are extraordinarily hard workers and demand a good day's work for a good day's pay. They run efficient meetings with a well-planned agenda, and they are briefed to the last detail. These managers typically interact formally and impersonally with others in the organization.

An organization that does not have some ST managers may not be run efficiently and effectively. Plant utilization may be inefficient, and there will probably be poor control of materials and organizational procedures. An organization without ST managers may find itself in a constant state of change without a base of sound, accepted policy and regulations from which to work.

POSSIBLE WEAKNESSES Sensation-thinker managers get impatient with projects that are delayed by complications. At times they may decide too quickly on a course of action and not notice new situations that need attention. Since they excel in preserving the procedures and rules of the organization, they may also preserve less successful ones to maintain stability in the organization. These responses may not be desirable when rapid change is necessary.

These managers often believe that some people are good and others bad, and that the bad should be punished. They often find tension in their relationships with others and blame others when things do not go their way. They are overly concerned about the possibility of negative consequences. They may repeatedly analyze situations and thus use up most of their energy anticipating having to deal with situations that never occur. They believe that all people can contribute to the company if only they work hard and long enough.

WAYS OF DEALING WITH OTHERS   Sensation-thinker managers want others to get to the point fast and stick to it. They want the facts presented in a highly organized fashion by logical thinkers. They enjoy dealing with data systems. When dealing with others, however, they may be frustrated by not always being able to get facts and figures. This manifests itself, for example, in an insistence that others follow formal procedures and policies.

These managers withhold rewards unless they believe the rewards are fully deserved. They may have difficulty giving symbolic rewards, such as honors and trophies, and are more comfortable giving verbal or monetary rewards based on measurable performance objectives.

OCCUPATIONS   Sensation-thinker managers are likely to be interested in occupations that deal with the details of the physical and impersonal side of the organization. These individuals may be attracted to occupations in fields such as accounting, production, market research, computer programming, clerical scheduling, copy editing, drafting, engineering, statistics, staff analysis, librarianship, assembling, and applied science. Their idea of organizational effectiveness tends to focus on such variables as sales per full-time salesperson, inventory cost per dollar of sales, scrap loss per unit produced, rate of return on invested capital, short-term profits, value of production per labor hour, and cost of goods sold. Most organizations, as well as the advanced industrialized societies and their educational systems, place considerable emphasis on developing and using the problem-solving style characteristic of sensation-thinkers.

Donald Nyrop of Northwest Airlines exhibits many of the characteristics of an ST. Consider how his style influences the running of this airline.

In Practice: Donald Nyrop, Northwest Airlines

Donald Nyrop, former chairman of Northwest Airlines, has been described as willing to stay on top of everything that affects the bottom line of the airline. It has had the best profit margins over the past decade (7.8 percent) despite having three strikes over the past six years of the 1,550 pilots who fly under the Northwest flag. Rising to the head of the CAB at the age of thirty-nine, Nyrop won the reputation of a formidable cost-cutter by delving into the minutest details. He likes to reduce everything to numbers and relate these to his airline. One former executive remembered that Nyrop commented that the cost of replacing one light bulb was the profit earned on a single passenger flying the Twin Cities–Chicago run. Nyrop's frugality has affected every facet of Northwest. The hangar-like structure that houses the airline's corporate offices has no windows and no pictures on the walls of the office; it leases for $1.75 per square foot compared with the more than $10.00 that most of Northwest's competitors pay.

Northwest doesn't spend much money on advertising either. Northwest ads just tell the customer when the airline flies and where. The management team is lean, with no committees and only fifteen vice-presidents. That means fewer assistant vice-presidents and secretaries. Nyrop believes in the Protestant work ethic and demands similar devotion from his staff. The leanness and efficiency of Northwest's operation lets it operate with the lowest break-even factor in the industry. Nyrop's great financial skills have enabled him to generate good profits through the sale of used planes. The commonality of aircraft and engines is reflected in the fact that Northwest flies two basic engines and three fuselages. The savings on maintenance and spare parts is staggering.[7]

Intuitive Thinkers

Managers who are NTs are the architects of progress and ideas. They are interested in the principles on which the organization is built and seek answers to why events occur. The ability to see relationships between various departments of the company enables them to make sense out of the activities that occur in the system. They focus on possibilities, but analyze them impersonally. For example, when they move into an organization, they are likely to analyze immediately the power base and structure and determine who holds the power. This type of manager is intellectually ingenious and an excellent pioneer in technical and administrative matters.

An organization that does not have NTs in management will undergo minimal change, and sooner or later organizational profits will decline. If NT managers perceive that the organization's goals are stability and the status quo, they drift off or form quiet pockets of passive resistance, being inclined to ignore rules and regulations out of sheer boredom.

They may prefer to work with other NT managers, but they also need to work with those who can persuade, conciliate, and negotiate cooperation. They should be supported by a staff who can carry out the details of projects and ideas. They value an administrative assistant who can read over contracts, keep track of details, check records, proofread, call attention to fine details, and patiently perform the same tasks repeatedly.

POSSIBLE WEAKNESSES Intuitive thinker managers involved in the creative process have enormous drive. Once a program is designed, however, they are more than willing to allow someone else to take over the implementation. Because they focus on principles and abstract thinking, at times they may not be aware of others' feelings. Such managers may not consider subordinates (or superiors) as valuable employees unless they are perceived to be intellectually competent.

These managers may encounter difficulty in their interpersonal relations because they believe that they (and others) should be as competent, adequate, and professional as possible. Thus they expect a great deal of themselves and others—often more than can be delivered. They need to remind themselves that people with strengths also have weaknesses. They often feel restless and unfulfilled, tending to escalate standards for themselves and others and often demonstrating an intolerance of mistakes and reflection after a decision has been made.

WAYS OF DEALING WITH OTHERS Intuitive thinker managers typically track the thought processes and ideas of others quite easily and enjoy doing so. They respond well to the new ideas of others, and they also are champions of their own causes. They enjoy solving new problems; when faced with a colleague's problem, they will be stimulated rather than feel weighted down by the prospect of having to solve it. They have the courage to stand behind their convictions, even if others believe they are wrong.

They like to make decisions, and employees know where their managers stand—but only if they ask, since NT managers believe that their position is quite obvious and therefore redundant to state. They answer questions about their opinions frankly. They admire reason, logic, and intelligence in others, and they do not feel a need to minimize the contributions of others.

In an organization, NT managers will be labeled as the "idea people." Since these managers easily conceptualize the outcomes of staff contributions, they are comfortable in organizations that focus on results rather than on procedures and rules.

They must consciously try to remember social rituals that others find important. While they may be the most appreciative of the ideas and contributions of others, they may fail to tell the other people this. They are most likely to respond to praise that involves recognition of accomplishments and will value recognition of the influence their work has had on others.

OCCUPATIONS Occupations that deal with an overall view and the impersonal side of the organization attract NT managers. Examples include middle and higher-level management; systems design and analysis; architectural design; pure scientific scholarship and teaching in such fields as economics, business and philosophy, and the physical sciences (caring more for the subject than perhaps the students); law; mathematics; and creative engineering. They probably determine organizational effectiveness by such variables as rate of new product development, market share, cost of capital, growth in earnings and long-run profits, new market development, and degree of action on and response to environmental changes.

Tom Landry, long-time coach of the Dallas Cowboys football team, displays many tendencies of an NT. However, when Dallas is in a close game and time is running out, he may choose a back-up style of an ST.

In Practice: **Tom Landry, Dallas Cowboys**

I believe in everything being well planned in my work. I believe that no stone should be left unturned. I want to gather facts and get answers. I relate this information to my coaches and then they relate it to the players. I want to be sure they understand the total picture. I don't want any coach or player not to understand the total game plan. Giving the big picture of what we need to do to win is critical.

In our defensive system, everybody has to work together. We rely on planning, preparation, systems, drill and logic, and not much on emotions. In defense, we don't strive for flair, but consistency and logic. We emphasize purpose, planning and excellence in execution.

On offense, we try to use more flair to achieve a surprise and the unexpected. The innovations, such as the shotgun and motions, are not done for innovations' or change's sake. They're done for a logical purpose. Our competitors will see what the Cowboys do on offense as "wide open," "daring," "gambling," perhaps. Sure, there's a lot of show to it, but there's a purpose to the show. We're trying to bring about the result of the opponent's defeat by means of the unexpected, the bold move, the unanticipated surprise stroke. Let's say that we are preparing to play the Pittsburgh Steelers. A given Cowboy player is preparing to play them. The coach reviews the player's job with him, exactly what he's expected to do. He has precise objectives. He must do these certain things to bring results. If he isn't prepared, he'll do the job in an imperfect way that will fail to achieve results. We do not want any player to fail. He must feel secure to succeed. If he fails to feel secure, he won't do his best. All our coaches use computer printouts. Hundreds of them. Every pattern, every stat of every team we play is on the computer. Each coach has one and uses it. It's analysis every step of the way. Football is a game of objectives. The Dallas Cowboys play football by objectives. We set team objectives, our offensive objectives, our defense objectives, our game objectives, and our play objectives. Every player has his own objectives.[8]

Sensation-Feelers

Managers who are SFs are pragmatists who can deal with concrete problems in a methodical fashion. These managers negotiate with ease and are natural troubleshooters or diplomats. They are good at putting out fires, at unsnarling messes, and getting it done quickly. They have the talent for getting people to cooperate with them and with each other on the basis of expediency. There is an attitude of sureness and damn-the-torpedoes, full-speed-ahead that causes others to be fully confident in the SF managers' decisions and directions. If they experience self-doubt, it is not transmitted to those around them. They can analyze a system and see how it works, find breakdowns and errors that occur, and determine the corrections needed.

As managers, SFs understand the organization better than any other type of manager because they astutely observe the details of how it is run. Subordinates working for SF managers say that things seem to happen effortlessly, without wasted time and motion. These managers do not fight the system; they use available means to solve problems rather than try to change the reality of the system.

They can spur action in a management team. Things are sure to happen with SF managers around. They are probably best at planning and decision making and good at producing written documents. Since they can spot troubles in an organization while the troubles are still minor and can prevent small problems from becoming larger ones, operations run smoothly. Productivity is apt to be high, and SF managers will be aware of employee comfort and working conditions. They are not likely to allow unnecessarily bad working conditions to exist for subordinates without attempting to do something about them.

POSSIBLE WEAKNESSES   Sensation-feeler managers may be reluctant to accept radical new theories and may become impatient with abstract ideas. They do not like the unfamiliar and tend to react negatively to extreme change. They view philosophical statements as mere academic exercises that are not relevant to solving problems in the real world. They are very adaptable until the system's rules and procedures are broken. They live fully for the moment and may experience difficulty in honoring commitments and decisions made in the past.

WAYS OF DEALING WITH OTHERS Sensation-feeler managers usually respond to the ideas of others only if those ideas are concrete. They are predictable in working with colleagues, who find them easy to get along with. The possibility of their own failure or that of others does not threaten SF managers, who take calculated risks and encourage others to do the same. These managers can change their position easily as facts change and new situations arise. They do not worry about what might have been; they deal with what is.

These managers typically do not judge their co-workers and accept their behaviors at face value rather than seek underlying motives and meanings. To motivate subordinates, SF managers reward them only when they have completed a task. They themselves prefer symbolic rewards such as plaques, lapel pins, and newspaper stories.

OCCUPATIONS Sensation-feeler managers are usually interested in jobs that require personal contact with others in the organization or with customers. They excel at selling, direct supervision, counseling, negotiating, teaching, preaching, personnel, interviewing, and many types of service work. These managers enjoy talking with other people. For them organizational effectiveness is determined by such factors as employee loyalty, attitudes, grievances, turnover, and absenteeism.

In Practice: **James McDonnell, McDonnell Douglas**

McDonnell Douglas, with sales over $8 billion, is now the leading defense contractor and the number 2 manufacturer of commercial transport planes. According to one Defense Department official, what sets McDonnell Douglas apart from their competition is top management's meticulous personal attention to detail. When James S. "Mr. Mac" McDonnell passed the baton to Sanford "Sandy" McDonnell in 1972, few, if any, companies of its size had witnessed such pervasive philosophy from one individual.

Nicknamed the "Practicing Scotsman," Mr. Mac was a brilliant engineer who built the company dominated by engineers with a penchant for penny-pinching. The infatuation with engineering penetrates every facet of the company's activities. Decision making is conducted with stress on quantitative analysis with everything broken down into small bits and analyzed. The company has a highly centralized management reporting and financial controls system; no minor points are overlooked. One former executive has commented that decision making takes forever because each decision is negotiated with facts and figures until the bitter end. The chairman's frugality and engineering orientation were even carried to a Christmas office party where he used a slide rule to figure out how much whiskey to put into the punch bowl. One vice-president describes the management style at McDonnell Douglas as measuring every risk carefully, being highly conservative, and being dedicated to technical approaches that produce a strategy without debating it around a table.

Most of the top management team have never worked anywhere else, and outsiders are rarely recruited for important jobs. Employees are encouraged to own shares of stock in the company and to participate in decisions. Sandy frequently takes to the plantwide public address system to inform all employees on contracts, awards and other vital matters. Face-to-face meetings dominate with only a minor regard for organizational protocol. According to Jerry Brown, vice-president and treasurer, "We're not rigidly constrained by an organization chart." Input from others is sought and respected at regularly scheduled meetings.[9]

Intuitive Feelers

Personal charisma and commitment to the people they lead highlight the problem-solving style of NFs. They usually use language well and through it communicate their caring and enthusiasm. They easily see abstract possibilities for their companies and particularly for the people in democratically run companies. They are very comfortable with an unstructured, group-centered management system that lets employees participate in decision-making processes. They are patient with complicated situations and can wait for the right time to move forward on an idea; they are like chemical catalysts.

The employees of an organization that does not have NF managers may find the environment cold, sterile, joyless, and dull. The NF managers focus on developing individuals within the organization. They are deeply committed to the career progress of subordinates and strive to enhance subordinates' personal growth. When NF managers are in leadership roles, their focus is primarily on developing the potentials of employees, with the development of the organization secondary. They look for and react to the best in others and give them feedback and coaching.

They head an organization well if they are given a free reign to manage, but they may rebel if they believe the system has placed too many constraints on them. To motivate others, NF managers give many psychological rewards. If they themselves receive sufficient praise, they are excellent managers; if not sufficiently praised, they can become ineffective, discouraged, and uninvolved—and they will look outside the organization for rewards.

POSSIBLE WEAKNESSES Intuitive feeler managers may find themselves making administrative decisions on the basis of their personal likes and dislikes rather than on the basis of performance measures. They work in great bursts of energy, powered by enthusiasm, but they need frequent rest periods to recharge their energy levels. They need the approval of both subordinates and superiors and at times may find themselves as the champion of two opposing groups. They understand the emotions of others so well that they are vulnerable to them and want to "please all the people all the time," which inevitably gets them into difficult situations as managers.

They are likely to feel pressured, because their belief system states that it is necessary for every person, especially significant others, to love and admire them. This belief may cause NF managers to spend too much time seeking approval and to constantly check with others until they show approval. Under these conditions, managers may become so responsive to the demands of others that they lose sight of their own values, beliefs, and goals.

WAYS OF DEALING WITH OTHERS Intuitive feeler managers relate well to others, who often vote them the most popular. They hunger for personal contact and go out of their way to find it. They are sociable and enjoy being where people are gathered. They frequently consult and maintain close personal contact with their boss. They find their office a source of social satisfaction as well as a place to work.

OCCUPATIONS Intuitive feeler managers, like SF managers, usually prefer occupations that deal with the human side of the organization. However, their jobs need not have as many personal and close contacts with others as SF managers prefer. They deal comfortably with groups of people either directly or indirectly. They excel in public relations work and shine as spokespersons for their company because they work well with all types of people, can "sell" an organization to its customers, and make the people who work for an organization feel good about themselves and the organization. They do well in such occupations as public relations, politics, advertising, personnel, some types of sales, art, and teaching. They believe organizational effectiveness is reflected in consumer satisfaction, social responsibility, ability to identify problems or new opportunities, quality of life, and community satisfaction with the organization.

Many of the characteristics of an NF can be found in John Emery, chairman of Emery Air Freight. Let us examine how he has transformed this company into a very successful business, relying on his NF administrative skills.

In Practice: **John C. Emery Jr., Emery Air Freight**

When John Emery became chairman of Emery Air Freight in 1981, this airfreight company was struggling. Federal Express had its own fleet of planes and was able to offer speedier service at a cheaper cost than Emery. The problems of Emery were further compounded by deregulation of airlines, which led to cutbacks in regional trunk routes and local air service. Since 1981, Emery has acquired its own fleet of more than 70 planes and built an automated hub for its shipments in Dayton, Ohio. The company has also gotten more heavily into the expanding market for overnight small-package deliveries. It now employs more than 5,000 people worldwide, and it has been reporting record profits.

The turnaround came when John created the Emery URGENT letter service, an idea which evolved from his discussions with employees. The idea was to deliver a package anywhere in the United States overnight for $14.00. John coined the term URGENT letter to promote it. For the Fortune 500 companies, one Emery truck would back up to the company's dock each day and pick up its letters, envelopes, small packages, computer printouts, and perform a total service job for them. Emery also expanded into international services. Prior to 1981, there had not been a company that provided true international door-to-door service for products. Emery created different levels of international service, in keeping with the customer's understanding of classes of service on an airline: first-class international door-to-door service and business class.

Emery describes his job as head cheerleader. In this capacity, he has been able to spark his people to get the business. As head cheerleader, he tries to reach out and touch people through his personal involvement in the firm. On a recent 31-city tour of Emery offices, one purpose was to make sure that the employees were in favor of the company's plans for reaching sales of $2 billion in 1990 (sales in 1984 were $1 billion). To show his interest in people, he shook hands and spent hours chatting with office managers, truck drivers and secretaries. He gets great pleasure out of dealing with people at all levels and having them understand that the job they're doing is very important.

Emery's greatest responsibilities are the manner in which he conducts his business. Integrity and morality are the foundation stones of his business. These are expressed in his personal belief statement, "People buy people first and companies second. They've got to believe in you before they believe in the company. They've got to believe in you, the Emery driver, before they believe in the company that stands behind you." As a result of this belief, Emery promotes from within whenever possible.

He has three personal priorities. First is the employee's personal health. Second is the employee's family. Emery believes that employees were not put on earth to work for Emery Air Freight, but to take care of that family that God gave you. If the family is not enthusiastic about Emery, if they think that their husband or wife is being taken advantage of, then Emery has troubles. Third is Emery.

When visiting Emery's headquarters, you get the feeling that there are high standards, enthusiasm for working at Emery, and a participative style of management. The result is that people at Emery are indeed trying to make ethical and moral decisions in their work that are consistent with John's personal beliefs. Employees are concerned about what will happen to people as a result of their decisions and are concerned about acting in concert with the 'spirit' of their company.[10]

Some Concluding Thoughts

The two ways of obtaining data and the two ways of evaluating data represent two independent dimensions of Jung's four psychological functions. A composite problem-solving model based on these functions results in the categories of (1) sensation-thinker (ST); (2) sensation-feeler (SF); (3) intuitive thinker (NT); and (4) intuitive feeler (NF). This model is consistent with a number of key assumptions and research findings, including the following:

■ Individuals differ in how they perceive or gather information from the environment and in how they evaluate it.

- Individual differences in judgments and decisions reflect the characteristic styles by which individuals perceive and organize their environment.[11]

- Differences in individual problem solving can also be influenced by a wide variety of other individual characteristics that were not discussed in this model of problem-solving styles, such as intelligence and values.[12]

- The environment in which individuals function can be as important or more important than their problem-solving styles.

SUMMARY

The discussion of problem-solving profiles focused on why and how individuals differ in gathering and evaluating information from the environment. This chapter, along with the preceding two chapters on personality, perception, and attitudes suggested ways of understanding how we affect others, view ourselves and others, and learn to appreciate and build on differences between ourselves and others.

The discussion of problem-solving styles concentrated on the four distinct styles for emphasis. However, most people exhibit characteristics of each style at times and in varying situations; they also tend to move toward a balance and integration of the four psychological functions. Each individual is rich in variety and complex in nature; therefore managers should not categorize individuals or infer that they cannot adapt to or learn from situations that do not fit their dominant style.

This chapter attempted to (1) provide insight into your own problem-solving style and how it might influence your actions and reactions in certain problem-solving situations; and (2) provide a framework for your individual growth and development. Although one problem-solving style is not necessarily better than another, the requirements of certain positions or roles in organizations may naturally favor one style over the others.

KEY WORDS AND CONCEPTS

Feeling type person	Sensation-feeler (SF)
Intuitive feeler (NF)	Sensation-thinker (ST)
Intuitive thinker (NT)	Sensation type person
Intuitive type person	Thinking type person

DISCUSSION QUESTIONS

1. How has your choice of academic courses been affected by your problem-solving style?

2. What is the likely influence of your problem-solving style on your career decision? List some managerial jobs and their likely corresponding problem-solving style.

3. If an organization is composed of managers representing all four problem-solving styles, why is achieving consensus so difficult?

4. What do you consider the most important feature of the ideal job?
   - (a.) Provides an opportunity to use my abilities.
   - (b.) Permits me to be creative and imaginative.
   - (c.) Provides me with a stable and secure future.
   - (d.) Provides me a chance to earn a great deal of money and status.
   - (e.) Gives me an opportunity to be of service to others.

   How has your problem-solving style influenced your answers?

5. The following stories were written by senior managers while attending an executive development program. Identify the problem-solving style of each and the reason behind your choice.

Story 1

The organization I would like to work for would need to be highly attentive to the personal needs of the employees. Also, I would need to produce a good product—one that society thinks is important. The organization should have a fine service department to service the product it sells. To keep moving forward, the company would need to be innovative and able to stay in front of the competition. These factors all lead to a more profitable organization.

Story 2

Organizations that have the greatest success in reaching established goals and objectives are those that have a staff of people who know what they are doing. Ideally, the organization would have a unique product, be a medium size (less than 1,000 employees), have formal lines of communication, and produce a return on investment of at least 12 percent on operating assets. The organization would be located in a single facility in the Sun Belt. The unique product line would have limited competition, and the competition would have relatively similar quality standards.

The organization would consist of a chief executive officer with a staff consisting of officers of marketing, finance, operations, personnel, and operations/services. The structure below these officers would allow a hands-on management style that would capitalize on the ideas of all personnel.

Story 3

Characteristics: (1) one product, (2) a highly centralized location, and (3) a small staff of professionals.

My organization operates through the efforts of several groups. Each group is loosely organized to achieve its goals and objectives and has professional personnel with the various skills required to produce our product. Each group has an adviser or consultant who functions to help the group in its task. He or she does not function as the group leader but knows all aspects of the job.

The groups set their own goals, choose their own leaders, and discipline and reward their members. Their production rates and quality are closely monitored and reported to the leaders. To some extent, the group is rewarded for high profitability. Leaders are elected by the group and change from time to time.

Story 4

My ideal organization would consist of people who are all dedicated to achieving the goals of the organization and who are willing to do so in a friendly, cooperative way. To be effective, all the people must have a servant attitude toward one another (that is, they must think not of their own interests first, but of the interests of others). An attitude of humility would prevail, and the needs of others would be met before our own.

I think of the New Testament church in its beginnings as an ideal organization. There was a structure, but it permitted everyone to share everything so no one was in need. As the organization grew and prospered, so did the people. People's needs come before the organization.

6. Should organizations attempt to select people for positions on the basis of their problem-solving styles? What would be the benefits of doing this? Would there be any dangers?

MANAGEMENT INCIDENTS AND CASES

Toughest Bosses in America

John Welch Jr., General Electric Company

Extraordinarily bright, penetrating in his questions, and determined to get results, John Welch, Jr., Chairman, General Electric, has carved out quite a reputation for himself since going to work for General Electric in 1960. According to former employees, Welch conducts meetings so aggressively that subordinates tremble. He criticizes, demeans, ridicules and humiliates people in meetings. "Jack comes on like a herd of elephants," says one former GE employee. Managers at GE used to hide out-of-favor employees from Welch's gunsights so they could keep their jobs. At one division that Welch was in charge of on his way to the top, these people were tagged "mummies."

Since taking over, Welch has announced the closing of 25 plants. This has earned him the nickname of "Neutron Jack." Employees joke that, like the aftermath of a neutron bomb, after Welch visits a plant the building is left standing but a lot of people are dead. A lot of people get shot up; the survivors go on to the next battle.

Most employees at GE agree that Welch is a doer, who doesn't want "I think" answers. Since taking over at GE, the stockholders' return on their money is around 18%, compared to 13.8% for other Fortune 500 companies. He is a person with many creative business ideas who has the ability to tap people's brains. Former employees at GE have said that at GE there had been more reviewers than doers until Welch's arrival. "I'd present plans to 35 people," says a veteran GE employee. "It was insane. And at times, incredibly provoking." For example, while head of GE's consumer products division, Welch instructed his general managers to cut inventories immediately. One month later he called a meeting to see what progress they had made. None had implemented his order. Welch then recessed the meeting and told the managers that he wanted action before the afternoon meeting. He got it.

Welch says that as chairman he is trying to promote risk-taking by making heroes out of risk-takers in the company, even if they have failed. He says, "the role for the mediocre is clearly short-lived." However, subordinates accuse him of missing the opportunity to get input from people who don't have the skill or courage to live up to his high standards. If you have a controversial idea, you must have the guts to put it forward.

John Smilow, Beatrice Companies, Inc.

John Smilow, a senior executive at Beatrice Companies, Inc., describes himself as tough but fair, and one who welcomes dissent and discussion. The long-time chairman of International Playtex division of Esmark has been described by subordinates as one who has all the answers and thinks that everyone else is wrong.

In the late 1970s and early 1980s, Playtex asked the Hay Associates, a consulting firm, to conduct two surveys to determine the level of satisfaction at Playtex. Both times, the firm got the same result: Morale was the lowest at Playtex that the firm had ever seen. Why? According to his subordinates, Smilow might have had something to do with the conditions. Former employees say that he has the uncanny ability to demoralize subordinates. As a former employee said, "He gives the impression that he thinks of employees as throwaways." Many of his subordinates have heard him use his favorite phrase, "Stupid is forever," behind an employee's back. According to a former Playtex manager, Smilow has little trust in people. He has risen to a senior executive because of his business knowledge and skills, not his interpersonal skills. When a former officer of Playtex was asked to characterize his boss's people skills, he replied, "The guy is a train wreck."

Smilow has been known to fire many people. Management turnover probably averaged somewhere in the high 30% range when Smilow ran Playtex. Under the former head of Playtex's International Division, Ralston Coffin, foreign sales and profits increased dramatically over four years. Smilow dumped him nonetheless. Once Smilow fired an employee with over 15 years of service and then refused to extend the man's medical insurance while he sought a job, even though he had a heart condition. After some discussion, personnel executives got Smilow to relent on the insurance and even allow the man to use a company office in his job search. Soon, however, Smilow forced the personnel department

to move the man's parking space. Smilow didn't want to see him in the parking lot.[13]

Questions

1. What are the problem-solving styles of these two men?
2. How would you like to work for either of them?
3. How can you account for their remarkable business success?

Roger Smith at General Motors

In 1980, the year before Roger Smith became the 10th Chief Executive Officer of General Motors, GM was in the red for the first time in more than 50 years. During 1981, Smith's in-house cost-cutting measures, including closing inefficient plants and the sale of the company's New York City office building, resulted in a profit of $33.4 million. In 1982, he consolidated and modernized GM plants, got wage concessions from the union, and saw GM's profits reach $926 million. In 1983, GM sold a record number of cars (4.1 million) and recorded record profits of $3.8 billion. In 1984, profits were slightly over $4.7 billion.

Smith began his GM career in the finance department at GM. "Being part of the finance staff," he says, "you're a little bit back from all the gung-ho spirit you normally get from other divisions, and you develop a more pragmatic attitude. Believe me, I've had my share of pet projects that just didn't fly. I've always felt that GM had not, in the past, quit early enough on some projects. One of my major roles is to manage change. Strategic planning is worthless without strategic management."

Traditionally, the word *change* has not been a commonly used term at GM. However, the radical reorganization of GM in late 1984 has changed this. Smith simplified GM's five separate car divisions (Cadillac, Buick, might hang up their harps on the willows. Ichabod! Ichabod! the glory of their house was departing from them.

Mr. Slope, great as he was with embryo grandeur, still came to see the signora. Indeed, he could not keep himself away. He dreamed of that soft hand which he had kissed so often, and of that imperial brow which his lips had once pressed, and he then dreamed also of further favours.

And Mr. Thorne was there also. It was the first visit he had ever paid to the signora, and he made it not without due preparation. Mr. Thorne was a gentleman usually precise in his dress, and prone to make the most of himself in an unpretending way. The grey hairs in his whiskers were eliminated perhaps once a month; those on his head were softened by a mixture which we will not call a dye; it was only a wash. His tailor lived in St. James's Street, and his bootmaker at the corner of that street and Piccadilly. He was particular in the article of gloves, and the getting up of his shirts was a matter not lightly thought of in the Ullathorne laundry. On the occasion of the present visit he had rather overdone his usual efforts, and caused some little uneasiness to his sister, who had not hitherto received very cordially the proposition for a lengthened visit from the signora at Ullathorne.

There were others also there—young men about the city who had not much to do, and who were induced by the lady's charms to neglect that little; but all gave way to Mr. Thorne, who was somewhat of a grand signior, as a country gentleman always is in a provincial city.

'Oh, Mr. Thorne, this is so kind of you!' said the signora. 'You promised to come; but I really did not expect it. I thought you country gentlemen never kept your pledges.'

'Oh, yes, sometimes,' said Mr. Thorne, looking rather sheepish, and making his salutations a little too much in the style of the last century.

'You deceive none but your consti—stit—stit; what do you call the people that carry you about in chairs and pelt you with eggs and apples when they make you a member of Parliament?'

'One another also, sometimes, signora,' said Mr. Slope, with a deanish sort of smirk on his face. 'Country gentlemen do deceive one another sometimes, don't they, Mr. Thorne?'

Mr. Thorne gave him a look which undeaned him completely for the moment; but he soon remembered his high hopes, and recovering himself quickly, sustained his probable coming dignity by a laugh at Mr. Thorne's expense.

'I never deceive a lady, at any rate,' said Mr. Thorne; 'especially when the gratification of my own wishes is so strong an inducement to keep me true, as it now is.'

Mr. Thorne went on thus awhile with antediluvian grimaces and compliments which he had picked up from Sir Charles Grandison, and the signora at every grimace and at every bow smiled a little smile and bowed a little bow. Mr. Thorne, however, was kept standing at the foot of the couch, for the new dean sat in the seat of honour near the table. Mr. Arabin the while was standing with his back to the fire, his coat tails under his arms, gazing at her with all his eyes—not quite in vain, for every now and again a glance came up at him, bright as a meteor out of heaven.

'Oh, Mr. Thorne, you promised to let me introduce my little girl to you. Can you spare a moment?—will you see her now?'

Mr. Thorne assured her that he could, and would see the young lady with the greatest pleasure in life. 'Mr. Slope, might I trouble you to ring the bell?' said she; and when Mr. Slope got up she looked at Mr. Thorne and pointed to the chair. Mr. Thorne, however, was much too slow to understand her, and Mr. Slope would have recovered his seat had not the signora, who never chose to be unsuccessful, somewhat summarily ordered him out of it.

'Oh, Mr. Slope, I must ask you to let Mr. Thorne sit here just for a moment or two. I am sure you will pardon me. We can take a liberty with you this week. Next week, you know, when you move into the dean's house, we shall all be afraid of you.'

Mr. Slope, with an air of much indifference, rose from his

seat, and, walking into the next room, became greatly interested in Mrs. Stanhope's worsted work.

And then the child was brought in. She was a little girl, about eight years of age, like her mother, only that her enormous eyes were black, and her hair quite jet. Her complexion, too, was very dark, and bespoke her foreign blood. She was dressed in the most outlandish and extravagant way in which clothes could be put on a child's back. She had great bracelets on her naked little arms, a crimson fillet braided with gold round her head, and scarlet shoes with high heels. Her dress was all flounces, and stuck out from her as though the object were to make it lie off horizontally from her little hips. It did not nearly cover her knees; but this was atoned for by a loose pair of drawers, which seemed made throughout of lace; then she had on pink silk stockings. It was thus that the last of the Neros was habitually dressed at the hour when visitors were wont to call.

'Julia, my love,' said the mother,—Julia was ever a favourite name with the ladies of that family. 'Julia, my love, come here. I was telling you about the beautiful party poor mamma went to. This is Mr. Thorne; will you give him a kiss, dearest?'

Julia put up her face to be kissed, as she did to all her mother's visitors; and then Mr. Thorne found that he had got her, and, which was much more terrific to him, all her finery, into his arms. The lace and starch crumpled against his waistcoat and trowsers, the greasy black curls hung upon his cheek, and one of the bracelet clasps scratched his ear. He did not at all know how to hold so magnificent a lady, nor holding her what to do with her. However, he had on other occasions been compelled to fondle little nieces and nephews, and now set about the task in the mode he always had used.

'Diddle, diddle, diddle, diddle,' said he, putting the child on one knee, and working away with it as though he were turning a knife-grinder's wheel with his foot.

'Mamma, mamma,' said Julia, crossly, 'I don't want to be diddle diddled. Let me go, you naughty old man, you.'

Poor Mr. Thorne put the child down quietly on the ground, and drew back his chair; Mr. Slope, who had returned to the pole star that attracted him, laughed aloud; Mr. Arabin winced and shut his eyes; and the signora pretended not to hear her daughter.

'Go to Aunt Charlotte, lovey,' said the mamma, 'and ask her if it is not time for you to go out.'

But little Miss Julia, though she had not exactly liked the nature of Mr. Thorne's attention, was accustomed to be played with by gentlemen, and did not relish the idea of being sent so soon to her aunt.

'Julia, go when I tell you, my dear.' But Julia still went pouting about the room. 'Charlotte, do come and take her,' said the signora. 'She must go out; and the days get so short now.' And thus ended the much-talked of interview between Mr. Thorne and the last of the Neros.

Mr. Thorne recovered from the child's crossness sooner than from Mr. Slope's laughter. He could put up with being called an old man by an infant, but he did not like to be laughed at by the bishop's chaplain, even though that chaplain was about to become a dean. He said nothing, but he showed plainly enough that he was angry.

The signora was ready enough to avenge him. 'Mr. Slope,' said she, 'I hear that you are triumphing on all sides.'

'How so?' said he, smiling. He did not dislike being talked to about the deanery, though, of course, he strongly denied the imputation.

'You carry the day both in love and war.' Mr. Slope hereupon did not look quite so satisfied as he had done.

'Mr. Arabin,' continued the signora, 'don't you think Mr. Slope is a very lucky man?'

'Not more so than he deserves, I am sure,' said Mr. Arabin.

'Only think, Mr. Thorne, he is to be our new dean; of course we all know that.'

'Indeed, signora,' said Mr. Slope, 'we all know nothing about it. I can assure you I myself——'

'He *is* to be the new dean—there is no manner of doubt of it, Mr. Thorne.'

'Hum!' said Mr. Thorne.

'Passing over the heads of old men like my father and Archdeacon Grantly——'

'Oh—oh!' said Mr. Slope.

'The archdeacon would not accept it,' said Mr. Arabin; whereupon Mr. Slope smiled abominably, and said, as plainly as a look could speak, that the grapes were sour.

'Going over all our heads,' continued the signora; 'for, of course, I consider myself one of the chapter.'

'If I am ever dean,' said Mr. Slope—'that is, were I ever to become so, I should glory in such a canoness.'

'Oh, Mr. Slope, stop; I haven't half done. There is another canoness for you to glory in. Mr. Slope is not only to have the deanery, but a wife to put in it.'

Mr. Slope again looked disconcerted.

'A wife with a large fortune too. It never rains but it pours, does it, Mr. Thorne?'

'No, never,' said Mr. Thorne, who did not quite relish talking about Mr. Slope and his affairs.

'When will it be, Mr. Slope?'

'When will what be?' said he.

'Oh, we know when the affair of the dean will be: a week will settle that. The new hat, I have no doubt, has already been ordered. But when will the marriage come off?'

'Do you mean mine or Mr. Arabin's?' said he, striving to be facetious.

'Well, just then I meant yours, though, perhaps, after all, Mr. Arabin's may be first. But we know nothing of him. He is too close for any of us. Now all is open and above board with you; which, by the bye, Mr. Arabin, I beg to tell you I like much the best. He who runs can read that Mr. Slope is a favoured lover. Come, Mr. Slope, when is the widow to be made Mrs. Dean?'

To Mr. Arabin this badinage was peculiarly painful; and yet he could not tear himself away and leave it. He believed,

still believed with that sort of belief which the fear of a thing
engenders, that Mrs. Bold would probably become the wife
of Mr. Slope. Of Mr. Slope's little adventure in the garden he
knew nothing. For aught he knew, Mr. Slope might have had
an adventure of quite a different character. He might have
thrown himself at the widow's feet, been accepted, and then
returned to town a jolly thriving wooer. The signora's jokes
were bitter enough to Mr. Slope, but they were quite as bitter
to Mr. Arabin. He still stood leaning against the fireplace,
fumbling with his hands in his trowsers pockets.

'Come, come, Mr. Slope, don't be so bashful,' continued
the signora. 'We all know that you proposed to the lady the
other day at Ullathorne. Tell us with what words she accepted
you. Was it with a simple "yes," or with two "no no's,"
which make an affirmative? or did silence give consent? or did
she speak out with that spirit which so well becomes a widow,
and say openly, "By my troth, sir, you shall make me Mrs.
Slope as soon as it is your pleasure to do so?"'

Mr. Slope had seldom in his life felt himself less at his ease.
There sat Mr. Thorne, laughing silently. There stood his old
antagonist, Mr. Arabin, gazing at him with all his eyes. There
round the door between the two rooms were clustered a little
group of people, including Miss Stanhope and the Rev. Messrs.
Grey and Green, all listening to his discomfiture. He knew
that it depended solely on his own wit whether or no he could
throw the joke back upon the lady. He knew that it stood him
to do so if he possibly could; but he had not a word. ''Tis conscience that makes cowards of us all.' He felt on his cheek the
sharp points of Eleanor's fingers, and did not know who
might have seen the blow, who might have told the tale to
this pestilent woman who took such delight in jeering him. He
stood there, therefore, red as a carbuncle and mute as a fish;
grinning just sufficiently to show his teeth; an object of pity.

But the signora had no pity; she knew nothing of mercy.
Her present object was to put Mr. Slope down, and she was
determined to do it thoroughly, now that she had him in her
power.

'What, Mr. Slope, no answer? Why it can't possibly be that the woman has been fool enough to refuse you? She can't surely be looking out after a bishop. But I see how it is, Mr. Slope. Widows are proverbially cautious. You should have let her alone till the new hat was on your head; till you could show her the key of the deanery.'

'Signora,' said he at last, trying to speak in a tone of dignified reproach, 'you really permit yourself to talk on solemn subjects in a very improper way.'

'Solemn subjects—what solemn subject? Surely a dean's hat is not such a solemn subject.'

'I have no aspirations such as those you impute to me. Perhaps you will drop the subject.'

'Oh, certainly, Mr. Slope; but one word first. Go to her again with the prime minister's letter in your pocket. I'll wager my shawl to your shovel she does not refuse you then.'

'I must say, signora, that I think you are speaking of the lady in a very unjustifiable manner.'

'And one other piece of advice, Mr. Slope; I'll only offer you one other;' and then she commenced singing—

'It's gude to be merry and wise, Mr. Slope;
  It's gude to be honest and true;
It's gude to be off with the old love—Mr. Slope,
  Before you are on with the new.—

'Ha, ha, ha!'

And the signora, throwing herself back on her sofa, laughed merrily. She little recked how those who heard her would, in their own imaginations, fill up the little history of Mr. Slope's first love. She little cared that some among them might attribute to her the honour of his earlier admiration. She was tired of Mr. Slope and wanted to get rid of him; and had ground for anger with him, and she chose to be revenged.

How Mr. Slope got out of that room he never himself knew. He did succeed ultimately, and probably with some assistance, in getting his hat and escaping into the air. At last his love for the signora was cured. Whenever he again thought of her in his dreams, it was not as of an angel with azure wings. He connected her rather with fire and brimstone, and though he could still believe her to be a spirit, he banished her entirely out of heaven, and found a place for her among the infernal gods. When he weighed in the balance, as he not seldom did, the two women to whom he had attached himself in Barchester, the pre-eminent place in his soul's hatred was usually allotted to the signora.

47

THE DEAN ELECT

During the entire next week Barchester was ignorant who was to be its new dean on Sunday morning. Mr. Slope was decidedly the favourite; but he did not show himself in the cathedral, and then he sank a point or two in the betting. On Monday, he got a scolding from the bishop in the hearing of the servants, and down he went till nobody would have him at any price; but on Tuesday he received a letter, in an official cover, marked private, by which he fully recovered his place in the public favour. On Wednesday, he was said to be ill, and that did not look well; but on Thursday morning he went down to the railway station, with a very jaunty air; and when it was ascertained that he had taken a first-class ticket for London, there was no longer any room for doubt on the matter.

While matters were in this state of ferment at Barchester, there was not much mental comfort at Plumstead. Our friend the archdeacon had many grounds for inward grief. He was much displeased at the result of Dr. Gwynne's diplomatic mission to the palace, and did not even scruple to say to his wife that had he gone himself, he would have managed the affair much better. His wife did not agree with him, but that did not mend the matter.

Mr. Quiverful's appointment to the hospital was, however, a *fait accompli*, and Mr. Harding's acquiescence in that appointment was not less so. Nothing would induce Mr. Harding to make a public appeal against the bishop; and the Master of Lazarus quite approved of his not doing so.

'I don't know what has come to the Master,' said the archdeacon over and over again. 'He used to be ready enough to stand up for his order.'

'My dear archdeacon,' Mrs. Grantly would say in reply, 'what is the use of always fighting? I really think the Master is right.' The Master, however, had taken steps of his own, of which neither the archdeacon nor his wife knew anything.

Then Mr. Slope's successes were henbane to Dr. Grantly; and Mrs. Bold's improprieties were as bad. What would be all the world to Archdeacon Grantly if Mr. Slope should become Dean of Barchester and marry his wife's sister! He talked of it, and talked of it till he was nearly ill. Mrs. Grantly almost wished that the marriage were done and over, so that she might hear no more about it.

And there was yet another ground of misery which cut him to the quick, nearly as closely as either of the others. That paragon of a clergyman, whom he had bestowed upon St. Ewold's, that college friend of whom he had boasted so loudly, that ecclesiastical knight before whose lance Mr. Slope was to fall and bite the dust, that worthy bulwark of the church as it should be, that honoured representative of Oxford's best spirit, was—so at least his wife had told him half a dozen times—misconducting himself!

Nothing had been seen of Mr. Arabin at Plumstead for the last week, but a good deal had, unfortunately, been heard of him. As soon as Mrs. Grantly had found herself alone with the archdeacon, on the evening of the Ullathorne party, she had expressed herself very forcibly as to Mr. Arabin's conduct on that occasion. He had, she declared, looked and acted and talked very unlike a decent parish clergyman. At first the archdeacon had laughed at this, and assured her that she need not trouble herself; that Mr. Arabin would be found to be quite safe. But by degrees he began to find that his wife's eyes had been sharper than his own. Other people coupled the signora's name with that of Mr. Arabin. The meagre little prebendary who lived in the close, told him to a nicety how often Mr. Arabin had visited at Dr. Stanhope's, and how long he had remained on the occasion of each visit. He had asked after Mr. Arabin at the cathedral library, and an officious little vicar choral had offered to go and see whether he could be found at Dr. Stanhope's. Rumour, when she has contrived to sound the first note on her trumpet, soon makes a loud peal audible enough. It was too clear that Mr. Arabin had succumbed to the Italian woman, and that the archdeacon's credit would suffer fearfully if something were not done to rescue the brand from the burning. Besides, to give the archdeacon his due, he was really attached to Mr. Arabin, and grieved greatly at his backsliding.

They were sitting, talking over their sorrows, in the drawing-room before dinner on the day after Mr. Slope's departure for London; and on this occasion Mrs. Grantly spoke out her mind freely. She had opinions of her own about parish clergymen, and now thought it right to give vent to them.

'If you would have been led by me, archdeacon, you would never have put a bachelor into St. Ewold's.'

'But, my dear, you don't mean to say that all bachelor clergymen misbehave themselves.'

'I don't know that clergymen are so much better than other men,' said Mrs. Grantly. 'It's all very well with a curate whom you have under your own eye, and whom you can get rid of if he persists in improprieties.'

'But Mr. Arabin was a fellow, and couldn't have had a wife.'

'Then I would have found some one who could.'

'But, my dear, are fellows never to get livings?'

'Yes, to be sure they are, when they get engaged. I never would put a young man into a living unless he were married, or engaged to be married. Now here is Mr. Arabin. The whole responsibility lies upon you.'

'There is not at this moment a clergyman in all Oxford more respected for morals and conduct than Arabin.'

'Oh, Oxford!' said the lady, with a sneer. 'What men choose to do at Oxford, nobody ever hears of. A man may do very well at Oxford who would bring disgrace on a parish; and, to tell you the truth, it seems to me that Mr. Arabin is just such a man.'

The archdeacon groaned deeply, but he had no further answer to make.

'You really must speak to him, archdeacon. Only think

what the Thornes will say if they hear that their parish clergy-man spends his whole time philandering with this woman.'

The archdeacon groaned again. He was a courageous man, and knew well enough how to rebuke the younger clergy-men of the diocese, when necessary. But there was that about Mr. Arabin which made the doctor feel that it would be very difficult to rebuke him with good effect.

'You can advise him to find a wife for himself, and he will understand well enough what that means,' said Mrs. Grantly.

The archdeacon had nothing for it but groaning. There was Mr. Slope; he was going to be made dean; he was going to take a wife; he was about to achieve respectability and wealth; an excellent family mansion, and a family carriage; he would soon be among the comfortable *élite* of the ecclesi-astical world of Barchester; whereas his own *protégé*, the true scion of the true church, by whom he had sworn, would be still but a poor vicar, and that with a very indifferent character for moral conduct! It might be all very well recommending Mr. Arabin to marry, but how would Mr. Arabin when mar-ried support a wife?

Things were ordering themselves thus in Plumstead draw-ing-room when Dr. and Mrs. Grantly were disturbed in their sweet discourse by the quick rattle of a carriage and pair of horses on the gravel sweep. The sound was not that of visitors, whose private carriages are generally brought up to country-house doors with demure propriety, but betokened rather the advent of some person or persons who were in a hurry to reach the house, and had no intention of immediately leaving it. Guests invited to stay a week, and who were conscious of arriving after the first dinner bell, would probably ap-proach in such a manner. So might arrive an attorney with the news of a granduncle's death, or a son from college with all the fresh honours of a double first. No one would have had himself driven up to the door of a country house in such a manner who had the slightest doubt of his own right to force an entry.

'Who is it?' said Mrs. Grantly, looking at her husband.

'Who on earth can it be?' said the archdeacon to his wife. He then quietly got up and stood with the drawing-room door open in his hand. 'Why, it's your father!'

It was indeed Mr. Harding, and Mr. Harding alone. He had come by himself in a post-chaise with a couple of horses from Barchester, arriving almost after dark, and evidently full of news. His visits had usually been made in the quietest manner; he had rarely presumed to come without notice, and had always been driven up in a modest old green fly, with one horse, that hardly made itself heard as it crawled up to the hall door.

'Good gracious, Warden, is it you?' said the archdeacon, forgetting in his surprise the events of the last few years. 'But come in; nothing the matter, I hope.'

'We are very glad you are come, papa,' said his daughter. 'I'll go and get your room ready at once.'

'I an't warden, archdeacon,' said Mr. Harding. 'Mr. Quiverful is warden.'

'Oh, I know, I know,' said the archdeacon, petulantly. 'I forgot all about it at the moment. Is anything the matter?'

'Don't go this moment, Susan,' said Mr. Harding; 'I have something to tell you.'

'The dinner bell will ring in five minutes,' said she.

'Will it?' said Mr. Harding. 'Then, perhaps, I had better wait.' He was big with news which he had come to tell, but which he knew could not be told without much discussion. He had hurried away to Plumstead as fast as two horses could bring him; and now, finding himself there, he was willing to accept the reprieve which dinner would give him.

'If you have anything of moment to tell us,' said the archdeacon, 'pray let us hear it at once. Has Eleanor gone off?'

'No, she has not,' said Mr. Harding, with a look of great displeasure.

'Has Slope been made dean?'

'No, he has not; but—'

'But what?' said the archdeacon, who was becoming very impatient.

'They have—'

'They have what?' said the archdeacon.

'They have offered it to me,' said Mr. Harding, with a modesty which almost prevented his speaking.

'Good heavens!' said the archdeacon, and sank back exhausted in an easy-chair.

'My dear, dear father,' said Mrs. Grantly, and threw her arms round her father's neck.

'So I thought I had better come out and consult with you at once,' said Mr. Harding.

'Consult!' shouted the archdeacon. 'But, my dear Harding, I congratulate you with my whole heart—with my whole heart; I do indeed. I never heard anything in my life that gave me so much pleasure;' and he got hold of both his father-in-law's hands, and shook them as though he were going to shake them off, and walked round and round the room, twirling a copy of the *Jupiter* over his head, to show his extreme exultation.

'But—' began Mr. Harding.

'But me no buts,' said the archdeacon. 'I never was so happy in my life. It was just the proper thing to do. Upon my honour, I'll never say another word against Lord —— the longest day I have to live.'

'That's Dr. Gwynne's doing, you may be sure,' said Mrs. Grantly, who greatly liked the Master of Lazarus, he being an orderly married man with a large family.

'I suppose it is,' said the archdeacon.

'Oh, papa, I am so truly delighted!' said Mrs. Grantly, getting up and kissing her father.

'But, my dear,' said Mr. Harding.—It was all in vain that he strove to speak; nobody would listen to him.

'Well, Mr. Dean,' said the archdeacon, triumphing; 'the deanery gardens will be some consolation for the hospital elms. Well, poor Quiverful! I won't begrudge him his good fortune any longer.'

'No, indeed,' said Mrs. Grantly. 'Poor woman, she has fourteen children. I am sure I am very glad they have got it.'

'So am I,' said Mr. Harding.

'I would give twenty pounds,' said the archdeacon, 'to see how Mr. Slope will look when he hears it.' The idea of Mr. Slope's discomfiture formed no small part of the archdeacon's pleasure.

At last Mr. Harding was allowed to go up-stairs and wash his hands, having, in fact, said very little of all that he had come out to Plumstead on purpose to say. Nor could anything more be said till the servants were gone after dinner. The joy of Dr. Grantly was so uncontrollable that he could not refrain from calling his father-in-law Mr. Dean before the men; and therefore it was soon matter of discussion in the lower regions how Mr. Harding, instead of his daughter's future husband, was to be the new dean, and various were the opinions on the matter. The cook and butler, who were advanced in years, thought that it was just as it should be; but the footman and lady's maid, who were younger, thought it was a great shame that Mr. Slope should lose his chance.

'He's a mean chap all the same,' said the footman; 'and it an't along of him that I says so. But I always did admire the missus's sister; and she'd well become the situation.'

While these were the ideas down-stairs, a very great difference of opinion existed above. As soon as the cloth was drawn and the wine on the table, Mr. Harding made for himself an opportunity of speaking. It was, however, with much inward troubling that he said:—

'It's very kind of Lord ——, very kind, and I feel it deeply, most deeply. I am, I must confess, gratified by the offer—'

'I should think so,' said the archdeacon.

'But, all the same, I am afraid that I can't accept it.'

The decanter almost fell from the archdeacon's hand upon the table; and the start he made was so great as to make his wife jump up from her chair. Not accept the deanship! If it really ended in this, there would be no longer any doubt that his father-in-law was demented. The question now was whether a clergyman with low rank, and preferment amounting to less than 200*l.* a year, should accept high rank, 1200*l.* a year, and one of the most desirable positions which his profession had to afford!

'What!' said the archdeacon, gasping for breath, and staring at his guest as though the violence of his emotion had almost thrown him into a fit. 'What!'

'I do not find myself fit for new duties,' urged Mr. Harding.

'New duties! what duties?' said the archdeacon, with unintended sarcasm.

'Oh, papa,' said Mrs. Grantly, 'nothing can be easier than what a dean has to do. Surely you are more active than Dr. Trefoil.'

'He won't have half as much to do as he has at present,' said Dr. Grantly.

'Did you see what the *Jupiter* said the other day about young men?'

'Yes; and I saw that the *Jupiter* said all that it could to induce the appointment of Mr. Slope. Perhaps you would wish to see Mr. Slope made dean.'

Mr. Harding made no reply to this rebuke, though he felt it strongly. He had not come over to Plumstead to have further contention with his son-in-law about Mr. Slope, so he allowed it to pass by.

'I know I cannot make you understand my feeling,' he said, 'for we have been cast in different moulds. I may wish that I had your spirit and energy and power of combating; but I have not. Every day that is added to my life increases my wish for peace and rest.'

'And where on earth can a man have peace and rest if not in a deanery?' said the archdeacon.

'People will say that I am too old for it.'

'Good heavens! people! what people? What need you care for any people?'

'But I think myself I am too old for any new place.'

'Dear papa,' said Mrs. Grantly, 'men ten years older than you are appointed to new situations day after day.'

'My dear,' said he, 'it is impossible that I should make you understand my feelings, nor do I pretend to any great virtue in the matter. The truth is, I want the force of character which might enable me to stand against the spirit of the times. The call on all sides now is for young men, and I have not the nerve to put myself in opposition to the demand. Were the *Jupiter*, when it hears of my appointment, to write article after article, setting forth my incompetency, I am sure it would cost me my reason. I ought to be able to bear with such things, you will say. Well, my dear, I own that I ought. But I feel my weakness, and I know that I can't. And, to tell you the truth, I know no more than a child what the dean has to do.'

'Pshaw!' exclaimed the archdeacon.

'Don't be angry with me, archdeacon: don't let us quarrel about it, Susan. If you knew how keenly I feel the necessity of having to disoblige you in this matter, you would not be angry with me.'

This was a dreadful blow to Dr. Grantly. Nothing could possibly have suited him better than having Mr. Harding in the deanery. Though he had never looked down on Mr. Harding on account of his recent poverty, he did fully recognise the satisfaction of having those belonging to him in comfortable positions. It would be much more suitable that Mr. Harding should be dean of Barchester than vicar of St. Cuthbert's and precentor to boot. And then the great discomfiture of that arch enemy of all that was respectable in Barchester, of that new low-church clerical *parvenu* that had fallen amongst them, that alone would be worth more, almost, than the situation itself. It was frightful to think that such unhoped-for good fortune should be marred by the absurd crotchets and unwholesome hallucinations by which Mr. Harding allowed himself to be led astray. To have the cup so near his lips and then to lose the drinking of it, was more than Dr. Grantly could endure.

And yet it appeared as though he would have to endure it. In vain he threatened and in vain he coaxed. Mr. Harding did not indeed speak with perfect decision of refusing the proffered glory, but he would not speak with anything like decision of accepting it. When pressed again and again, he would again and again allege that he was wholly unfitted to new duties. It was in vain that the archdeacon tried to insinuate, though he could not plainly declare, that there were no new duties to perform. It was in vain he hinted that in all cases of difficulty he, the archdeacon, was willing and able to guide a weak-minded dean. Mr. Harding seemed to have a foolish idea, not only that there were new duties to do, but that no one should accept the place who was not himself prepared to do them.

The conference ended in an understanding that Mr. Harding should at once acknowledge the letter he had received from the minister's private secretary, and should beg that he might be allowed two days to make up his mind; and that during those two days the matter should be considered.

On the following morning the archdeacon was to drive Mr. Harding back to Barchester.

48

MISS THORNE SHOWS HER TALENT
AT MATCHMAKING

On Mr. Harding's return to Barchester from Plumstead, which was effected by him in due course in company with the archdeacon, more tidings of a surprising nature met him. He was, during the journey, subjected to such a weight of unanswerable argument, all of which went to prove that it was his bounden duty not to interfere with the paternal government that was so anxious to make him a dean, that when he arrived at the chemist's door in High Street, he hardly knew which way to turn himself in the matter. But, perplexed as he was, he was doomed to further perplexity. He found a note there from his daughter begging him most urgently to come to her immediately. But we must again go back a little in our story.

Miss Thorne had not been slow to hear the rumours respecting Mr. Arabin, which had so much disturbed the happiness of Mrs. Grantly. And she, also, was unhappy to think that her parish clergyman should be accused of worshipping a strange goddess. She, also, was of opinion, that rectors and vicars should all be married, and with that good-natured energy which was characteristic of her, she put her wits to work to find a fitting match for Mr. Arabin. Mrs. Grantly, in this difficulty, could think of no better remedy than a lecture from the archdeacon. Miss Thorne thought that a young lady, marriageable, and with a dowry, might be of more efficacy. In looking through the catalogue of her unmarried friends, who might possibly be in want of a husband, and might also be fit for such promotion as a country parsonage affords, she could think of no one more eligible than Mrs. Bold; and, consequently, losing no time, she went into Barchester on the day of Mr. Slope's discomfiture, the same day that her brother had had his interesting interview with the last of the Neros, and invited Mrs. Bold to bring her nurse and baby to Ullathorne and make them a protracted visit.

Miss Thorne suggested a month or two, intending to use her influence afterwards in prolonging it so as to last out the winter, in order that Mr. Arabin might have an opportunity of becoming fairly intimate with his intended bride. 'We'll have Mr. Arabin too,' said Miss Thorne to herself; 'and before the spring they'll know each other; and in twelve or eighteen months' time, if all goes well, Mrs. Bold will be domiciled at St. Ewold's;' and then the kind-hearted lady gave herself some not undeserved praise for her match-making genius.

Eleanor was taken a little by surprise, but the matter ended in her promising to go to Ullathorne for at any rate a week or two; and on the day previous to that on which her father drove out to Plumstead, she had had herself driven out to Ullathorne.

Miss Thorne would not perplex her with her embryo lord on that same evening, thinking that she would allow her a few hours to make herself at home; but on the following morning Mr. Arabin arrived. 'And now,' said Miss Thorne to herself,

'I must contrive to throw them in each other's way.' That same day, after dinner, Eleanor, with an assumed air of dignity which she could not maintain, with tears that she could not suppress, with a flutter which she could not conquer, and a joy which she could not hide, told Miss Thorne that she was engaged to marry Mr. Arabin, and that it behoved her to get back home to Barchester as quick as she could.

To say simply that Miss Thorne was rejoiced at the success of the scheme, would give a very faint idea of her feelings on the occasion. My readers may probably have dreamt before now that they have had before them some terribly long walk to accomplish, some journey of twenty or thirty miles, an amount of labour frightful to anticipate, and that immediately on starting they have ingeniously found some accommodating short cut which has brought them without fatigue to their work's end in five minutes. Miss Thorne's waking feelings were somewhat of the same nature. My readers may perhaps have had to do with children, and may on some occasion have promised to their young charges some great gratification intended to come off, perhaps at the end of the winter, or at the beginning of summer. The impatient juveniles, however, will not wait, and clamorously demand their treat before they go to bed. Miss Thorne had a sort of feeling that her children were equally unreasonable. She was like an inexperienced gunner, who has ill calculated the length of the train that he has laid. The gunpowder exploded much too soon, and poor Miss Thorne felt that she was blown up by the strength of her own petard.

Miss Thorne had had lovers of her own, but they had been gentlemen of old-fashioned and deliberate habits. Miss Thorne's heart also had not always been hard, though she was still a virgin spinster; but it had never yielded in this way at the first assault. She had intended to bring together a middle-aged studious clergyman, and a discreet matron who might possibly be induced to marry again; and in doing so she had thrown fire among tinder. Well, it was all as it should be, but she did feel perhaps a little put out by the precipitancy of her own success; and perhaps a little vexed at the readiness of Mrs. Bold to be wooed.

She said, however, nothing about it to any one, and ascribed it all to the altered manners of the new age. Their mothers and grandmothers were perhaps a little more deliberate; but it was admitted on all sides that things were conducted very differently now than in former times. For aught Miss Thorne knew of the matter, a couple of hours might be quite sufficient under the new régime to complete that for which she in her ignorance had allotted twelve months.

But we must not pass over the wooing so cavalierly. It has been told, with perhaps tedious accuracy, how Eleanor disposed of two of her lovers at Ullathorne; and it must also be told with equal accuracy, and if possible with less tedium, how she encountered Mr. Arabin.

It cannot be denied that when Eleanor accepted Miss Thorne's invitation, she remembered that Ullathorne was in the parish of St. Ewold's. Since her interview with the signora she had done little else than think about Mr. Arabin, and the appeal that had been made to her. She could not bring herself to believe or try to bring herself to believe, that what she had been told was untrue. Think of it how she would, she could not but accept it as a fact that Mr. Arabin was fond of her; and then when she went further, and asked herself the question, she could not but accept it as a fact also that she was fond of him. If it were destined for her to be the partner of his hopes and sorrows, to whom could she look for friendship so properly as to Miss Thorne? This invitation was like an ordained step towards the fulfilment of her destiny, and when she also heard that Mr. Arabin was expected to be at Ullathorne on the following day, it seemed as though all the world were conspiring in her favour. Well, did she not deserve it? In that affair of Mr. Slope, had not all the world conspired against her?

She could not, however, make herself easy and at home. When in the evening after dinner Miss Thorne expatiated on the excellence of Mr. Arabin's qualities, and hinted that any little rumour which might be ill-naturedly spread abroad concerning him really meant nothing, Mrs. Bold found herself unable to answer. When Miss Thorne went a little further and declared that she did not know a prettier vicarage-house in the county than St. Ewold's, Mrs. Bold remembering the projected bow-window and the projected priestess still held her tongue; though her ears tingled with the conviction that all the world knew that she was in love with Mr. Arabin. Well; what would that matter if they could only meet and tell each other what each now longed to tell?

And they did meet. Mr. Arabin came early in the day, and found the two ladies together at work in the drawing-room. Miss Thorne, who had she known all the truth would have vanished into air at once, had no conception that her immediate absence would be a blessing, and remained chatting with them till luncheon-time. Mr. Arabin could talk about nothing but the Signora Neroni's beauty, would discuss no people but the Stanhopes. This was very distressing to Eleanor, and not very satisfactory to Miss Thorne. But yet there was evidence of innocence in his open avowal of admiration.

And then they had lunch, and then Mr. Arabin went out on parish duty, and Eleanor and Miss Thorne were left to take a walk together.

'Do you think the Signora Neroni is so lovely as people say?' Eleanor asked as they were coming home.

'She is very beautiful certainly, very beautiful,' Miss Thorne answered; 'but I do not know that any one considers her lovely. She is a woman all men would like to look at; but few I imagine would be glad to take her to their hearths, even were she unmarried and not afflicted as she is.'

There was some little comfort in this. Eleanor made the most of it till she got back to the house. She was then left alone in the drawing-room, and just as it was getting dark Mr. Arabin came in.

It was a beautiful afternoon in the beginning of October, and Eleanor was sitting in the window to get the advantage of the last daylight for her novel. There was a fire in the comfortable room, but the weather was not cold enough to make it attractive; and as she could see the sun set from where she sat, she was not very attentive to her book.

Mr. Arabin when he entered stood awhile with his back to the fire in his usual way, merely uttering a few common-place remarks about the beauty of the weather, while he plucked up courage for more interesting converse. It cannot probably be said that he had resolved then and there to make an offer to Eleanor. Men we believe seldom make such resolves. Mr. Slope and Mr. Stanhope had done so, it is true; but gentlemen generally propose without any absolutely defined determination as to their doing so. Such was now the case with Mr. Arabin.

'It is a lovely sunset,' said Eleanor, answering him on the dreadfully trite subject which he had chosen.

Mr. Arabin could not see the sunset from the hearth-rug, so he had to go close to her.

'Very lovely,' said he, standing modestly so far away from her as to avoid touching the flounces of her dress. Then it appeared that he had nothing further to say; so after gazing for a moment in silence at the brightness of the setting sun, he returned to the fire.

Eleanor found that it was quite impossible for herself to commence a conversation. In the first place she could find nothing to say; words, which were generally plenty enough with her, would not come to her relief. And, moreover, do what she would, she could hardly prevent herself from crying.

'Do you like Ullathorne?' said Mr. Arabin, speaking from the safely distant position which he had assumed on the hearth-rug.

'Yes, indeed, very much!'

'I don't mean Mr. and Miss Thorne. I know you like them; but the style of the house. There is something about old-fashioned mansions, built as this is, and old-fashioned gardens, that to me is especially delightful.'

'I like everything old-fashioned,' said Eleanor; 'old-fashioned things are so much the honestest.'

'I don't know about that,' said Mr. Arabin, gently laughing. 'That is an opinion on which very much may be said on either side. It is strange how widely the world is divided on a subject which so nearly concerns us all, and which is so close beneath our eyes. Some think that we are quickly progressing towards perfection, while others imagine that virtue is disappearing from the earth.'

'And you, Mr. Arabin, what do you think?' said Eleanor. She felt somewhat surprised at the tone which his conversation was taking, and yet she was relieved at his saying something which enabled herself to speak without showing her own emotion.

'What do I think, Mrs. Bold?' and then he rumbled his money with his hands in his trowsers pockets, and looked and spoke very little like a thriving lover. 'It is the bane of my life that on important subjects I acquire no fixed opinion. I think, and think, and go on thinking; and yet my thoughts are running ever in different directions. I hardly know whether or no we do lean more confidently than our fathers did on those high hopes to which we profess to aspire.'

'I think the world grows more worldly every day,' said Eleanor.

'That is because you see more of it than when you were younger. But we should hardly judge by what we see,—we see so very very little.' There was then a pause for a while, during which Mr. Arabin continued to turn over his shillings and half-crowns. 'If we believe in Scripture, we can hardly think that mankind in general will now be allowed to retrograde.'

Eleanor, whose mind was certainly engaged otherwise than on the general state of mankind, made no answer to this. She felt thoroughly dissatisfied with herself. She could not force her thoughts away from the topic on which the signora had spoken to her in so strange a way, and yet she knew that she could not converse with Mr. Arabin in an unrestrained natural tone till she did so. She was most anxious not to show to him any special emotion, and yet she felt that if he looked at her he would at once see that she was not at ease.

But he did not look at her. Instead of doing so, he left the fire-place and began walking up and down the room. Eleanor took up her book resolutely; but she could not read, for there was a tear in her eye, and do what she would it fell on her cheek. When Mr. Arabin's back was turned to her she wiped it away; but another was soon coursing down her face in its place. They would come; not a deluge of tears that would have betrayed her at once, but one by one, single monitors. Mr. Arabin did not observe her closely, and they passed unseen.

Mr. Arabin, thus pacing up and down the room, took four or five turns before he spoke another word, and Eleanor sat

equally silent with her face bent over her book. She was afraid that her tears would get the better of her, and was preparing for an escape from the room, when Mr. Arabin in his walk stood opposite to her. He did not come close up, but stood exactly on the spot to which his course brought him, and then, with his hands under his coat tails, thus made his confession.

'Mrs. Bold,' said he, 'I owe you retribution for a great offence of which I have been guilty towards you.' Eleanor's heart beat so that she could not trust herself to say that he had never been guilty of any offence. So Mr. Arabin thus went on.

'I have thought much of it since, and I am now aware that I was wholly unwarranted in putting to you a question which I once asked you. It was indelicate on my part, and perhaps unmanly. No intimacy which may exist between myself and your connection, Dr. Grantly, could justify it. Nor could the acquaintance which existed between ourselves.' This word acquaintance struck cold on Eleanor's heart. Was this to be her doom after all? 'I therefore think it right to beg your pardon in a humble spirit, and I now do so.'

What was Eleanor to say to him? She could not say much, because she was crying, and yet she must say something. She was most anxious to say that something graciously, kindly, and yet not in such a manner as to betray herself. She had never felt herself so much at a loss for words.

'Indeed I took no offence, Mr. Arabin.'

'Oh, but you did! And had you not done so, you would not have been yourself. You were as right to be offended, as I was wrong so to offend you. I have not forgiven myself, but I hope to hear that you forgive me.'

She was now past speaking calmly, though she still continued to hide her tears, and Mr. Arabin, after pausing a moment in vain for her reply, was walking off towards the door. She felt that she could not allow him to go unanswered without grievously sinning against all charity; so, rising from her seat, she gently touched his arm and said: 'Oh, Mr. Arabin, do not go till I speak to you! I do forgive you. You know that I forgive you.'

He took the hand that had so gently touched his arm, and then gazed into her face as if he would peruse there, as though written in a book, the whole future destiny of his life; and as

he did so, there was a sober sad seriousness in his own countenance, which Eleanor found herself unable to sustain. She
could only look down upon the carpet, let her tears trickle as
they would, and leave her hand within his.

It was but for a minute that they stood so, but the duration
of that minute was sufficient to make it ever memorable to
them both. Eleanor was sure now that she was loved. No
words, be their eloquence what it might, could be more im-
pressive than that eager, melancholy gaze.

Why did he look so into her eyes? Why did he not speak
to her? Could it be that he looked for her to make the first sign?

And he, though he knew but little of women, even he knew
that he was loved. He had only to ask and it would be all his
own, that inexpressible loveliness, those ever speaking but
yet now mute eyes, that feminine brightness and eager loving
spirit which had so attracted him since first he had encountered it at St. Ewold's. It might, must all be his own now. On
no other supposition was it possible that she should allow her
hand to remain thus clasped within his own. He had only to
ask. Ah! but that was the difficulty. Did a minute suffice for
all this? Nay, perhaps it might be more than a minute.

'Mrs. Bold—' at last he said, and then stopped himself.

If he could not speak, how was she to do so? He had called
her by her name, the same name that any merest stranger
would have used! She withdrew her hand from his, and moved
as though to return to her seat. 'Eleanor!' he then said, in his
softest tone, as though the courage of a lover were as yet but
half assumed, as though he were still afraid of giving offence
by the freedom which he took. She looked slowly, gently,
almost piteously up into his face. There was at any rate no
anger there to deter him.

'Eleanor!' he again exclaimed; and in a moment he had
her clasped to his bosom. How this was done, whether the
doing was with him or her, whether she had flown thither
conquered by the tenderness of his voice, or he with a violence
not likely to give offence had drawn her to his breast, neither
of them knew; nor can I declare. There was now that sym-

pathy between them which hardly admitted of individual motion. They were one and the same,—one flesh,—one spirit,—
one life.

'Eleanor, my own Eleanor, my own, my wife!' She ventured to look up at him through her tears, and he, bowing
his face down over hers, pressed his lips upon her brow; his
virgin lips, which since a beard first grew upon his chin, had
never yet tasted the luxury of a woman's cheek.

She had been told that her yea must be yea, or her nay,
nay; but she was called on for neither the one nor the other.
She told Miss Thorne that she was engaged to Mr. Arabin,
but no such words had passed between them, no promises had
been asked or given.

'Oh, let me go,' said she; 'let me go now. I am too happy
to remain,—let me go, that I may be alone.' He did not try to
hinder her; he did not repeat the kiss; he did not press another
on her lips. He might have done so had he been so minded.
She was now all his own. He took his arm from round her
waist, his arm that was trembling with a new delight, and let
her go. She fled like a roe to her own chamber, and then,
having turned the bolt, she enjoyed the full luxury of her love.
She idolised, almost worshipped this man who had so meekly
begged her pardon. And he was now her own. Oh, how she
wept and cried and laughed, as the hopes and fears and miser-
ies of the last few weeks passed in remembrance through
her mind.

Mr. Slope! That any one should have dared to think that
she who had been chosen by him could possibly have mated
herself with Mr. Slope! That they should have dared to tell
him, also, and subject her bright happiness to such needless
risk! And then she smiled with joy as she thought of all the
comforts that she could give him; not that he cared for comforts, but that it would be so delicious for her to give.

She got up and rang for her maid that she might tell her
little boy of his new father; and in her own way she did tell
him. She desired her maid to leave her, in order that she might
be alone with her child; and then, while he lay sprawling on

the bed, she poured forth the praises, all unmeaning to him, of the man she had selected to guard his infancy.

She could not be happy, however, till she had made Mr. Arabin take the child to himself, and thus, as it were, adopt him as his own. The moment the idea struck her she took the baby up in her arms, and, opening the door, ran quickly down to the drawing-room. She at once found, by his step still pacing on the floor, that he was there; and a glance within the room told her that he was alone. She hesitated a moment, and then hurried in with her precious charge.

Mr. Arabin met her in the middle of the room. 'There,' said she, breathless with her haste; 'there, take him—take him and love him.'

Mr. Arabin took the little fellow from her, and kissing him again and again, prayed God to bless him. 'He shall be all as my own—all as my own,' said he. Eleanor, as she stooped to take back her child, kissed the hand that held him, and then rushed back with her treasure to her chamber.

It was thus that Mr. Harding's younger daughter was won for the second time. At dinner neither she nor Mr. Arabin were very bright, but their silence occasioned no remark. In the drawing-room, as we have before said, she told Miss Thorne what had occurred. The next morning she returned to Barchester, and Mr. Arabin went over with his budget of news to the archdeacon. As Doctor Grantly was not there, he could only satisfy himself by telling Mrs. Grantly how that he intended himself the honour of becoming her brother-in-law. In the ecstasy of her joy at hearing such tidings, Mrs. Grantly vouchsafed him a warmer welcome than any he had yet received from Eleanor.

'Good heavens!' she exclaimed—it was the general exclamation of the rectory. 'Poor Eleanor! Dear Eleanor! What a monstrous injustice has been done her!—Well, it shall all be made up now.' And then she thought of the signora. 'What lies people tell,' she said to herself.

But people in this matter had told no lies at all.

49

THE BELZEBUB COLT

WHEN Miss Thorne left the dining-room, Eleanor had formed no intention of revealing to her what had occurred; but when she was seated beside her hostess on the sofa the secret dropped from her almost unawares. Eleanor was but a bad hypocrite, and she found herself quite unable to continue talking about Mr. Arabin as though he were a stranger, while her heart was full of him. When Miss Thorne, pursuing her own scheme with discreet zeal, asked the young widow whether, in her opinion, it would not be a good thing for Mr. Arabin to get married, she had nothing for it but to confess the truth. 'I suppose it would,' said Eleanor, rather sheepishly. Whereupon Miss Thorne amplified on the idea. 'Oh, Miss Thorne,' said Eleanor, 'he is going to be married: I am engaged to him.'

Now Miss Thorne knew very well that there had been no such engagement when she had been walking with Mrs. Bold in the morning. She had also heard enough to be tolerably sure that there had been no preliminaries to such an engagement. She was, therefore, as we have before described, taken a little by surprise. But, nevertheless, she embraced her guest, and cordially congratulated her.

Eleanor had no opportunity of speaking another word to Mr. Arabin that evening, except such words as all the world might hear; and these, as may be supposed, were few enough. Miss Thorne did her best to leave them in privacy; but Mr. Thorne, who knew nothing of what had occurred, and another guest, a friend of his, entirely interfered with her good intentions. So poor Eleanor had to go to bed without one sign of affection. Her state, nevertheless, was not to be pitied.

The next morning she was up early. It was probable, she thought, that by going down a little before the usual hour of breakfast, she might find Mr. Arabin alone in the dining-room. Might it not be that he also would calculate that an interview would thus be possible? Thus thinking, Eleanor was dressed a full hour before the time fixed in the Ullathorne household for morning prayers. She did not at once go down. She was afraid to seem to be too anxious to meet her lover; though, heaven knows, her anxiety was intense enough. She therefore sat herself down at her window, and repeatedly looking at her watch, nursed her child till she thought she might venture forth.

When she found herself at the dining-room door, she stood a moment, hesitating to turn the handle; but when she heard Mr. Thorne's voice inside she hesitated no longer. Her object was defeated, and she might now go in as soon as she liked without the slightest imputation on her delicacy. Mr. Thorne and Mr. Arabin were standing on the hearth-rug, discussing the merits of the Belzebub colt; or rather, Mr. Thorne was discussing, and Mr. Arabin was listening. That interesting animal had rubbed the stump of his tail against the wall of his stable, and occasioned much uneasiness to the Ullathorne master of the horse. Had Eleanor but waited another minute, Mr. Thorne would have been in the stables.

Mr. Thorne, when he saw his lady guest, repressed his anxiety. The Belzebub colt must do without him. And so the three stood, saying little or nothing to each other, till at last the master of the house, finding that he could no longer bear his present state of suspense respecting his favourite young steed, made an elaborate apology to Mrs. Bold, and escaped. As he shut the door behind him, Eleanor almost wished that he had remained. It was not that she was afraid of Mr. Arabin, but she hardly yet knew how to address him.

He, however, soon relieved her from her embarrassment. He came up to her, and taking both her hands in his, he said: 'So, Eleanor, you and I are to be man and wife. Is it so?'

She looked up into his face, and her lips formed themselves into a single syllable. She uttered no sound, but he could read the affirmative plainly in her face.

'It is a great trust,' said he; 'a very great trust.'

'It is—it is,' said Eleanor, not exactly taking what he had said in the sense that he had meant. 'It is a very, very great trust, and I will do my utmost to deserve it.'

'And I also will do my utmost to deserve it,' said Mr. Arabin, very solemnly. And then, winding his arm round her waist, he stood there gazing at the fire, and she with her head leaning on his shoulder, stood by him, well satisfied with her position. They neither of them spoke, or found any want of speaking. All that was needful for them to say had been said. The yea, yea, had been spoken by Eleanor in her own way— and that way had been perfectly satisfactory to Mr. Arabin.

And now it remained to them each to enjoy the assurance of the other's love. And how great that luxury is! How far it surpasses any other pleasure which God has allowed to his creatures! And to a woman's heart how doubly delightful!

When the ivy has found its tower, when the delicate creeper has found its strong wall, we know how the parasite plants grow and prosper. They were not created to stretch forth their branches alone, and endure without protection the summer's sun and the winter's storm. Alone they but spread themselves on the ground, and cower unseen in the dingy shade. But when they have found their firm supporters, how wonderful is their beauty; how all pervading and victorious! What is the turret without its ivy, or the high garden-wall without the jasmine which gives it its beauty and fragrance? The hedge without the honeysuckle is but a hedge.

There is a feeling still half existing, but now half conquered by the force of human nature, that a woman should be ashamed of her love till the husband's right to her compels her to acknowledge it. We would fain preach a different doctrine. A woman should glory in her love; but on that account let her take the more care that it be such as to justify her glory.

Eleanor did glory in hers, and she felt, and had cause to feel, that it deserved to be held as glorious. She could have stood there for hours with his arm round her, had fate and Mr. Thorne permitted it. Each moment she crept nearer to his bosom, and felt more and more certain that there was her home. What now to her was the archdeacon's arrogance, her sister's coldness, or her dear father's weakness? What need she care for the duplicity of such friends as Charlotte Stanhope? She had found the strong shield that should guard her from all wrongs, the trusty pilot that should henceforward guide her through the shoals and rocks. She would give up the heavy burden of her independence, and once more assume the position of a woman, and the duties of a trusting and loving wife.

And he, too, stood there fully satisfied with his place. They were both looking intently on the fire, as though they could read there their future fate, till at last Eleanor turned her face towards his. 'How sad you are,' she said, smiling; and indeed his face was, if not sad, at least serious. 'How sad you are, love!'

'Sad,' said he, looking down at her; 'no, certainly not sad.' Her sweet loving eyes were turned towards him, and she smiled softly as he answered her. The temptation was too strong even for the demure propriety of Mr. Arabin, and, bending over her, he pressed his lips to hers.

Immediately after this, Mr. Thorne appeared, and they were both delighted to hear that the tail of the Belzebub colt was not materially injured.

It had been Mr. Harding's intention to hurry over to Ullathorne as soon as possible after his return to Barchester, in order to secure the support of his daughter in his meditated revolt against the archdeacon as touching the deanery; but he was spared the additional journey by hearing that Mrs. Bold had returned unexpectedly home. As soon as he had read her note he started off, and found her waiting for him in her own house.

How much each of them had to tell the other, and how certain each was that the story which he or she had to tell would astonish the other!

'My dear, I am so anxious to see you,' said Mr. Harding, kissing his daughter.

'Oh, papa, I have so much to tell you!' said the daughter, returning the embrace.

'My dear, they have offered me the deanery!' said Mr. Harding, anticipating by the suddenness of the revelation the tidings which Eleanor had to give him.

'Oh, papa,' said she, forgetting her own love and happiness in her joy at the surprising news; 'oh, papa, can it be possible? Dear papa, how thoroughly, thoroughly happy that makes me!'

'But, my dear, I think it best to refuse it.'

'Oh, papa!'

'I am sure you will agree with me, Eleanor, when I explain it to you. You know, my dear, how old I am. If I live, I——'

'But, papa, I must tell you about myself.'

'Well, my dear.'

'I do so wonder how you'll take it.'

'Take what?'

'If you don't rejoice at it, if it doesn't make you happy, if you don't encourage me, I shall break my heart.'

'If that be the case, Nelly, I certainly will encourage you.'

'But I fear you won't. I do so fear you won't. And yet you can't but think I am the most fortunate woman living on God's earth.'

'Are you, dearest? Then I certainly will rejoice with you. Come, Nelly, come to me, and tell me what it is.'

'I am going——'

He led her to the sofa, and seating himself beside her, took both her hands in his. 'You are going to be married, Nelly. Is not that it?'

'Yes,' she said, faintly. 'That is if you will approve;' and then she blushed as she remembered the promise which she had so lately volunteered to him, and which she had so utterly forgotten in making her engagement with Mr. Arabin.

Mr. Harding thought for a moment who the man could be whom he was to be called upon to welcome as his son-in-law. A week since he would have had no doubt whom to name. In that case he would have been prepared to give his sanction, although he would have done so with a heavy heart. Now he knew that at any rate it would not be Mr. Slope, though he was perfectly at a loss to guess who could possibly have filled the place. For a moment he thought that the man might be Bertie Stanhope, and his very soul sank within him.

'Well, Nelly?'

'Oh, papa, promise that, for my sake, you will love him.'

'Come, Nelly, come; tell me who it is.'

'But will you love him, papa?'

'Dearest, I must love any one that you love.' Then she turned her face to his, and whispered into his ear the name of Mr. Arabin.

No man that she could have named could have more surprised or more delighted him. Had he looked round the world for a son-in-law to his taste, he could have selected no one whom he would have preferred to Mr. Arabin. He was a clergyman; he held a living in the neighbourhood; he was of a set to which all Mr. Harding's own partialities most closely adhered; he was the great friend of Dr. Grantly; and he was, moreover, a man of whom Mr. Harding knew nothing but what he approved. Nevertheless, his surprise was so great as to prevent the immediate expression of his joy. He had never thought of Mr. Arabin in connection with his daughter; he had never imagined that they had any feeling in common. He had feared that his daughter had been made hostile to clergymen of Mr. Arabin's stamp by her intolerance of the archdeacon's pretensions. Had he been put to wish, he might have wished for Mr. Arabin for a son-in-law; but had he been put to guess, the name would never have occurred to him.

'Mr. Arabin!' he exclaimed; 'impossible!'

'Oh, papa, for heaven's sake don't say anything against him! If you love me, don't say anything against him. Oh, papa, it's done, and mustn't be undone—oh, papa!'

Fickle Eleanor! where was the promise that she would make no choice for herself without her father's approval? She had chosen, and now demanded his acquiescence. 'Oh, papa, isn't he good? isn't he noble? isn't he religious, highminded, everything that a good man possibly can be?' and she clung to her father, beseeching him for his consent.

'My Nelly, my child, my own daughter! He is; he is noble

and good and highminded; he is all that a woman can love and a man admire. He shall be my son, my own son. He shall be as close to my heart as you are. My Nelly, my child, my happy, happy child!'

We need not pursue the interview any further. By degrees they returned to the subject of the new promotion. Eleanor tried to prove to him, as the Grantlys had done, that his age could be no bar to his being a very excellent dean; but those arguments had now even less weight on him than before. He said little or nothing, but sat meditative. Every now and then he would kiss his daughter, and say 'yes,' or 'no,' or 'very true,' or 'well, my dear, I can't quite agree with you there,' but he could not be got to enter sharply into the question of 'to be, or not to be' dean of Barchester. Of her and her happiness, of Mr. Arabin and his virtues, he would talk as much as Eleanor desired; and, to tell the truth, that was not a little; but about the deanery he would now say nothing further. He had got a new idea into his head—Why should not Mr. Arabin be the new dean?

Barchester Towers

50

THE ARCHDEACON IS SATISFIED
WITH THE STATE OF AFFAIRS

THE archdeacon, in his journey into Barchester, had been assured by Mr. Harding that all their prognostications about Mr. Slope and Eleanor were groundless. Mr. Harding, however, had found it very difficult to shake his son-in-law's faith in his own acuteness. The matter had, to Dr. Grantly, been so plainly corroborated by such patent evidence, borne out by such endless circumstances, that he at first refused to take as true the positive statement which Mr. Harding made to him of Eleanor's own disavowal of the impeachment. But at last he yielded in a qualified way. He brought himself to admit that he would at the present regard his past convictions as a mistake; but in doing this he so guarded himself, that if, at any future time, Eleanor should come forth to the world as Mrs. Slope, he might still be able to say: 'There, I told you so. Remember what you said and what I said; and remember also for coming years, that I was right in this matter,—as in all others.'

He carried, however, his concession so far as to bring himself to undertake to call at Eleanor's house, and he did call accordingly, while the father and daughter were yet in the middle of their conference. Mr. Harding had had so much to hear and to say that he had forgotten to advertise Eleanor of the honour that awaited her, and she heard her brother-in-law's voice in the hall, while she was quite unprepared to see him.

'There's the archdeacon,' she said, springing up.

'Yes, my dear. He told me to tell you that he would come and see you; but, to tell the truth, I had forgotten all about it.'

Eleanor fled away, regardless of all her father's entreaties. She could not now, in the first hours of her joy, bring herself to bear all the archdeacon's retractions, apologies, and congratulations. He would have so much to say, and would be so tedious in saying it; consequently, the archdeacon, when he was shown into the drawing-room, found no one there but Mr. Harding.

'You must excuse Eleanor,' said Mr. Harding.

'Is anything the matter?' asked the doctor, who at once anticipated that the whole truth about Mr. Slope had at last come out.

'Well, something is the matter. I wonder now whether you will be much surprised?'

The archdeacon saw by his father-in-law's manner that after all he had nothing to tell him about Mr. Slope. 'No,' said he, 'certainly not—nothing will ever surprise me again.' Very many men now-a-days, besides the archdeacon, adopt or affect to adopt the *nil admirari* doctrine; but nevertheless, to judge from their appearance, they are just as subject to sudden emotions as their grandfathers and grandmothers were before them.

'What do you think Mr. Arabin has done?'

'Mr. Arabin! It's nothing about that daughter of Stanhope's, I hope?'

'No, not that woman,' said Mr. Harding, enjoying his joke in his sleeve.

'Not that woman! Is he going to do anything about any woman? Why can't you speak out if you have anything to say? There is nothing I hate so much as these sort of mysteries.'

'There shall be no mystery with you, archdeacon; though of course, it must go no further at present.'

'Well.'

'Except Susan. You must promise me you'll tell no one else.'

'Nonsense!' exclaimed the archdeacon, who was becoming angry in his suspense. 'You can't have any secret about Mr. Arabin.'

'Only this—that he and Eleanor are engaged.'

It was quite clear to see, by the archdeacon's face, that he did not believe a word of it. 'Mr. Arabin! It's impossible!'

'Eleanor, at any rate, has just now told me so.'

'It's impossible,' repeated the archdeacon.

'Well, I can't say I think it impossible. It certainly took me by surprise; but that does not make it impossible.'

'She must be mistaken.'

Mr. Harding assured him that there was no mistake; that he would find, on returning home, that Mr. Arabin had been at Plumstead with the express object of making the same declaration, that even Miss Thorne knew all about it; and that, in fact, the thing was as clearly settled as any such arrangement between a lady and a gentleman could well be.

'Good heavens!' said the archdeacon, walking up and down Eleanor's drawing-room. 'Good heavens! Good heavens!'

Now, these exclamations certainly betokened faith. Mr. Harding properly gathered from it that, at last, Dr. Grantly did believe the fact. The first utterance clearly evinced a certain amount of distaste at the information he had received; the second, simply indicated surprise; in the tone of the third, Mr. Harding fancied that he could catch a certain gleam of satisfaction.

The archdeacon had truly expressed the workings of his mind. He could not but be disgusted to find how utterly astray he had been in all his anticipations. Had he only been lucky enough to have suggested this marriage himself when he first brought Mr. Arabin into the country, his character for judgment and wisdom would have received an addition which would have classed him at any rate next to Solomon. And why had he not done so? Might he not have foreseen that Mr. Arabin would want a wife in his parsonage? He had foreseen that Eleanor would want a husband; but should he not also have perceived that Mr. Arabin was a man much more likely to attract her than Mr. Slope? The archdeacon found that he had been at fault, and of course could not immediately get over his discomfiture.

Then his surprise was intense. How sly this pair of young turtle doves had been with him. How egregiously they had hoaxed him. He had preached to Eleanor against her fancied attachment to Mr. Slope, at the very time that she was in love with his own protégé, Mr. Arabin; and had absolutely taken that same Mr. Arabin into his confidence with reference to his dread of Mr. Slope's alliance. It was very natural that the archdeacon should feel surprise.

But there was also great ground for satisfaction. Looking at the match by itself, it was the very thing to help the doctor out of his difficulties. In the first place, the assurance that he should never have Mr. Slope for his brother-in-law, was in itself a great comfort. Then Mr. Arabin was, of all men, the one with whom it would best suit him to be so intimately connected. But the crowning comfort was the blow which this marriage would give to Mr. Slope. He had now certainly lost his wife; rumour was beginning to whisper that he might possibly lose his position in the palace; and if Mr. Harding would only be true, the great danger of all would be surmounted. In such case it might be expected that Mr. Slope would own himself vanquished, and take himself altogether away from Barchester. And so the archdeacon would again be able to breathe pure air.

'Well, well,' said he. 'Good heavens! good heavens!' and the tone of the fifth exclamation made Mr. Harding fully aware that content was reigning in the archdeacon's bosom.

And then slowly, gradually, and craftily Mr. Harding propounded his own new scheme. Why should not Mr. Arabin be the new dean?

Slowly, gradually, and thoughtfully Dr. Grantly fell into his father-in-law's views. Much as he liked Mr. Arabin, sincere as was his admiration for that gentleman's ecclesiastical abilities, he would not have sanctioned a measure which would rob his father-in-law of his fairly-earned promotion, were it at all practicable to induce his father-in-law to accept the promotion which he had earned. But the archdeacon had, on a former occasion, received proof of the obstinacy with which Mr. Harding could adhere to his own views in opposition to the advice of all his friends. He knew tolerably well that nothing would induce the meek, mild man before him to take the high place offered to him, if he thought it wrong to do so.

Knowing this, he also said to himself more than once: 'Why should not Mr. Arabin be Dean of Barchester?' It was at last arranged between them that they would together start to London by the earliest train on the following morning, making a little *détour* to Oxford on their journey. Dr. Gwynne's counsels, they imagined, might perhaps be of assistance to them.

These matters settled, the archdeacon hurried off, that he might return to Plumstead and prepare for his journey. The day was extremely fine, and he came into the city in an open gig. As he was driving up the High Street he encountered Mr. Slope at a crossing. Had he not pulled up rather sharply, he would have run over him. The two had never spoken to each other since they had met on a memorable occasion in the bishop's study. They did not speak now; but they looked each other full in the face, and Mr. Slope's countenance was as impudent, as triumphant, as defiant as ever. Had Dr. Grantly not known to the contrary, he would have imagined that his enemy had won the deanship, the wife, and all the rich honours, for which he had been striving. As it was, he had lost everything that he had in the world, and had just received his *congé* from the bishop.

In leaving the town the archdeacon drove by the well-remembered entrance of Hiram's Hospital. There, at the gate, was a large, untidy, farmer's wagon, laden with untidy-looking furniture; and there, inspecting the arrival, was good Mrs. Quiverful—not dressed in her Sunday best—not very clean in her apparel—not graceful as to her bonnet and shawl; or, indeed, with many feminine charms as to her whole appearance. She was busy at domestic work in her new house, and had just ventured out, expecting to see no one on the arrival of the family chattels. The archdeacon was down upon her before she knew where she was.

Her acquaintance with Dr. Grantly or his family was very slight indeed. The archdeacon, as a matter of course, knew every clergyman in the archdeaconry, it may almost be said in the diocese, and had some acquaintance, more or less intimate, with their wives and families. With Mr. Quiverful he had been concerned on various matters of business; but of Mrs. Q. he had seen very little. Now, however, he was in too gracious a mood to pass her by unnoticed. The Quiverfuls, one and all, had looked for the bitterest hostility from Dr. Grantly; they knew his anxiety that Mr. Harding should return to his old home at the hospital, and they did not know that a new home had been offered to him at the deanery. Mrs. Quiverful was therefore not a little surprised and not a little rejoiced also, at the tone in which she was addressed.

'How do you do, Mrs. Quiverful?—how do you do?' said he, stretching his left hand out of the gig, as he spoke to her. 'I am very glad to see you employed in so pleasant and useful a manner; very glad indeed.'

Mrs. Quiverful thanked him, and shook hands with him, and looked into his face suspiciously. She was not sure whether the congratulations and kindness were or were not ironical.

'Pray tell Mr. Quiverful from me,' he continued, 'that I am rejoiced at his appointment. It's a comfortable place, Mrs. Quiverful, and a comfortable house, and I am very glad to see you in it. Good-bye—good-bye.' And he drove on, leaving the lady well pleased and astonished at his good-nature. On the whole things were going well with the archdeacon, and he could afford to be charitable to Mrs. Quiverful. He looked forth from his gig smilingly on all the world, and forgave every one in Barchester their sins, excepting only Mrs. Proudie and Mr. Slope. Had he seen the bishop, he would have felt inclined to pat even him kindly on the head.

He determined to go home by St. Ewold's. This would take him some three miles out of his way; but he felt that he could not leave Plumstead comfortably without saying one word of good fellowship to Mr. Arabin. When he reached the parsonage the vicar was still out; but, from what he had heard, he did not doubt but that he would meet him on the road between their two houses. He was right in this, for about half-way home, at a narrow turn, he came upon Mr. Arabin, who was on horseback.

'Well, well, well, well;' said the archdeacon, loudly, joyously, and with supreme good humour; 'well, well, well, well; so, after all, we have no further cause to fear Mr. Slope.'

'I hear from Mrs. Grantly that they have offered the deanery to Mr. Harding,' said the other.

'Mr. Slope has lost more than the deanery, I find,' and then the archdeacon laughed jocosely. 'Come, come, Arabin, you have kept your secret well enough. I know all about it now.'

'I have had no secret, archdeacon,' said the other with a quiet smile. 'None at all—not for a day. It was only yesterday that I knew my own good fortune, and to-day I went over to Plumstead to ask your approval. From what Mrs. Grantly has said to me, I am led to hope that I shall have it.'

'With all my heart, with all my heart,' said the archdeacon cordially, holding his friend fast by the hand. 'It's just as I would have it. She is an excellent young woman; she will not come to you empty-handed; and I think she will make you a good wife. If she does her duty by you as her sister does by me, you'll be a happy man; that's all I can say.' And as he finished speaking, a tear might have been observed in each of the doctor's eyes.

Mr. Arabin warmly returned the archdeacon's grasp, but he said little. His heart was too full for speaking, and he could not express the gratitude which he felt. Dr. Grantly understood him as well as though he had spoken for an hour.

'And mind, Arabin,' said he, 'no one but myself shall tie the knot. We'll get Eleanor out to Plumstead, and it shall come off there. I'll make Susan stir herself, and we'll do it in style. I must be off to London to-morrow on special business. Harding goes with me. But I'll be back before your bride has got her wedding dress ready.' And so they parted.

On his journey home the archdeacon occupied his mind with preparations for the marriage festivities. He made a great resolve that he would atone to Eleanor for all the injury he had done her by the munificence of his future treatment. He would show her what was the difference in his eyes between a Slope and an Arabin. On one other thing also he decided with a firm mind: if the affair of the dean should not be settled in Mr. Arabin's favour, nothing should prevent him putting a new front and bow-window to the dining-room at St. Ewold's parsonage.

'So we're sold after all, Sue,' said he to his wife, accosting her with a kiss as soon as he entered his house. He did not call his wife Sue above twice or thrice in a year, and these occasions were great high days.

'Eleanor has had more sense than we gave her credit for,' said Mrs. Grantly.

And there was great content in Plumstead rectory that evening; and Mrs. Grantly promised her husband that she would now open her heart, and take Mr. Arabin into it. Hitherto she had declined to do so.

51

MR. SLOPE BIDS FAREWELL
TO THE PALACE AND ITS INHABITANTS

We must now take leave of Mr. Slope, and of the bishop also, and of Mrs. Proudie. These leave-takings in novels are as disagreeable as they are in real life; not so sad, indeed, for they want the reality of sadness; but quite as perplexing, and generally less satisfactory. What novelist, what Fielding, what Scott, what George Sand, or Sue, or Dumas, can impart an interest to the last chapter of his fictitious history? Promises of two children and superhuman happiness are of no avail, nor assurance of extreme respectability carried to an age far exceeding that usually allotted to mortals. The sorrows of our heroes and heroines, they are your delight, oh public! their sorrows, or their sins, or their absurdities; not their virtues, good sense, and consequent rewards. When we begin to tint our final pages with *couleur de rose*, as in accordance with fixed rule we must do, we altogether extinguish our own powers of pleasing. When we become dull we offend your intellect; and we must become dull or we should offend your taste. A late writer, wishing to sustain his interest to the last page, hung his hero at the end of the third volume. The consequence was, that no one would read his novel. And who can apportion out and dovetail his incidents, dialogues, characters, and descriptive morsels, so as to fit them all exactly into 439 pages, without either compressing them unnaturally, or extending them artificially at the end of his labour? Do I not myself know that I am at this moment in want of a dozen pages, and that I am sick with cudgelling my brains to find them? And then when everything is done, the kindest-hearted critic of them all invariably twits us with the incompetency and lameness of our conclusion. We have either become idle and neglected it, or tedious and over-laboured it. It is insipid or unnatural, over-strained or imbecile. It means nothing, or attempts too much. The last scene of all, as all last scenes we fear must be,

Is second childishness, and mere oblivion,
Sans teeth, sans eyes, sans taste, sans everything.

I can only say that if some critic, who thoroughly knows his work, and has laboured on it till experience has made him perfect, will write the last fifty pages of a novel in the way they should be written, I, for one, will in future do my best to copy the example. Guided by my own lights only, I confess that I despair of success.

For the last week or ten days, Mr. Slope had seen nothing of Mrs. Proudie, and very little of the bishop. He still lived in the palace, and still went through his usual routine work; but the confidential doings of the diocese had passed into other hands. He had seen this clearly, and marked it well; but it had not much disturbed him. He had indulged in other hopes till the bishop's affairs had become dull to him, and he was moreover aware that, as regarded the diocese, Mrs. Proudie had checkmated him. It has been explained, in the beginning of these pages, how three or four were contending together as to who, in fact, should be bishop of Barchester. Each of these had now admitted to himself (or boasted to herself) that

Mrs. Proudie was victorious in the struggle. They had gone through a competitive examination of considerable severity, and she had come forth the winner, *facile princeps*. Mr. Slope had, for a moment, run her hard, but it was only for a moment. It had become, as it were, acknowledged that Hiram's hospital should be the testing point between them, and now Mr. Quiverful was already in the hospital, the proof of Mrs. Proudie's skill and courage.

All this did not break down Mr. Slope's spirit, because he had other hopes. But, alas, at last there came to him a note from his friend Sir Nicholas, informing him that the deanship was disposed of. Let us give Mr. Slope his due. He did not lie prostrate under this blow, or give himself up to vain lamentations; he did not henceforward despair of life, and call upon gods above and gods below to carry him off. He sat himself down in his chair, counted out what monies he had in hand for present purposes, and what others were coming in to him, bethought himself as to the best sphere for his future exertions, and at once wrote off a letter to a rich sugar-refiner's wife in Baker Street, who, as he well knew, was much given to the entertainment and encouragement of serious young evangelical clergymen. He was again, he said, 'upon the world, having found the air of a cathedral town, and the very nature of cathedral services, uncongenial to his spirit;' and then he sat awhile, making firm resolves as to his manner of parting from the bishop, and also as to his future conduct.

At last he rose, and twitched his mantle blue (black),
To-morrow to fresh woods and pastures new.

Having received a formal command to wait upon the bishop, he rose and proceeded to obey it. He rang the bell and desired the servant to inform his master that if it suited his lordship, he, Mr. Slope, was ready to wait upon him. The servant, who well understood that Mr. Slope was no longer in the ascendant, brought back a message, saying that 'his lordship desired that Mr. Slope would attend him immediately in his study.' Mr. Slope waited about ten minutes more to prove his independence, and then he went into the bishop's room. There, as he had expected, he found Mrs. Proudie, together with her husband.

'Hum, ha,—Mr. Slope, pray take a chair,' said the gentleman bishop.

'Pray be seated, Mr. Slope,' said the lady bishop.

'Thank ye, thank ye,' said Mr. Slope, and walking round to the fire, he threw himself into one of the arm-chairs that graced the hearth-rug.

'Mr. Slope,' said the bishop, 'it has become necessary that I should speak to you definitively on a matter that has for some time been pressing itself on my attention.'

'May I ask whether the subject is in any way connected with myself?' said Mr. Slope.

'It is so,—certainly,—yes, it certainly is connected with yourself, Mr. Slope.'

'Then, my lord, if I may be allowed to express a wish, I would prefer that no discussion on the subject should take place between us in the presence of a third person.'

'Don't alarm yourself, Mr. Slope,' said Mrs. Proudie, 'no discussion is at all necessary. The bishop merely intends to express his own wishes.'

'I merely intend, Mr. Slope, to express my own wishes,— no discussion will be at all necessary,' said the bishop, reiterating his wife's words.

'That is more, my lord, than we any of us can be sure of,' said Mr. Slope; 'I cannot, however, force Mrs. Proudie to leave the room; nor can I refuse to remain here if it be your lordship's wish that I should do so.'

'It is his lordship's wish, certainly,' said Mrs. Proudie.

'Mr. Slope,' began the bishop, in a solemn, serious voice, 'it grieves me to have to find fault. It grieves me much to have to find fault with a clergyman; but especially so with a clergyman in your position.'

'Why, what have I done amiss, my lord?' demanded Mr. Slope, boldly.

'What have you done amiss, Mr. Slope?' said Mrs. Proudie, standing erect before the culprit, and raising that terrible forefinger. 'Do you dare to ask the bishop what you have done amiss? does not your conscience——'

'Mrs. Proudie, pray let it be understood, once for all, that I will have no words with you.'

'Ah, sir, but you will have words,' said she; 'you must have words. Why have you had so many words with that Signora Neroni? Why have you disgraced yourself, you a clergyman too, by constantly consorting with such a woman as that,—with a married woman—with one altogether unfit for a clergyman's society?'

'At any rate, I was introduced to her in your drawing-room,' retorted Mr. Slope.

'And shamefully you behaved there,' said Mrs. Proudie, 'most shamefully. I was wrong to allow you to remain in the house a day after what I then saw. I should have insisted on your instant dismissal.'

'I have yet to learn, Mrs. Proudie, that you have the power to insist either on my going from hence or on my staying here.'

'What!' said the lady; 'I am not to have the privilege of saying who shall and who shall not frequent my own drawing-room! I am not to save my servants and dependents from having their morals corrupted by improper conduct! I am not to save my own daughters from impurity! I will let you see, Mr. Slope, whether I have the power or whether I have not. You will have the goodness to understand that you no longer fill any situation about the bishop; and as your room will be immediately wanted in the palace for another chaplain, I must ask you to provide yourself with apartments as soon as may be convenient to you.'

'My lord,' said Mr. Slope, appealing to the bishop, and so turning his back completely on the lady, 'will you permit me to ask that I may have from your own lips any decision that you may have come to on this matter?'

'Certainly, Mr. Slope, certainly,' said the bishop; 'that is but reasonable. Well, my decision is that you had better look for some other preferment. For the situation which you have lately held I do not think that you are well suited.'

'And what, my lord, has been my fault?'

'That Signora Neroni is one fault,' said Mrs. Proudie; 'and a very abominable fault she is; very abominable and very disgraceful. Fie, Mr. Slope, fie! You an evangelical clergyman indeed!'

'My lord, I desire to know for what fault I am turned out of your lordship's house.'

'You hear what Mrs. Proudie says,' said the bishop.

'When I publish the history of this transaction, my lord, as I decidedly shall do in my own vindication, I presume you will not wish me to state that you have discarded me at your wife's bidding—because she has objected to my being acquainted with another lady, the daughter of one of the prebendaries of the chapter?'

'You may publish what you please, sir,' said Mrs. Proudie. 'But you will not be insane enough to publish any of your doings in Barchester. Do you think I have not heard of your kneelings at that creature's feet—that is if she has any feet—and of your constant slobbering over her hand? I advise you to beware, Mr. Slope, of what you do and say. Clergymen have been unfrocked for less than what you have been guilty of.'

'My lord, if this goes on I shall be obliged to indict this woman—Mrs. Proudie I mean—for defamation of character.'

'I think, Mr. Slope, you had better now retire,' said the bishop. 'I will enclose to you a cheque for any balance that may be due to you; and, under the present circumstances, it will of course be better for all parties that you should leave the palace at the earliest possible moment. I will allow you for your journey back to London, and for your maintenance in Barchester for a week from this date.'

'If, however, you wish to remain in this neighbourhood,' said Mrs. Proudie, 'and will solemnly pledge yourself never again to see that woman, and will promise also to be more circumspect in your conduct, the bishop will mention your name to Mr. Quiverful, who now wants a curate at Pudding-

dale. The house is, I imagine, quite sufficient for your requirements: and there will moreover be a stipend of fifty pounds
a year.'

'May God forgive you, madam, for the manner in which
you have treated me,' said Mr. Slope, looking at her with a
very heavenly look; 'and remember this, madam, that you
yourself may still have a fall;' and he looked at her with a very
worldly look. 'As to the bishop, I pity him!' And so saying,
Mr. Slope left the room. Thus ended the intimacy of the
Bishop of Barchester with his first confidential chaplain.

Mrs. Proudie was right in this: namely, that Mr. Slope
was not insane enough to publish to the world any of his
doings in Barchester. He did not trouble his friend Mr. Towers with any written statement of the iniquity of Mrs. Proudie,
or the imbecility of her husband. He was aware that it would
be wise in him to drop for the future all allusions to his doings
in the cathedral city. Soon after the interview just recorded,
he left Barchester, shaking the dust off his feet as he entered
the railway carriage; and he gave no longing lingering look
after the cathedral towers, as the train hurried him quickly
out of their sight.

It is well known that the family of the Slopes never starve:
they always fall on their feet like cats, and let them fall where
they will, they live on the fat of the land. Our Mr. Slope did
so. On his return to town he found that the sugar-refiner had
died, and that his widow was inconsolable: or, in other words,
in want of consolation. Mr. Slope consoled her, and soon found
himself settled with much comfort in the house in Baker Street.
He possessed himself, also, before long, of a church in the
vicinity of the New Road, and became known to fame as one
of the most eloquent preachers and pious clergymen in that
part of the metropolis. There let us leave him.

Of the bishop and his wife very little further need be said.
From that time forth nothing material occurred to interrupt
the even course of their domestic harmony. Very speedily, a
further vacancy on the bench of bishops gave to Dr. Proudie
the seat in the House of Lords, which he at first so anxiously

longed for. But by this time he had become a wiser man. He did certainly take his seat, and occasionally registered a vote in favour of Government views on ecclesiastical matters. But he had thoroughly learnt that his proper sphere of action lay in close contiguity with Mrs. Proudie's wardrobe. He never again aspired to disobey, or seemed even to wish for auto-cratic diocesan authority. If ever he thought of freedom, he did so, as men think of the millennium, as of a good time which may be coming, but which nobody expects to come in their day. Mrs. Proudie might be said still to bloom, and was, at any rate, strong; and the bishop had no reason to apprehend that he would be speedily visited with the sorrows of a widow-er's life.

He is still Bishop of Barchester. He has so graced that throne, that the Government has been averse to translate him, even to higher dignities. There may he remain, under safe pupilage, till the new-fangled manners of the age have dis-covered him to be superannuated, and bestowed on him a pension. As for Mrs. Proudie, our prayers for her are that she may live for ever.

52

THE NEW DEAN

TAKES POSSESSION OF THE DEANERY,

AND THE NEW WARDEN OF THE HOSPITAL

Mr. HARDING and the archdeacon together made their way to Oxford, and there, by dint of cunning argument, they induced the Master of Lazarus also to ask himself this mo-mentous question: 'Why should not Mr. Arabin be Dean of Barchester?' He of course, for a while tried his hand at per-suading Mr. Harding that he was foolish, over-scrupulous, self-willed, and weak-minded; but he tried in vain. If Mr. Harding would not give way to Dr. Grantly, it was not likely he would give way to Dr. Gwynne; more especially now that so admirable a scheme as that of inducting Mr. Arabin into the deanery had been set on foot. When the master found that his eloquence was vain, and heard also that Mr. Arabin was about to become Mr. Harding's son-in-law, he confessed that he also would, under such circumstances, be glad to see his old friend and protégé, the fellow of his college, placed in the comfortable position that was going a-begging.

'It might be the means, you know, Master, of keeping Mr. Slope out,' said the archdeacon with grave caution.

'He has no more chance of it,' said the master, 'than our college chaplain. I know more about it than that.'

Mrs. Grantly had been right in her surmise. It was the Master of Lazarus who had been instrumental in representing in high places the claims which Mr. Harding had upon the Government, and he now consented to use his best endeavours towards getting the offer transferred to Mr. Arabin. The three of them went on to London together, and there they remained a week, to the great disgust of Mrs. Grantly, and most probably also of Mrs. Gwynne. The minister was out of town in one direction, and his private secretary in another. The clerks who remained could do nothing in such a matter as this, and all was difficulty and confusion. The two doctors seemed to have plenty to do; they bustled here and they bustled there, and complained at their club in the evenings that they had been driven off their legs; but Mr. Harding had no occupation. Once or twice he suggested that he might perhaps return to Barchester. His request, however, was peremptorily refused, and he had nothing for it but to while away his time in Westminster Abbey.

At length an answer from the great man came. The Master of Lazarus had made his proposition through the Bishop of Belgravia. Now this bishop, though but newly gifted with his diocesan honours, was a man of much weight in the clerico-political world. He was, if not as pious, at any rate as wise as St. Paul, and had been with so much effect all things to all men, that though he was great among the dons of Oxford, he had been selected for the most favourite seat on the bench

by a Whig Prime Minister. To him Dr. Gwynne had made
known his wishes and his arguments, and the bishop had made
them known to the Marquis of Kensington Gore. The marquis, who was Lord High Steward of the Pantry Board, and
who by most men was supposed to hold the highest office out
of the cabinet, trafficked much in affairs of this kind. He not
only suggested the arrangement to the minister over a cup
of coffee, standing on a drawing-room rug in Windsor Castle,
but he also favourably mentioned Mr. Arabin's name in the
ear of a distinguished person.

And so the matter was arranged. The answer of the great
man came, and Mr. Arabin was made Dean of Barchester.
The three clergymen who had come up to town on this important mission dined together with great glee on the day on
which the news reached them. In a silent, decent, clerical
manner, they toasted Mr. Arabin with full bumpers of claret.
The satisfaction of all of them was supreme. The Master of
Lazarus had been successful in his attempt, and success is dear
to us all. The archdeacon had trampled upon Mr. Slope, and
had lifted to high honours the young clergyman whom he had
induced to quit the retirement and comfort of the university.
So at least the archdeacon thought; though, to speak sooth,
not he, but circumstances, had trampled on Mr. Slope. But
the satisfaction of Mr. Harding was, of all, perhaps, the most
complete. He laid aside his usual melancholy manner, and
brought forth little quiet jokes from the inmost mirth of his
heart; he poked his fun at the archdeacon about Mr. Slope's
marriage, and quizzed him for his improper love for Mrs.
Proudie. On the following day they all returned to Barchester.

It was arranged that Mr. Arabin should know nothing of
what had been done till he received the minister's letter from
the hands of his embryo father-in-law. In order that no time
might be lost, a message had been sent to him by the preceding night's post, begging him to be at the deanery at the hour
that the train from London arrived. There was nothing in
this which surprised Mr. Arabin. It had somehow got about
through all Barchester that Mr. Harding was the new dean,

and all Barchester was prepared to welcome him with pealing bells and full hearts. Mr. Slope had certainly had a party; there had certainly been those in Barchester who were prepared to congratulate him on his promotion with assumed sincerity, but even his own party was not broken-hearted by his failure. The inhabitants of the city, even the high-souled ecstatic young ladies of thirty-five, had begun to comprehend that their welfare, and the welfare of the place, was connected in some mysterious manner with daily chants and bi-weekly anthems. The expenditure of the palace had not added much to the popularity of the bishop's side of the question; and, on the whole, there was a strong reaction. When it became known to all the world that Mr. Harding was to be the new dean, all the world rejoiced heartily.

Mr. Arabin, we have said, was not surprised at the summons which called him to the deanery. He had not as yet seen Mr. Harding since Eleanor had accepted him, nor had he seen him since he had learnt his future father-in-law's preferment. There was nothing more natural, more necessary, than that they should meet each other at the earliest possible moment. Mr. Arabin was waiting in the deanery parlour when Mr. Harding and Dr. Grantly were driven up from the station.

There was some excitement in the bosoms of them all, as they met and shook hands; by far too much to enable either of them to begin his story and tell it in a proper equable style of narrative. Mr. Harding was some minutes quite dumbfounded, and Mr. Arabin could only talk in short, spasmodic sentences about his love and good fortune. He slipped in, as best he could, some sort of congratulation about the deanship, and then went on with his hopes and fears,—hopes that he might be received as a son, and fears that he hardly deserved such good fortune. Then he went back to the dean; it was the most thoroughly satisfactory appointment, he said, of which he had ever heard.

'But! but! but——' said Mr. Harding; and then failing to get any further, he looked imploringly at the archdeacon.

'The truth is, Arabin,' said the doctor, 'that, after all, you

are not destined to be son-in-law to a dean. Nor am I either:
more's the pity.'

Mr. Arabin looked at him for explanation. 'Is not Mr.
Harding to be the new dean?'

'It appears not,' said the archdeacon. Mr. Arabin's face
fell a little, and he looked from one to the other. It was plainly
to be seen from them both that there was no cause of unhappiness in the matter, at least not of unhappiness to them; but
there was as yet no elucidation of the mystery.

'Think how old I am,' said Mr. Harding, imploringly.

'Fiddlestick!' said the archdeacon.

'That's all very well, but it won't make a young man of
me,' said Mr. Harding.

'And who is to be dean?' asked Mr. Arabin.

'Yes, that's the question,' said the archdeacon. 'Come, Mr.
Precentor, since you obstinately refuse to be anything else,
let us know who is to be the man. He has got the nomination
in his pocket.'

With eyes brim full of tears, Mr. Harding pulled out the
letter and handed it to his future son-in-law. He tried to make
a little speech, but failed altogether. Having given up the
document, he turned round to the wall, feigning to blow his
nose, and then sat himself down on the old dean's dingy horse-
hair sofa. And here we find it necessary to bring our account
of the interview to an end.

Nor can we pretend to describe the rapture with which
Mr. Harding was received by his daughter. She wept with
grief and wept with joy; with grief that her father should, in
his old age, still be without that rank and worldly position
which, according to her ideas, he had so well earned; and with
joy in that he, her darling father, should have bestowed on
that other dear one the good things of which he himself would
not open his hand to take possession. And here Mr. Harding
again showed his weakness. In the *mêlée* of this exposal of
their loves and reciprocal affection, he found himself unable
to resist the entreaties of all parties that the lodgings in the
High Street should be given up. Eleanor would not live in

the deanery, she said, unless her father lived there also. Mr. Arabin would not be dean, unless Mr. Harding would be co-dean with him. The archdeacon declared that his father-in-law should not have his own way in everything, and Mrs. Grantly carried him off to Plumstead, that he might remain there till Mr. and Mrs. Arabin were in a state to receive him in their own mansion.

Pressed by such arguments as these, what could a weak old man do but yield?

But there was yet another task which it behoved Mr. Harding to do before he could allow himself to be at rest. Little has been said in these pages of the state of those remaining old men who had lived under his sway at the hospital. But not on this account must it be presumed that he had forgotten them, or that in their state of anarchy and in their want of due government he had omitted to visit them. He visited them constantly, and had latterly given them to understand that they would soon be required to subscribe their adherence to a new master. There were now but five of them, one of them having been but quite lately carried to his rest,— but five of the full number, which had hitherto been twelve, and which was now to be raised to twenty-four, including women. Of these old Bunce, who for many years had been the favourite of the late warden, was one; and Abel Handy, who had been the humble means of driving that warden from his home, was another.

Mr. Harding now resolved that he himself would introduce the new warden to the hospital. He felt that many circumstances might conspire to make the men receive Mr. Quiverful with aversion and disrespect; he felt also that Mr. Quiverful might himself feel some qualms of conscience if he entered the hospital with an idea that he did so in hostility to his predecessor. Mr. Harding therefore determined to walk in, arm in arm with Mr. Quiverful, and to ask from these men their respectful obedience to their new master.

On returning to Barchester, he found that Mr. Quiverful had not yet slept in the hospital house, or entered on his new duties. He accordingly made known to that gentleman his wishes, and his proposition was not rejected.

It was a bright clear morning, though in November, that Mr. Harding and Mr. Quiverful, arm in arm, walked through the hospital gate. It was one trait in our old friend's character that he did nothing with parade. He omitted, even in the more important doings of his life, that sort of parade by which most of us deem it necessary to grace our important doings. We have housewarmings, christenings, and gala days; we keep, if not our own birthdays, those of our children; we are apt to fuss ourselves if called upon to change our residences, and have, almost all of us, our little state occasions. Mr. Harding had no state occasions. When he left his old house, he went forth from it with the same quiet composure as though he were merely taking his daily walk; and now that he re-entered it with another warden under his wing, he did so with the same quiet step and calm demeanour. He was a little less upright than he had been five years, nay, it was nearly six years ago; he walked perhaps a little slower; his footfall was perhaps a thought less firm; otherwise one might have said that he was merely returning with a friend under his arm.

This friendliness was everything to Mr. Quiverful. To him, even in his poverty, the thought that he was supplanting a brother clergyman so kind and courteous as Mr. Harding, had been very bitter. Under his circumstances it had been impossible for him to refuse the proffered boon; he could not reject the bread that was offered to his children, or refuse to ease the heavy burden that had so long oppressed that poor wife of his; nevertheless, it had been very grievous to him to think that in going to the hospital he might encounter the ill will of his brethren in the diocese. All this Mr. Harding had fully comprehended. It was for such feelings as these, for the nice comprehension of such motives, that his heart and intellect were peculiarly fitted. In most matters of worldly import the archdeacon set down his father-in-law as little better than a fool. And perhaps he was right. But in some other matters, equally important if they be rightly judged, Mr. Harding,

had he been so minded, might with as much propriety have
set down his son-in-law for a fool. Few men, however, are
constituted as was Mr. Harding. He had that nice appreciation of the feelings of others which belongs of right exclusively
to women.

Arm in arm they walked into the inner quadrangle of the
building, and there the five old men met them. Mr. Harding
shook hands with them all, and then Mr. Quiverful did the
same. With Bunce Mr. Harding shook hands twice, and Mr.
Quiverful was about to repeat the same ceremony, but the old
man gave him no encouragement.

'I am very glad to know that at last you have a new
warden,' said Mr. Harding in a very cheery voice.

'We be very old for any change,' said one of them; 'but
we do suppose it be all for the best.'

'Certainly—certainly it is for the best,' said Mr. Harding.
'You will again have a clergyman of your own church under
the same roof with you, and a very excellent clergyman you
will have. It is a great satisfaction to me to know that so good
a man is coming to take care of you, and that it is no stranger,
but a friend of my own, who will allow me from time to time
to come in and see you.'

'We be very thankful to your reverence,' said another of
them.

'I need not tell you, my good friends,' said Mr. Quiverful,
'how extremely grateful I am to Mr. Harding for his kindness
to me,—I must say his uncalled for, unexpected kindness.'

'He be always very kind,' said a third.

'What I can do to fill the void which he left here, I will do.
For your sake and my own I will do so, and especially for his
sake. But to you who have known him, I can never be the
same well-loved friend and father that he has been.'

'No, sir, no,' said old Bunce, who hitherto had held his
peace; 'no one can be that. Not if the new bishop sent a hangel
to us out of heaven. We doesn't doubt you'll do your best,
sir, but you'll not be like the old master; not to us old ones.'

'Fie, Bunce, fie! how dare you talk in that way?' said Mr.

Harding; but as he scolded the old man he still held him by his arm, and pressed it with warm affection.

There was no getting up any enthusiasm in the matter. How could five old men tottering away to their final resting-place be enthusiastic on the reception of a stranger? What could Mr. Quiverful be to them, or they to Mr. Quiverful? Had Mr. Harding indeed come back to them, some last flicker of joyous light might have shone forth on their aged cheeks; but it was in vain to bid them rejoice because Mr. Quiverful was about to move his fourteen children from Puddingdale into the hospital house. In reality they did no doubt receive advantage, spiritual as well as corporal; but this they could neither anticipate nor acknowledge.

It was a dull affair enough, this introduction of Mr. Quiverful; but still it had its effect. The good which Mr. Harding intended did not fall to the ground. All the Barchester world, including the five old bedesmen, treated Mr. Quiverful with the more respect, because Mr. Harding had thus walked in arm in arm with him, on his first entrance to his duties.

And here in their new abode we will leave Mr. and Mrs. Quiverful and their fourteen children. May they enjoy the good things which Providence has at length given to them!

53

CONCLUSION

THE end of a novel, like the end of a children's dinner-party, must be made up of sweetmeats and sugar-plums. There is now nothing else to be told but the gala doings of Mr. Arabin's marriage, nothing more to be described than the wedding dresses, no further dialogue to be recorded than that which took place between the archdeacon who married them, and Mr. Arabin and Eleanor who were married. 'Wilt thou have this woman to thy wedded wife,' and 'Wilt thou have this man to thy wedded husband, to live together according to God's ordinance?' Mr. Arabin and Eleanor each answered,

'I will.' We have no doubt that they will keep their promises; the more especially as the Signora Neroni had left Barchester before the ceremony was performed.

Mrs. Bold had been somewhat more than two years a widow before she was married to her second husband, and little Johnnie was then able with due assistance to walk on his own legs into the drawing-room to receive the salutations of the assembled guests. Mr. Harding gave away the bride, the archdeacon performed the service, and the two Miss Grantlys, who were joined in their labours by other young ladies of the neighbourhood, performed the duties of bridesmaids with equal diligence and grace. Mrs. Grantly superintended the breakfast and bouquets, and Mary Bold distributed the cards and cake. The archdeacon's three sons had also come home for the occasion. The eldest was great with learning, being regarded by all who knew him as a certain future double first. The second, however, bore the palm on this occasion, being resplendent in a new uniform. The third was just entering the university, and was probably the proudest of the three.

But the most remarkable feature in the whole occasion was the excessive liberality of the archdeacon. He literally made presents to everybody. As Mr. Arabin had already moved out of the parsonage of St. Ewold's, that scheme of elongating the dining-room was of course abandoned; but he would have refurnished the whole deanery had he been allowed. He sent down a magnificent piano by Erard, gave Mr. Arabin a cob which any dean in the land might have been proud to bestride, and made a special present to Eleanor of a new pony chair that had gained a prize in the Exhibition. Nor did he even stay his hand here; he bought a set of cameos for his wife, and a sapphire bracelet for Miss Bold; showered pearls and workboxes on his daughters, and to each of his sons he presented a cheque for 20*l.* On Mr. Harding he bestowed a magnificent violoncello with all the new-fashioned arrangements and expensive additions, which, on account of these novelties, that gentleman could never use with satisfaction to his audience or pleasure to himself.

Those who knew the archdeacon well, perfectly understood the cause of his extravagance. 'Twas thus that he sang his song of triumph over Mr. Slope. This was his pæan, his hymn of thanksgiving, his loud oration. He had girded himself with his sword, and gone forth to the war; now he was returning from the field laden with the spoils of the foe. The cob and the cameos, the violoncello and the pianoforte, were all as it were trophies reft from the tent of his now conquered enemy.

The Arabins after their marriage went abroad for a couple of months, according to the custom in such matters now duly established, and then commenced their deanery life under good auspices. And nothing can be more pleasant than the present arrangement of ecclesiastical affairs in Barchester. The titular bishop never interfered, and Mrs. Proudie not often. Her sphere is more extended, more noble, and more suited to her ambition than that of a cathedral city. As long as she can do what she pleases with the diocese, she is willing to leave the dean and chapter to themselves. Mr. Slope tried his hand at subverting the old-established customs of the close, and from his failure she has learnt experience. The burly chancellor and the meagre little prebendary are not teased by any application respecting Sabbath-day schools, the dean is left to his own dominions, and the intercourse between Mrs. Proudie and Mrs. Arabin is confined to a yearly dinner given by each to the other. At these dinners Dr. Grantly will not take a part; but he never fails to ask for and receive a full account of all that Mrs. Proudie either does or says.

His ecclesiastical authority has been greatly shorn since the palmy days in which he reigned supreme as mayor of the palace to his father, but nevertheless such authority as is now left to him he can enjoy without interference. He can walk down the Main Street of Barchester without feeling that those who see him are comparing his claims with those of Mr. Slope. The intercourse between Plumstead and the deanery is of the most constant and familiar description. Since Eleanor has been married to a clergyman, and especially to a dignitary of the church, Mrs. Grantly has found many more points of sympathy with her sister; and on a coming occasion, which is much looked forward to by all parties, she intends to spend a month or two at the deanery. She never thought of spending a month in Barchester when little Johnny Bold was born!

The two sisters do not quite agree on matters of church doctrine, though their differences are of the most amicable description. Mr. Arabin's church is two degrees higher than that of Mrs. Grantly. This may seem strange to those who will remember that Eleanor was once accused of partiality to Mr. Slope; but it is no less the fact. She likes her husband's silken vest, she likes his adherence to the rubric, she specially likes the eloquent philosophy of his sermons, and she likes the red letters in her own prayer-book. It must not be presumed that she has a taste for candles, or that she is at all astray about the real presence; but she has an inkling that way. She sent a handsome subscription towards certain very heavy ecclesiastical legal expenses which have lately been incurred in Bath, her name of course not appearing; she assumes a smile of gentle ridicule when the Archbishop of Canterbury is named, and she has put up a memorial window in the cathedral.

Mrs. Grantly, who belongs to the high and dry church, the high church as it was some fifty years since, before tracts were written and young clergymen took upon themselves the highly meritorious duty of cleaning churches, rather laughs at her sister. She shrugs her shoulders, and tells Miss Thorne that she supposes Eleanor will have an oratory in the deanery before she has done. But she is not on that account a whit displeased. A few high church vagaries do not, she thinks, sit amiss on the shoulders of a young dean's wife. It shows at any rate that her heart is in the subject; and it shows moreover that she is removed, wide as the poles asunder, from that cesspool of abomination in which it was once suspected that she would wallow and grovel. Anathema maranatha! Let anything else be held as blessed, so that that be well cursed. Welcome kneelings and bowings, welcome matins and complines, welcome bell, book, and candle, so that Mr. Slope's dirty surplices and ceremonial Sabbaths be held in due execration!

If it be essentially and absolutely necessary to choose between the two, we are inclined to agree with Mrs. Grantly that the bell, book, and candle are the lesser evil of the two. Let it however be understood that no such necessity is admitted in these pages.

Dr. Arabin (we suppose he must have become a doctor when he became a dean) is more moderate and less outspoken on doctrinal points than his wife, as indeed in his station it behoves him to be. He is a studious, thoughtful, hard-working man. He lives constantly at the deanery, and preaches nearly every Sunday. His time is spent in sifting and editing old ecclesiastical literature, and in producing the same articles new. At Oxford he is generally regarded as the most promising clerical ornament of the age. He and his wife live together in perfect mutual confidence. There is but one secret in her bosom which he has not shared. He has never yet learned how Mr. Slope had his ears boxed.

The Stanhopes soon found that Mr. Slope's power need no longer operate to keep them from the delight of their Italian villa. Before Eleanor's marriage they had all migrated back to the shores of Como. They had not been resettled long before the signora received from Mrs. Arabin a very pretty though very short epistle, in which she was informed of the fate of the writer. This letter was answered by another, bright, charming, and witty, as the signora's letters always were; and so ended the friendship between Eleanor and the Stanhopes.

One word of Mr. Harding, and we have done.

He is still Precentor of Barchester, and still pastor of the little church of St. Cuthbert's. In spite of what he has so often said himself, he is not even yet an old man. He does such duties as fall to his lot well and conscientiously, and is thankful that he has never been tempted to assume others for which he might be less fitted.

Barchester Towers

The Author now leaves him in the hands of his readers; not as a hero, not as a man to be admired and talked of, not as a man who should be toasted at public dinners and spoken of with conventional absurdity as a perfect divine, but as a good man without guile, believing humbly in the religion which he has striven to teach, and guided by the precepts which he has striven to learn.